Together Again

Twin Souls Reunite in Love and Life

A True Story

Dennis Jackson and Alice Best

Published by
DenAliLove Publications
P.O. Box 83-2106
Miami, Florida 33283-2106
(877) 595-4111
http://www.denalilove.com

Library of Congress Cataloging-in-Publication Data
Jackson, Dennis. - Best, Alice.
  Together Again : *Twin Souls Reunite in Love and Life* / Dennis Jackson and Alice Best.
    ISBN 0-9673752-0-7 : $15.95
  1.Relationships 2. Twin Souls 3. New Age
I. Title
  1999   99-90754
                                          CIP

Printed in the United States of America
Printed on acid free paper

10 9 8 7 6 5 4 3 2 1

Book Concept and Design by Dennis Jackson
Cover Design by Dennis Jackson
Authors' Photo by J. Brian King

This book is dedicated
to all the people
who helped bring us

"*Together Again*"

and to all the people
who are still looking for
the perfect relationship...
May your search be moved
ever forward by this story,
and may Love and Light be with you

always...

All Ways.

About the rings...

Credit is given to **Patricia Joudry** and **Dr. Maurie Pressman**, co-authors of the book, *Twin Souls: A guide to meeting your spiritual partner.* We honor them for bringing the world their message. As stated in their book, *"The Sufi symbol for twin souls is that of two interlocking rings that cannot be pulled apart."* We took that idea and expanded on it by creating a set of our own twin soul rings, which we have worn since 1996. They are, for us, the symbol of our love and commitment to each other and it is only appropriate that they be a part of this book.

Preface

Alice Best

Our book is written in three parts: "Dennis", "Alice", and "The Love". "The Love" is written by both of us, and often in responsive format. Dennis' words are in regular type, and mine are in bold and italics.

I knew that my life's purpose was not being fulfilled prior to the time I met Dennis in 1996. I was searching for something or someone, but I didn't know what or who, or even why. I just knew that there had to be something more "out there" for me than being a divorce lawyer. When I met Dennis, it was as though I suddenly knew what life was all about, and I finally understood the term "unconditional love".

When we began writing "Together Again", we thought we would just be telling our own story of how we met and came to recognize that we had been together before in many lifetimes. As friends read the initial drafts in manuscript form, they told us how much they had learned and how much they were touched by the stories and messages we'd presented. The book soon became a "how-to" book on preparing yourself to meet and recognize your own twin soul.

As twin souls, we had found the other half of ourselves. In finding that other half, we enhanced the person we each had already become. That is an important part of knowing that you have truly connected with your twin soul. The partnership is not a completion, but an enhancement of who you already are. You are already perfect! Your twin soul brings to the relationship whatever energy is needed to empower you to create your own choices and realize your dreams, and is there to celebrate with you when they happen! Twin souls are mirrors of each other; they are not an exact duplication. In fact, they may even be complete opposites, or may have had vast differences in life styles and life choices.

In the three years that Dennis and I have been lecturing and teaching others about twin souls, the questions we are most often asked include, "How do you know when you've met your twin soul?" "What if your twin soul doesn't recognize you?" "What if I never find my twin soul?" We trust that you will find the answers to those questions and others within the pages of this book.

✳ ✳ ✳

Dennis Jackson

In April of 1997 I was just beginning to completely realize "who I really am". I was becoming more tuned into my psychic gifts and had been doing many private personal readings. My communication with the other side was becoming more intense and acute. People who had passed on were showing themselves to me and communicating directly with me. Ho, a Zuni Indian with whom I had shared a past life and who had become my personal guide, was making it known to me that I was to write the book I had been told about in various psychic readings. In those readings I wasn't told what the subject would be, but that it would be very obvious at the time that I was to write it. So I began looking, watching and listening to everyone for a sign as to what I was to write.

I was a computer technician the first time I heard about

a "book" that I was supposed to write, so I figured it would have to do with computers or something like that. At that time I had no idea what a "twin soul" was. I really didn't want to write a technical book about computers, but I thought, if that is what it is supposed to be, oh well. So I resigned myself to writing a computer "how-to".

After Alice and I got together, we would be at social functions and people would often ask us how we met. As we would begin to enthusiastically relate our story, people would say, "...you should write this down...your story about your recognition, meeting and evolvement together is incredible...it could be a guide for other people who are searching for their own twin soul." We listened, we heard, but we didn't really know how to go about writing down a single story, let alone an entire book. We knew how to tell our stories, but nothing about writing them down in a readable form, so I consulted Ho and asked how to go about getting this done.

The vision I was given at that time consisted of a book of three parts. The first part would be my story about my evolvement and spiritual journey to the place where I met Alice. The second part would be Alice's story of evolvement and her spiritual journey to where we met, and the third section would be the story of how we came to be living a life together.

Having never written a book or an article of any kind, I had to go within and ask for even more guidance in this task. What I was given were visions about the success of this book. I was shown that it was to be read by many people and would become a how-to guidebook for people in search of their own twin soul. I was shown that it was divinely guided and that it was becoming an entity in itself. It was taking on a life of its own. We were merely the vehicles for it to be introduced into the world. I was shown that it would have the support of many well known and highly respected people who were also writers.

Little did we know that we would come to meet and get to know James Redfield, author of *The Celestine Prophecy*, his wife Salle, and Alan Cohen, author of *The Dragon Doesn't Live Here Anymore*, three of the most wonderful and "real" people on the planet today. These people truly walk their talk and I am proud to have made their acquaintance.

***

We started this journey that April and it has continued for over two years. Writing and re-writing, editing and re-editing every chapter and every word, making sure that nothing was left out and that nothing was missed. Making sure that this child that Alice and I have borne into this world truly is the best it can be.

We know that you will enjoy and gain insight from the words on these pages. They are meant to tell the story of a love that began many lifetimes ago. A love that endures and has no end: a love that withstands the tests of time…and time again…a love that has come...

"Together Again"

Acknowledgements

Perhaps even more difficult than writing a book is writing the acknowledgements. There are so many people who have touched our lives, and who have assisted us in making our dream become reality.

All of the "characters" in this book are real. We especially thank each and every one of them for being a part of our lives, in whatever role was played. Each person helped us to create that which we chose to experience in our lives, and in so doing, each person was an integral tool toward our finding each other as twin souls.

We thank the special people who have been with us throughout the birthing of our book: Tom and Dale Chasteen, Judith Conrad of KEST radio in San Francisco, Robert Diaz, Dee Dee and Jerry Gardner, Allan (Al) Jensen, Vicki Lawrence, Kristen and Robert Malfara, Susan and Bob Roth, Kathleen Schramm, Dr. Holly Schwartztol, Michael Von Zamft, and our four wonderful children, Justin Best, and Joel, Leo, and Andrea Jackson.

I (Alice) wish to honor my parents, Marcia & David Rabinowitz. I know that my mother is watching over us and has given us her blessings to go forward with the publication of this book. I also honor my three sisters, Diane Parker, Linda Zack Faber, and Norma Greenstein. I cherish the relationships we have rediscovered, and I at last know that I am blessed to be a part of this family.

My love goes out to my friends, Sherril Siegel and Sandra Von Zamft, both of whom left this planet at a young age, but who have remained in my heart and my thoughts ever since. It is because of them that I searched for reasons for my own existence, and in so doing, I discovered spirituality, peace, and true love.

I (Dennis) wish to acknowledge a few special people that have touched my life in this incarnation. Sylvia Browne, who was my launching pad into the psychic world. Neale Donald Walsch, for having his "Conversations With God," and putting himself out there. If not for his book, I might never have met Alice as soon as I did.

I want to thank all the people that I met in the chat rooms of Prodigy and America Online, without whom I might never have been able to strengthen my psychic abilities and move on into the work that I now do in reaching loved ones that have passed on.

Finally, I wish to thank my mother, Billie Jean Evers, for giving me the words when I was younger that have helped me build a foundation for the life I now lead as a psychic medium. She always said, "Don't worry, I know everything will work out perfectly!"

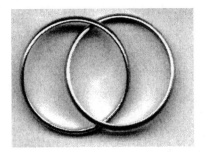

Table of Contents

Dennis

Alice

The Love

14.   Decision Making Time

15.   The Journey to Paradise

***

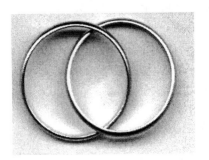

Dennis

Chapter One

Past Lives Revisited

- *Reginald May* -

"I see clouds, I can't..." I said as if I was going to continue.

"Ok..." Moria said. Then coaxing me on she continued, "It's ok, go through the clouds." After a long pause she said, "Go through the clouds to the land below. You're still, you're just above..."

I broke in with an almost inaudible whisper, "Yeah, I'm still... I can't get down." Then, realizing what was happening I said, "I'm flying. I can't... can't get out of the clouds."

"Ok, can you get a time or a feeling?" Moria questioned,

"Umm, it's a plane. It's a... it has propellers."

"Ok, so you're flying in a plane," she repeated. Then she asked, "Are you flying in it, are you the pilot?"

"It's like I'm outside looking at it. It's like, a DC-9. That's the first thought, I, I don't know. It could be some other kind of plane."

"Ok, why is this plane important to you?"

I couldn't answer her question because at that moment I had no idea why this airplane was important. The answers to this and many other questions were about to be given to me in a profound and very exciting way. However, it would be some time before I would be able to really understand them.

This was the first few minutes of a past life regression that I was experiencing. I had been directed during this regression to travel through a tunnel into an area that held the memories of all my past lives. This occurred on May 28th, 1993. During this regression I was having visions that I didn't understand. I realized when listening to this tape afterward, that I was being given a clear vision of the events I had experienced in that life. I had just begun, I was to find out later, the beginning of the end. I was beginning a path that would change the course of my life and turn it into something that is now wonderful and totally fulfilling.

However, I was still halfway between my life now and the past life that I was visiting, which is why the thought of a DC-9 came into it. As we progressed further, and I went deeper into the hypnotic state, the visions became much clearer and the information started to flow more freely and became more precise.

This first life that I found myself in was that of a pilot whose name was Reginald May. He appeared to be a Wing Commander or the Commander of a bomber group in WWII. It seemed, from the information I was able to collect, that he was an American flying the giant four-engine "Flying Fortress" bomber out of Great Britain. During the regression, I began connecting to that life while on a mission over the South Pacific.

I continued, talking over but not answering the question that Moria had just asked about the plane's importance to me. "And, and another plane. I'm looking at the plane from another, from another plane. I'm flying another plane."

"Now, are you the pilot of this other plane or are you just a passenger?"

"Yeah, the pilot."

Then I said, to no one in particular, the word "control." I don't even think that Moria heard me, at least she didn't say anything if she did, but I remember thinking, "It's about control." My life then and now was about control, always being in control. Wanting to be in charge. I think that control was my theme in that life, and it has carried over into this life.

Moria went on by questioning me, "Can you look at what you're wearing?"

"A hat, um, a uniform of some kind."

"Is it...?"

I broke in, "Wings, on the left lapel. It's like a... stripes on the sleeve. It's a flight suit."

"If there are stripes, would you say you were in the service, or was it...?"

"Yeah, I think that's what... it's like a...42."

"You're, you're about 42, or there's 42 stripes?"

"Nineteen forty...no it was 1942," I said, again talking over her.

"And where are you? Where in the air are you?" Her interest now piqued, she gently helped me through this experience.

"I don't know, I'm escorting a plane."

"Ok, to where? Destination? Country?"

"Iwo Jima."

"1942, Iwo Jima. Ok, what color is your uniform?"

"Wow, I've got a chill, it's cold." I was physically shivering.

"It's cold up there, huh?" Moria questioned.

Moria got my coat and laid it over me which helped me to warm up. She told me to stay relaxed and to tell her what was happening then. I told her that I was having trouble getting a clear picture. It was at this point in the regression that I was getting images that were confusing. I was seeing myself flying planes over water and over land. It was unclear at that moment as to where I was flying, but I know that I flew many missions in WWII and the visions were all coming at me at the same time. I was having trouble distinguishing which was which. After a few minutes they became much clearer and I was able to focus in on one particular event.

"I'm in control of the plane, I know that," I stated matter-of-factly.

"Ok, and you're escorting. Who are you escorting, is it another service man, a commander or something?"

"No, the other plane has four engines, and it's a large plane and I know that there's, there are soldiers in it. There are people in it, and they have to get somewhere."

Then Moria burst into my statement finishing it for me, "And so you're protecting them to make sure they get where they're going. Do you know wha…you're going to Iwo Jima?"

Then I was stammering. I remember at this moment not being really clear as to where I was while in this plane. As I saw the images in my head change, I was actually moving forward in time while watching events flash past.

"Um, that's… that's the area, we're…"

"Ok."

"South Pacific, that area."

As soon as the words "South Pacific" were out of my mouth, I was instantly transported to another part of the world. It was as if I was supposed to know that I had flown many missions all over the world, but the healing I was to go through was best served by remembering a particular mission that I flew over Europe. I could see the checkerboard land below and I was feeling all the fear that Reginald was feeling at that moment. I knew that we had been on a bombing mission over Germany and we were limping home.

Leaning in closer, Moria questioned, "Ok. Can you see what nationality you are?"

"Uh, I see a, no, I see English writing. Reginald, Reginald May, that's my name tag. That's my name, yeah," I stammered and then continued, "Yeah, that's my name tag."

"Are you British?"

"Uhm, no, I don't think so." I wasn't sure. I felt that I could be English or American, but I came to the conclusion that I was not British. I continued by saying, "R.A.F." I said this meaning the Royal Air Force.

Moria repeated, "R.A.F., ok."

"Yeah." I'm sure that I was flying for the R.A.F. I feel that I was an American dispatched to the R.A.F.

I started shivering again and Moria asked, "You cold?"

"Yeah, chills, and I'm worried about being attacked."

"About how old would you say you are?"

"Thirty, thirty…two," I said, letting it hang in the air.

"Is there anybody in your plane with you?"

"There's one other person on the right, I think...I think we're bombing."

"So you're bombing..." Moria started but I cut her off, finally realizing where I was and what I was doing.

Excitedly I said, "It's a bomber, that's what it is, it's a bomber. It's not, it's not a troop carrier."

"Ok, you're guarding the bomber?"

"Yeah, we're flying along with the other bombers. We're a bomber, too. It's not protection. Uhm, we're bombing somewhere over Germany is what I get. And we're being attacked, I'm scared."

Moria broke in, "They're firing at you?"

"Yeah, that's why I'm scared."

When I flashed into this life I saw other bombers flying with me. I had quickly moved forward in time and saw myself flying over Germany, returning from a mission. Of the planes flying with me, some were smoking, some were flying in with less than four engines running, and some were just fine.

"Ok, and anything else you can see right now?"

"Smoke," I stated flatly.

"Are you hit, or is this smoke coming from the ground?"

"No, the other plane is smoking."

"Ok, go forward with me a little bit," she coaxed, "What happens to the other plane?"

"It goes down...it's going down...yeah, it's going down. I can't... I can't help them."

"And you can't do anything," she said with some sadness in her voice.

I repeated as if I couldn't believe what I was seeing, "I can't help them, they're going down."

"Ok, release that," she softly instructed.

It was then that I was overcome with my emotions and began to weep for those men who had died some 50 years before. I felt it like it was happening right then but Moria, being very skilled, helped me work through the emotions

She then continued, "And I want you to realize that as we do this, this will cleanse, and once you've experienced something, especially something traumatic you don't have to go through it again." Because I had begun to weep Moria grew concerned and said, "Ok, what's happening now, Dennis?"

Speaking through tears, I managed to say in a voice a little above a whisper, "They...they're all dead!"

"They're all dead in the other plane?"

"Yeah."

"Ok, it's ok," she soothed, but it was still traumatic.

I was weeping profusely for these men. Men that I had reconnected with and watched plummet to their deaths. Tears for their families, for their loved ones and for me. I was reliving the feelings of that day. More was to come.

"I'm right here," Moria assured me.

"I can't ...I can't save them," I said, still weeping.

"Were you a commander, was it your...?" she asked.

"Yes, I'm so afraid..." Then in a barely audible whisper, "It's my fault."

Moria quickly saw that I was in the middle of this life when I should have been an observer. She directed me, "Ok, I want you to release that. I want you to back up from the situation just a little bit. Just back up and look at it, and realize…"

I broke in while still sniffling and weeping, "I don't know what happened, I…I can't see everything; that's why…"

"Ok, now do you still feel this is your fault? Looking at it now, looking at it backed up a little bit as Dennis, do you still feel that this was your fault?"

I realized then that I was not physically there but that I was now in this life. I was not there living it again, I was just observing the events as they happened.

"No, there was nothing that I could do." Then whispering again, "There was nothing I could do."

"Ok, I want you to realize that."

Coming to yet another realization, I said, "I've always needed to control the situation and I can't." Then, softly, "Oh… I hate war. God I hate it!" Still in whispering tones, "…don't want to be here."

Then Moria moved me forward with a question, "Ok, anything else about this situation, as you go forward now a little bit, do you make it to your destination?"

"Yeah," I sighed, "we make it to land… we go down… we don't have any… one wheel… only one wheel." I was seeing these events in my mind's eye.

As we descended toward the runway, I realized that one landing gear wheel was still retracted. Trying to keep the plane level for as long as I could, it was apparent that it would be impossible to make a normal landing and keep one wing from hitting the ground. With great effort I was able to control the plane long enough for it to slow before the wing slammed into the runway. When it caught, the plane went into a spin and began a twisting, turning motion before crashing into the ground.

Moria then went into a teaching lesson with me. She said, "Ok, now I want you to draw a parallel, taking just that one situation that came up." Then she asked, "Do you think your need to always be in control might have anything to do with this situation that you just went through where you had no control?"

I quickly answered, "Yes, if I'm in control, everything's ok."

"Because you were a commander? And you were responsible for those troops?"

"They died."

"But you couldn't stop them from dying."

"No, no. But I feel so helpless."

"Ok, but let's look at the bigger picture for a second." Then she reminded me about the philosophy that I had been studying.

Moria was a minister in a church that psychic Sylvia Browne founded in the Seattle area. I was a member of Sylvia's organization at the time, and was working as a videographer at her seminars.

I had just started on this spiritual path about a year before and had begun to understand that we all planned our own lives before we got here. We lay them out from the beginning to the end and then we live them. Our only job here, on this earth, in this life, is to experience what we planned.

I believe that we are all one and all are a part of God, and since we truly are a part of God we have nothing to learn. If God really is an all-knowing, all-seeing entity, and we are a part of that, then we already know all there is to know; at least conceptually. I also believe that everything is perfect, therefore, it makes perfect sense, and , that we have no lessons to learn, only experiences to experience.

One of the biggest hurdles that I was to overcome and to accept during this life is that I have control over nothing. I can't control another's life and the other can't control mine. That is what this book is about: learning to watch for the signs, recognizing and understanding them, and experiencing the outcome of following them.

Moria continued, "Do you see that just as you planned that life (for yourself), and it can be pulled up now, they also planned that they would go then?"

"Yeah," I whispered still half-crying. "Yes I do." Then I continued brokenly while catching my breath, "But the human inside of me wants to control it... I need to feel... like I... I..."

Moria jumped in to help me, "Of course you did, you wanted them to survive, because when you're a commander, you're responsible for everybody under your command. Isn't that what they tell you?"

"Yes, I needed to protect them, that's what I felt, the protection. That I needed to protect them, and that I couldn't do it."

"But didn't you do your best?"

"Yes, but I felt like I had failed."

"Ok, let's move forward, you've landed." Moria was moving me onward. I think that she felt there would be more answers coming and more experiences to help me through this traumatic time in that life.

"Four of my crew were killed in the plane attack," I continued by telling her what I'd just observed. "We were attacked by fighters. My co-pilot was killed, and he was sitting right beside me."

While I was describing the plane and the surroundings in my regression, I looked to my right at my co-pilot, and found that he had been killed. He was leaning over, limp, with blood coming out of his ear. He had taken a bullet or a fragment of shrapnel. Even though I was taking the viewpoint of an observer, it was hard to detach and not get into the emotional feelings that were a natural part of these sad events.

Then I asked almost whispering, "Why not me? That was my question, why not me?"

"It's worse when you feel responsible for people, to see the people you care about being hurt. You'd almost rather see it happen to yourself, wouldn't you?" Moria had paraphrased the feelings I was having at that moment. "I mean you'd save them if you could and let it be you."

"Jim was killed," I whispered. I had remembered my co-pilot's name in the emotions of the moment.

"And was he a good friend?"

"Yeah, my best friend," I sobbed.

Again Moria reinforced the knowledge with "There was nothing you could do about any of this."

"They shot him!" I whispered out and broke into tears. "Oh... oh man..."

I was feeling the emotions of these traumatic events as

if I were watching it happen all over again. Because of Moria's guidance, I was observing rather than participating in the events unfolding before me. It would have been even more emotionally traumatic had I been reliving it all as a participant again.

Moria quietly asked me, "Is there anything else that you want to see about this life? Do you want to explore anything else? Anything that comes to mind, let the images just flow through your mind. You can move forward..."

"I just need to tell him I'm sorry," I said, again cutting her off with my thoughts turned into statements.

"You can do that. Why don't you tell him now? Why don't you tell his soul?"

So, talking to the soul of my co-pilot who died so long ago I said, "I did my best. I'm sorry, Jim. I'm so sorry I wasn't able to protect you."

Then a feeling came over me and I said to Moria, "I'm spinning. A lot of emotions are coming up."

She calmly said to me, "Sure they are, you're touching a very emotional time. It's called 'morphic resonance'. It's affecting your life now in some way."

There was a healing taking place then. I didn't realize it then, but my life would go through that same type of loss of control just a few short years in the future. I was starting down a path that was resonating with a past life. I was being prepared for events that were to come up very soon.

Moria started to continue, "But I want you to..."

I broke in, "I'm going home now. I'm going home." A vision had come over me and I just blurted out the feeling that I was going home.

"Ok, so is the war over?"

"They sent me home; I was wounded. I didn't realize it, but I was wounded."

When I had landed the plane on the single landing gear and it crashed, I was knocked unconscious. I awoke in a hospital with a broken leg.

Then another vision appeared and I said to Moria, "I didn't make it home." Then almost whispering, "I didn't make it home. I don't know, I just didn't make it home."

"Can you see how you died? Do you want to explore that issue?"

"Yeah, I need to know that."

"Ok, I want you to go up to the point at which you died," she directed me with a gentle push, then continued, "and tell me how you died."

This is the part of the regression that is a bit foggy. I am not sure if I was being flown home or just to another place in Great Britain to board a ship headed for home. I was on a plane when, much to my dismay, it developed engine trouble and crashed. In this crash everyone, including me, died. As an observer, I, as Dennis, felt no pain. My soul was ejected out of Reginald May's body and I joined a group of about 8 to 10 other souls who had been on the plane.

"I'm spinning, and the plane crashed. The plane crashed, oh… going down, I can feel myself spinning. I'm not in control. It's just like before. I'm not controlling it and it's going down."

Suddenly I jerked. My whole body went through a sudden movement that I couldn't explain then. I now realize that I was reliving the crash and experiencing my soul's exit from my body.

Moria then helped me get through what I was feeling and helped guide me to a place that was safe so that I could experience the events again from the perspective of an observer and not a participant. She then took me to the point just past the death of Reginald to where my soul was ejected from the body and released.

"Tell me what you're feeling now."

"Floating," I said, a bit in disbelief.

It was a feeling of total freedom. It was very strange to have this feeling of lightness. I felt like I could go anywhere or be anything that I wanted, instantaneously. I was floating on air with no heaviness of the body to encumber me. I realized that everything was perfect. I was pure energy.

"Ok, what are the emotions?"

"Peaceful, I just feel like I'm floating…and spinning, I can't seem to stop the spinning. I don't know why I'm spinning."

"You are probably still in the plane. I just want you to let go, release, and realize that you charted this to happen. Realize that the control was when you were on the other side and you were charting, and that was when you had the control. You, with God, had the say-so of what you would write in your script, what you would experience and when you would take an exit point."

"That was my exit point," I said matter-of-factly, "that was my natural end and I had planned another life after that one, the one I'm in now."

"That was a really close life to this one, as far as time goes, so that is why you are picking up a lot of it," Moria explained. "So now I want you to say with me, 'let me release all the negativity from the experience, and let me hold onto what I learned from the experience. Let me be cleansed of the particular fear or phobia and let it be wiped clean, and let only the positive remain.'"

I repeated those words.

"Ok, good, Dennis."

"I am really hot now."

"Ok, let's take that jacket off now."

She took off the jacket that she had placed over me when I got the chills and then told me to relax for a couple moments before we continued. She took me through an exercise to rejuvenate me and connected me to the other side for an energy transfer. This was to replenish any loss of energy I may have had.

The name Reginald May would be with me for a long while. He had come to me for a healing. A healing of a fear of flying that I had. Once I had seen that he died in a plane crash, and having been there and having experienced it again, I was able to get past that fear. I was able to look at it and say to myself, "I have done this once before, so I don't have to experience it again." I was able to understand that if in fact I did choose my life, I would not choose to die in this manner again. This life would come back to me at a later date when I connected the self of today with Reginald in a profound, intricate, unusual and even more personal way.

- *Joshua Abram* -

Then Moria directed me back into the tunnel with, "Ok, now let's go through the tunnel again, and let's explore another life that is pertinent to this life."

"Ok, I've stopped spinning now that I have reentered

the tunnel." Then with a quiet rush of air out of my lungs and an almost awestruck sound I exclaimed, "Wow."

After a few moments I burst out of the darkness and into another life. It took only a matter of seconds for me to realize this was a very different life.

"I'm on a wagon train," I stated, and we were off again.

"Ok, and tell me about what that feels like."

"Tired, very tired," I said, feeling totally fatigued. I know that I was tired from the regression, but this feeling was coming through from the life I was now entering.

"Have you been on it a long time?" she asked.

"The date I see is 1876. My name is Josh, Joshua, but they call me Josh."

Everything was so clear. The year was 1876 and this time I found myself on a horse. Someone was riding up to me. It was a man, wearing old dirty clothes that hadn't been washed in quite a few days, maybe even weeks. Because they were so dirty, I couldn't even tell what color they were.

He seemed to be a friend because as he rode up on his horse he said, "Ya' wanna circle up the wagons, Josh?"

I heard myself reply, "Yeah, let's make camp here and get the lookouts set up before dark." Then almost as an aside I added, "Thanks, Jonah." He then rode off and went about setting up camp.

And then, in the distance, I heard Moria's voice, "And where are you heading?"

I started laughing out loud. The feeling I was having was one of lightness. I knew I was going to a new land, a new life. I knew exactly where I was going, "We're going to California," I told her.

We both laughed then. Moria, being from San Jose, got a kick out of it, too. "Cali-for-ni-a," she laughed, using the term from back in the gold rush days.

"Where are you right now?"

"I'm on a horse, I'm riding a horse."

"Where did you come from?"

"St. Louis."

"And why are you going to California?" she asked, continuing to make me look at that life in greater detail.

Laughing I said, "I'm a wagon master, ha ha ha, I'm in charge again. Oh, no! I'm sorry, but I just…"

Moria jumped in laughing herself, "You not getting away from that are you?" she asked.

Still laughing I said, "No, I'm leading the wagons and we're going…" Then recognizing where I was I said, "I recognize this place…wow…oh man, it's…it's Idaho. That's the Snake River I see. Oh wow, I'm in a place called…I don't know what it's called now, but I know what it's called in the future. I can't think of the name now, but I will remember it. I'm on wagon train, there are three wagon trains that I know of, and we're all about a day apart. We're being attacked by Indians and we've lost one person. We're in Idaho along the Snake River, it's a place called uh, crater, uh no not crater, um crater rocks or something like that. I can't think of the name of the place, I recognize it though." I was still struggling with remembering the name of this significant spot.

"Have you been there in this lifetime?" Moria questioned.

"Yes, yeah, yeah, that's why I recognize it. It's like all of a sudden I know why I felt so familiar about this place," I excitedly said.

Moria started, "Cause in this life…"

And I finished, "…Yeah, I've been there."

At the time I couldn't remember the name, but it did come to me later. It's known as "Massacre Rocks State Park." When my family had stopped there overnight, on a motorhome trip, I had experienced a warmth, a familiar closeness. I felt that I had been there before. After this regression, when on another trip, we traveled past Massacre Rocks State Park and stopped again. While we were there, I gathered some information and it confirmed with what I had gotten in the regression. It was named Massacre Rocks after a wagon train was completely wiped out in the late 1800's.

I continued on giving Moria details of what I was seeing, "I was going down the Oregon Trail. Just beyond this point the trail splits, one leg goes north and the other goes south…to California, and we're going south to California."

"So that is your job? To bring people on wagon trains to California, and then will you be going back to St. Louis?"

I answered yes to all these questions then, but the true story was to be revealed later in this regression. I was dealing with the thoughts of Joshua. At the time he really thought that he would go back to St. Louis and bring other wagon trains loaded with people to California.

I knew my name was Joshua and I was around 45 years old. I also realized that I had been a printer in St. Louis,

Missouri. I am not sure how I died, but it is my feeling that I froze to death up in some mountainous area. Joshua had sold everything he owned to finance this wagon train to go to California.

Moria then directed me back to the moment we were in, "So what happens during the attack? You say you're being attacked by Indians."

"We lost one person, one man, Jeremiah was his name. All the wagon trains were attacked, at different times. All on the same day or within a day of each other, some were wiped out."

Moria dug further, "Do you know the name or the type of Indians, the tribe?"

"Nez Pierce, but they weren't really hostile, we were mistaken. We thought they were attacking, but they weren't. We fought them and they had to protect themselves. Everybody was afraid so they shot one of them saying, 'the savages'. But they're not really, we just don't understand them. Again somebody dies because I couldn't control it. Whoa."

The emotions were surfacing again. I was reliving the feeling of not being able to control the situation and being responsible for someone dying. I was again overwhelmed with the feeling of inadequacy. The messages about letting go seemed to be what I was supposed to understand. It was time to start letting go.

Moria started to guide me again, but she realized I was already going in a direction of healing and let me go with it, "Ok so…go ahead."

"I can't…I can't… I feel horrible. I can't … I can't cry… shows weakness."

"But even though you feel really sad, you don't want to let them see that…any weakness."

"That I'm scared…can't let them see that. Gotta get these people through safely."

"And do you get them through safely?"

"Yeah, we only lose five more. Through pneumonia, and some other disease, but we can't figure out what it is. It's some kind of a…they just kind of dwindle away. They get sick and they have a really high fever. I think it's what we now know as the flu."

"Influenza," she said stating the real name.

"Yeah, five of them died. There are a hundred people on the train."

"Ok, I want you to go forward in time…" Moria had started to guide me on. But as if a message had flashed from the heavens for me to know, I added something. This would give me solid information to look into later when I searched for documentation to prove this life.

"My name's Joshua Abram."

"Joshua Abram, ok." Moria repeated the name.

"That's it, yeah." I then continued on not really realizing how significant that name was. I wouldn't understand the significance of either of these lives until a few years later. "We get to this really high pass," I was describing a pass through the mountains that we were to traverse. "Lots of snow."

"Where are you?"

"Going to California."

"You're going through the Sierra Nevada's then?" Moria

asked, naming the mountains on the border between California and Nevada. "Are you that far west?"

"It's a very high pass that we have to get over before winter comes. The snow's about a foot and a half deep. It's not really bad; it's just that there is a lot of it. We're going to get through it ok. Just have to get over this pass and down the other side. We're running late in the year. That's where the people died, on top. Because we couldn't get them down soon enough." I had just described the trip over what is known as Donner's Pass. We had lost some people to an influenza outbreak and my feeling was that if we could have gotten down to warmer weather they might have lived. The control issue arose again.

I continued narrating and describing the scenes before my eyes. "The Indians were not hostile, they were friendly."

"Is this in the Sierra's or in California or...?"

"After we got past the snow," I explained, "the Indians there are very friendly, very helpful, Mexican... they are Mexican...Spanish. Hard to tell, they look like a combination. The wagons... it's so hard in this... 'cause there's no road, just a very hard trail; we make it ok."

"Ok, is there anything else you want to explore about this time?"

"I...I'm really getting a message about this control thing. It's like they are telling me, I'm not responsible for everything in the world, and I'm not responsible for the people that die around me or who are around me. That was too hard, I couldn't do that again. Couldn't do that war thing again. When I went into the service, in this life, I didn't want to go to the war in Viet Nam, so I avoided it by joining the Coast Guard. I had this burning need to not go to war."

The Universe was taking control and moving me ever closer to a path of total spirituality. At the time, I was just becoming aware of a force much greater than myself but I was still trying to control the path and direction of my life. The experiences that I had during this time have become a way of life for me now. I was being shown, in a not-so-subtle way, that I would be moving in a very different direction soon. What I was beginning to see was that I had to let go and get out of my own way because then things could move more smoothly.

I knew that somehow I would be able to document this life and find even more information out about this man. I didn't know how or when that would happen, but one year later, I would be able to do just that and more.

Moria went on with some thoughts about why these lives were coming to me and she helped me to move on from there with a better feeling about what I was dealing with in this life. I was not to learn what these lives were all about until a few years later.

- *The Other Side* -

The next place we visited was a place we all go to when we leave this plane known as Earth. When Moria mentioned going to the other side, I got an incredible chill that went up and down my body. This was a sign to me that I was about to enter an area that would give me an insight into what lay ahead in this life. As I burst out into the light again after moving through the tunnel I began describing what I saw.

"Stars, I see stars, billions and billions of stars. The light's really bright from somewhere. I can't tell where it is coming from."

"Ok, just ask that your eyes be shaded a little bit,

because over there the colors are very intense." Moria guided me in what to ask for. "Now let's go toward the light, almost as if you're walking over a bridge, and then walk down. Like you're bridging through the two worlds..."

"It's beautiful, so beautiful," I exclaimed while Moria was still talking.

"And bridge over, and tell me what you see," she said, completing her instructions.

"Right now I see lights, thousands and thousands of sparkling little sparkling lights. And I'm just going to go toward them."

"What do you see when you get over there?"

I began laughing with joy and told her, "Everybody's saying hi to me."

"Are you seeing people you know?"

"Yeah, I see Elmo, one of my spirit guides. I had never been able to see what he looked like before." I had a vision of the guide I knew as Elmo. He was the Saint Elmo that had guided sailors with his light. I later came to know an even closer guide, Ho, who is with me in my work as a psychic/medium, helping to bring information to me from the other side.

"Now you can; describe him a little bit."

I went on to describe him to her, "Ah, looks like about six foot, sandy blonde hair, mustache, big smile. He's welcoming me, putting his arm around me saying 'come on, walk with me.' Trees, it's just trees; it's like all of nature that I have never seen before. The light's really bright. It almost hurts my eyes. It kind of reminds me of the valleys of Hawaii, with all of the lush green hills. They're really steep. It's like valleys, really beautiful valleys. We're up on top of them. I want to just look around."

"Does this hold any significance to you that you can think of?"

I explained that it looked familiar, "It looks like Hawaii; it looks like this spot in Hawaii. I was there once many years ago."

"Ok, anything else, anybody else? Since you were saying hi to people, did you see anybody else you know from a life?"

I am overcome with many emotions, happiness and joy, all the sides of love as I start to recognize someone coming toward me.

"Um, ah, I see somebody that I recognize, but I don't know who it is. I'm getting a real strong feeling of knowing this person really well. Oh my God, *it's like looking at myself.*"

Moria acknowledged my statement, "Ok."

"I know her, yeah, I know who she is." This was the first time I actually got a glimpse of my true twin soul.I saw no facial features or body. What I saw was the essence of my twin soul. Then she was speaking to me through thought and energy, without audibly saying anything.This was simply to let me know that we would be meeting and connecting again, in this life. On the tape of this regression, I only quietly say, "Ok"; I know that I was acknowledging her and what she had just said to me.

As the session ended, a realization came over me, "This is so cool. Now I understand, I finally understand." Just as I said that, a new experience was set in motion. A new phase of my life and a new path was opened.

Chapter Two

The New Beginning

- *The Messages* -

My regression was wonderful and I received some very important information. It wasn't until a few years later that I really understood what had happened that day and just how important that information would turn out to be.

During the regression I had been given a glimpse of two very distinct lives with very specific messages in each. Had I been more aware at the time I could have followed the signs and not had to endure as much pain as I did in the following years. But as I have come to realize, without pain, there is no gain; and everything in life is perfect, even though it may not seem that way at the time.

A few of the messages that came through during that regression were as plain as the nose on my face. To use a phrase that I have heard before, they were hiding in plain sight. But the hidden messages that weren't so obvious were the ones that I received during deep meditations. These were the most profound and life changing. The most obvious of the messages were related to the first life that I found.

I had been working for a company in Seattle in 1987 which required air travel once a month. I had to fly to Atlanta, Georgia, taking the "red eye" on Saturday night and returning the following Friday night. I had been working there for about eight months when one night I had a nightmare. I woke up in a cold sweat after dreaming that I was in a plane that had crashed and I died. It was so real that the next day I went into work and asked to speak to my boss, who happened to be the owner, to ask about not flying for awhile. When I was told that this was not a possibility, I told him about my dream and that I was so upset about it that I just couldn't fly again. I then said I was sorry but that I couldn't continue working for him.

After the regression in 1993, Reginald May gave me back my ability to get on a plane again. I knew that because I had died in a plane crash in that life, I would not have chosen to die that way in this life. I also had a fear of dying at that time and had to work through that in my spiritual journey. Reginald also gave me a sense that dying was not an ending, but a continuing of another, but much different, existence.

There is only one minor problem. Try as I might, I have not been able to confirm nor deny by any formal proof, the existence of Reginald May. It is my belief that this is the reason that I was given the vision of my life as Joshua Abram. I have been able to document proof of his existence in this world, and the journey to that proof is detailed later in this chapter.

The vision of my twin soul on the other side was also a very profound message. It was telling me that my twin soul was not there but that she was on this plane. The reason I could give no details of how she appeared was that I was only seeing her energy, the essence of her soul. This was also a glimpse of a future event. An event where I would actually meet and be with "the other half of me", my twin soul, in this life. The fact that I saw a vision of Hawaii in it is also very profound because of the awakening and onion peeling process that Alice would go through in Hawaii.

However, the most profound of these came at a much later date, about three or four years later. During many deep meditations, my personal spirit guides brought visions to me that connected my life as Reginald May to my life as Dennis Jackson.

It was the fall of 1996 and I was quickly realizing that my path was to be that of service to people. That service was taking the shape of teaching and helping people get in touch with their own intuitive abilities and helping them find who they really are. But my first mission was to get in deeper touch with who I am, and really use the psychic and intuitive abilities that had been developing within me over the last 5 years.

I was in the process of going into deep meditations to find out what my life was all about and what I was supposed to be "doing" with it. It was during one of my deep meditations and knowledge gathering missions that the following information was given to me.

My past life regression had shown me that during WWII, I was a pilot and commander of a wing flying missions over Europe. My circle of friends included only the people that I flew with or knew from missions that I had flown. One of these men was a bombardier that I had flown with. We had become good friends and made a pact that if either of us was killed, the survivor would go to the other's family and do what he could for them, and help in any way that he could.

I couldn't figure out why this was coming to me in this way. No name was given at first and it took a few months for this much to come out, but when the time became right for me to know, the Universe opened the doors and let me have it. Afterward, I was stunned.

I must come back to this life for a moment. I was married for over 22 years to a woman named Jackie and we had three children. Joel Wesley was named after my father and was born on 2/14/82. Leo Keller, who was named after

Jackie's dad and her mother's only brother who died in WWII, was born 7/2/84. Andrea Evelyn, named after Jackie's mother, was born on 8/20/86.

Continuing on with the search, I was trying to figure out why my life had taken the direction that it had. I was trying to understand why my marriage ended after such a long time. Then the details started coming. The friend that I had made a pact with was none other than Leo Levander, my former mother-in-law's only brother.

As I worked through the shock, I remembered that I had once seen a picture of Leo, who was killed in WWII and realized that I had recognized him and I didn't know why. Now the veil was being lifted and I was being allowed to see more details. It was precisely because of the pact that I had made with Leo that I was in this life and the events were transpiring as they were.

I came into this life in 1950, met and married Jackie who was Leo's neice. My agreement with Leo was fulfilled as I had done my part to take care of his sister and in fact, had been with her when she passed on to the other side. After her death all that was left was to sell her house and everything would be completed. As you will see later, the sale of her house was a major turning point in my life as I am living it now and a sign to me that my life was changing in a very drastic way.

- Finding Proof -

It was in the summer of 1994 when I decided to go to the National Archives Center in Seattle to research the information that I had received in the regression. I went specifically to find out about Joshua Abram and the life that I had lived in the late 1800's, and what I found astounded me.

The volunteer at the center had directed me to the correct places to look saying all the while, "It is probably going to take you a few weeks to find this person." You see, I had told him that I was looking for a relative and any information that I could find.

We started in the books where the census records of specific people are kept. It was a listing of the census of 1870 in St. Louis. As I scanned down the page of alphabetical names, I saw "Abram, Joshua." It was the only one in the list, so I figured he must be the one. The volunteer said, "This is the fastest I have ever seen anyone find someone since I have been here." I don't know if he was just being nice or hadn't really seen anyone find someone that fast. It didn't matter, because it felt good to me.

I didn't know what to do then so I asked the volunteer. He explained that the next thing I could do was go to another book and look up the number for the correct roll of microfilm to view. A microfilm record was kept of each of the census polls since the first one was recorded. All the hand written records were kept on microfilm and could be viewed in a microfiche machine.

I went over to look through the book and found the number of the correct roll of film. I retrieved the film, took it to the microfiche and began to view it. There were many names to go through, but I finally found him. There, in the record book was Joshua Abram. As I rolled the film forward it showed his age, 45, his address and that he was not married. I had to roll it to the next page to see the rest of the information. There on the page it said, "occupation: printer." I had really found him! I was ecstatic. I couldn't have been happier. It was like finding another part of myself.

What an incredible feeling to know that at that very same moment, I had crossed another threshold. Another part of my journey was completed. I was heading toward discovery.

- *The Psychic Path Begins* -

Life at that time was changing for me and I was going through some very painful experiences. I had been searching for something for a long time. I just didn't know what it was. In the 2½ years following the regression, many events took place to shake up my world. There were many losses. I lost my father, my mother-in-law (who had been a very good friend), a house, and a job that paid very well. I had friends that started pulling away. It felt as though everything that I had ever known was detaching and setting me adrift. I felt as if I didn't belong here and at the time I felt that my life was falling apart. It was kind of a long downward spiraling effect. I now know that this was the perfect way for things to happen. I was going through drastic changes in my life.

Sylvia Browne is a famous psychic who hails from the San Francisco Bay area. She is very gifted and has been able to "see" things since early childhood. She is an author, lecturer, and television personality who has appeared on such national shows as *Unsolved Mysteries*, *Montel Williams* and many local area shows in the Northwest. She has also helped solve many missing persons cases.

I met Sylvia in early 1993. Jackie had seen her on TV and wanted to get a reading from her. I really was off in another world at that time but for some reason, I was also drawn to this woman. She seemed so "real" to me. She seemed almost like a mother figure, and I really liked her. I just knew that I "knew" her. I later learned about soul recognition and I understand why we feel that we "know" people in this life even though we have just met them or have just seen them. I now know that there are no "coincidences" at all. Every event in our lives is either created or planned and co-created by us for our own experience.

"Dennis, the world is waiting," Sylvia said to me.

I was attending one of Sylvia's seminars and I had just asked her a question about the feelings I was having concerning my psychic abilities.

"You have much to give the world and much work ahead of you, so get out there and do it," she ordered.

She continued with, "You know you are very psychic. Everyone has psychic abilities, but you are moving forward with yours and the world is waiting."

She had repeated the statement again. I had known Sylvia for about a year when she told me this. At that time I didn't really know what she meant. I had been trying to be a "rock and roll star" for years and I was hoping she was talking about my musical abilities. Somehow I knew that she wasn't, because music was just not in my path as a vehicle to perform the work I needed to complete. I didn't know then what this work was to be, but I did know that it was not through rock and roll. I had always felt that I was "different" from everyone else, but I didn't think of it in a spiritual sense.

Sylvia was the key for me to begin the steps toward a path of psychic phenomena and spirituality that had eluded me over the years. During my childhood years I had been very involved in the church and because of the hypocrisies that I witnessed there, I was turned off by organized religion from then on. I know now that everything that happened to me was perfect and with each event, I was a step closer to finding Alice, my twin soul.

- *The Psychic Muscle* -

When Sylvia and I met, we hit it off very well. I really wanted to be involved with her and what she was doing. My soul knew that this is what I was supposed to do, and Sylvia was the "kick in the pants" that I needed to get me moving in the right direction. I learned from her that we all are psychic, which I already knew, but just didn't realize. I also learned our psychic ability is like a muscle that needs to be exercised.

I had always known that I was a little different but I just didn't know what that difference was until I met Sylvia.

To be able to learn as much as I could from her, I volunteered to videotape all of her Seattle area lectures. We agreed that I would videotape on two tapes so that I could send one to her and keep one for myself as payment for taping. I was able to learn much and I continued doing this for about a year to a year and a half. I felt that I was progressing along with my psychic ability very quickly.

During this same period, I was attending groups that were studying Sylvia's channelings about information on life here and on the other side. We were left alone to set-up and run the study groups as we saw fit. Because Sylvia's messages were about developing psychic abilities and contacting guides and angels, we started each meeting with a meditation and a psychic exercise. After a deep meditation, we would go around the room and each person would ask a question. The other people would write down the answer that they received psychically and each would give his or her psychic feeling on each question. This really worked and it helped each one of us tune into that part of our own self that is intuitive. This process continued for a year or so and we went from having one group with between ten and eighteen people showing up, to two groups with some of the same people meeting two nights a week.

At one particular meeting, I went into a deep meditative state and started doing a reading for one of the members. She asked a variety of questions and the answers were coming very clearly. Afterward I felt like I had run a marathon. I was so tired and so completely drained that I had to sit and collect myself before I could leave to go home. At the same time I was incredibly ecstatic with what had just happened because I had just done a completely channeled reading for the very first time. It was such a wonderful feeling and I felt very relaxed. A quiet calm had come over me. The woman that I read for was very impressed and stated that she had just gotten a reading from Sylvia, and that some of the answers that I had brought through for her were even more detailed than the ones from Sylvia.

Well, as you can guess, that felt wonderful because I respected Sylvia so much and really admired her to the point I think I had placed her up on a pedestal. She could do no wrong! We are all human but I feel that I had just made Sylvia a god or something like that. I was always in awe of her gift and the ability she had for giving such detailed answers to people. I always thought, "I wish I could do that." Little did I know that the answers she was getting are available to anyone who really wants to take the time to practice and "exercise" that psychic muscle.

-The Turning Point-

This is where Sylvia and I parted ways. She was giving a two-hour lecture in Seattle at a local hotel near the airport. I was videotaping. The lecture was all about guardian angels and such, and was an incredible hit. There were about 700 people there and many were interested in Sylvia's study groups and how to join.

After each lecture she always invited interested people

to stay and get information on joining her organization or study groups. This was usually overseen by her husband and some of the ministers in her organization, but on this particular day, Sylvia herself stayed to address the audience. Most of the people were feeling particularly happy and kind of special to have Sylvia talk to them personally. I was not as happy because I sensed that something was wrong. I wasn't sure what it was, but I just knew something negative was going to happen. Of course I had no idea it would have me in the center of what Sylvia saw as a "problem".

She began explaining to the crowd what the study groups are all about and how easy it would be to join or start a group if none was in their particular area. Then she digressed into a mini-tirade about some guy who was trying to "steal" her members and who was touting his ability as a channeler in her San Jose' area groups. She explained how she would not stand for that, and if it ever happened it would be terrible for her organization.

Then she was focusing on some guy in the Seattle area (where I lived) who was claiming to channel. She was saying that he was not really channeling and she explained that there was only one psychic in her organization and that person was she. When I finally understood what was happening, it was too late.

She suddenly looked directly at me and said, "Do you have a problem with this, Dennis?"

I was, to say the least, caught completely off guard. She was talking about me. I was so stunned that I could only stammer, "No."

Then she turned back to the audience and went on to say, "Good, now that we have settled that, have a wonderful day and love to you all."

I was struggling with emotions that I couldn't understand. I didn't know quite how to react and so I went up to her and said, "Sylvia, I am sorry that you took what I did wrong, I didn't mean any harm to you and I am not trying to "move in" on your organization."

She replied something to the effect, "Well, we can't have readings going on in our groups because I do all the readings in my organization, period."

I was devastated. I felt like I had just been beaten up. I felt betrayed and completely let down. Sylvia had shown another side of herself and it was a major turning point in my life.

I must say that she did me a favor because she was just a stepping stone in my soul's evolution. I was moving quickly down a particular path. I realized that if I had stayed in Sylvia's organization I would have had to stop all of my growth and be a follower or a pawn and being neither, I needed to move on.

For the next year and a half, I really didn't experience much noticeable growth along my psychic path. Most of the time I was watching Jackie doing all sorts of what I referred to as "psychic stuff", but I did do some little non-eventful readings such as when a friend of ours was buying a house.

Mary is the woman that introduced me to Jackie in 1972. Mary had been through much in her life, but she was pretty much what I would call a non-believer. When Jackie or I would mention anything remotely associated with the metaphysical, I could see Mary sort of rolling her eyes. I could feel her saying to herself, "These people have gone over the edge. They have really gone off the deep end."

So one spring day we had gotten together with Mary and she was talking about buying a house by summer.

I just blurted out, "No you won't, you'll find the house and buy it in December, this year, and you will move in, in February." It just sort of jumped out of my mouth and I couldn't stop it, not that I wanted to.

She replied, "No way, I am not waiting until winter to find a house. I am ready now and I want it by the end of summer".

Needless to say, she found the house in December, and moved in around the first of February. I was elated and it gave me back my hope of becoming a full-fledged psychic, which is what I felt that I would eventually be.

- Feeling Out Of Place -

My life had changed so drastically at this point that I had grown to expect anything. I felt that nothing that could happen would surprise me. In the previous three years, I had lost a good job, had to sell a house and moved into a motor home. So when more events occurred that could only be read as signs we should leave the area, we listened closely.

When Jackie's mother died, our family moved into her house and out of our motorhome. After we moved out of the motorhome, I spent hundreds of dollars fixing it up only to have the brakes fail while driving it to my friend's house to complete the repairs. I crashed it into a telephone pole while my son Joel was with me. We were both strapped to backboards and taken to the hospital by ambulance. At least we both rode in the same ambulance so I was with him and we knew each of us was ok. It was very traumatic for me, let alone a 12-year-old child. I felt terrible that I had put him through that.

Then just two weeks later, dogs that were owned by Jackie's childhood friends attacked Joel. Andrea, who was 8 years old at the time, was with him. She wasn't attacked but was traumatized by the scene she had witnessed.

The dogs, which were Golden Retrievers, are normally very docile but something snapped in the youngest dog and he led the attack. They knocked Joel down, but only the one dog continued the attack. He went for the face and throat but when Joel threw up his arm in protection, the dog grabbed hold, shook him and did some major damage to his upper arm. Joel was very lucky in that the injuries he suffered could have been life-threatening, but were not. As a result of the attack and the way it was handled by the dog's owners, Jackie's lifelong friendship was severed. This was yet another sign that we were not supposed to be here.

I had applied for at least twenty-five jobs that I was well qualified for with no positive results. I had gone on a few interviews, but all in all I was feeling like I should be somewhere else. I felt as though I didn't belong. It would seem that the messages were coming through loud and clear.

Unfortunately, we couldn't just leave because after my mother-in-law died, we had agreed to live there and be caretakers until the house sold.

- Selling the Past -

Living in this house was a tough thing to do. There were five siblings in Jackie's family, all with keys to the house. They felt as though the house was open for them to come into at any time they wanted. It had been that way for their whole lives, why should it change now? We had the feeling that we were being watched at all times. We had no privacy or guarantee that anyone wouldn't just walk into the house, without knocking, at any moment.

It was listed for sale for about two years, so during that time we also had to put up with real estate agents not calling and just stopping in. We never knew when someone might just come to the door to "show" the house, so we could never really relax. It was a living hell of a nightmare. It was very hard not to feel a little depressed about life. However, there was one good thing about living there. Since Jackie was part owner of the house and we had agreed to be the caretakers, we didn't have to pay a mortgage or rent to anyone, so it made it a little easier.

I was able to get a job as a computer technician at a nearby high school and had just enough income to get by. We also went to garage sales, bought select used clothes and then sold them to an exporter to make extra money. We took all of this as signs that when the house was sold we would not be sticking around the Seattle area. So when I quit trying to get a job to keep me there, things began to happen.

The first thing that happened was the house sold. We decided that when it closed we would buy a bigger motorhome than the one we had before. We would sell most of the "junk", put everything we wanted to keep into storage, except our clothes and some personal stuff, and take off to points unknown.

Not knowing exactly where to go, we left that up to the Universe. We were becoming more convinced that our lives were being divinely guided. We decided and agreed that we would take the kids out of public school and homeschool them until we decided on a place to settle.

We would just hit the road with no expectations and take whatever came to us. This could be a disaster or it could be something that would be wonderful. We had no way of knowing which way it would go, but we had faith in

God. So we planned to head out and not make any decisions as to where we would go but just follow whatever came to us. This was really our beginning to opening up to a spiritual way of life.

Between the time the house actually sold and the closing, we went through the process of setting up the homeschooling for our kids. We went to each of their schools, to many meetings, and filed all the papers needed. We all looked forward to the experience we were about to have.

- Leaving Town -

When the house closed, we paid off all of our bills and bought the motorhome we had picked out. We had searched all over the Northwest for the right one. We should have just sat back and waited because we ended up finding the right one practically in our back yard.

When we actually headed out on the road, sometime during the last part of October 1995, I began to feel like Christopher Columbus sailing off to points unknown. We took the kids out of school, left Seattle and headed south, just wanting to relax and figure out where to go. I said to Jackie, "I see us in Texas," and she answered back, "I don't want to go to Texas, I have no desire to go to Texas. Been there, done that." She had been to Dallas in the mid 1970's to help her sister move back to Seattle. She said Texas is "hot and humid and I never want to go back."

So we went to many of the tourist stops along the way. We saw the beautiful coasts of Oregon and northern California, San Francisco and the Golden Gate Bridge, then on down the coast to the Hearst Castle and San Simeon and on into Los Angeles. We visited Universal Studios, Disneyland and Knotts Berry Farm. Our kids were having a ball and learning a lot about life at the same time. We continued on down the coast to San Diego to visit the San Diego Zoo and Sea World. We were having a wonderful time all along the way and enjoying life to the fullest.

At San Diego we headed east on I-10 with the intention of going to Yuma to see my mom and stepfather, John. They were living in their motorhome out on the Arizona desert, and they were among the "snowbirds" that winter in the Southwest and then go back up north for the summer.

I had not seen my mom in a while and she had not seen her grandkids, so we decided to spend some time with them. We had fun there; we played cards and just relaxed while the kids explored. We were there about a week until we couldn't take the desert heat and dryness anymore. We decided to move on eastward, again not knowing where we were going, just heading east.

We decided that we would go through Phoenix since none of us had been there and then head north to Flagstaff. I still felt we were supposed to go to Texas, but Jackie was also still adamant about going north and across the upper part of New Mexico. So, feeling frustrated about my psychic visions not being taken seriously, I gave in.

When we got to Phoenix, there was a temperature inversion and all the smog and carbon monoxide from the cars was hanging near the ground. It was so thick that when I got out to fill up the motorhome with gas, my eyes started burning.

Even though it was close to 10:00 PM, I decided to drive on north toward Flagstaff to see if we could find someplace to stay that was out of this inversion. We had to drive almost to Flagstaff before we were finally out of the smog. We pulled into a rest area and went to sleep.

The next morning when we awoke, Jackie was deathly

ill. She had a major migraine headache and couldn't keep any food down. We headed on to Flagstaff to get something to help her but as we climbed higher in altitude, she became even more sick.

Pretty soon she was saying, "Ok, ok, so I am wrong, let's head south. I am too sick up here. Let's head for Texas, maybe you're right, Den." Even though she was deathly ill, and could barely sit up, she was still not convinced that we should be going the opposite direction. I feel that was the start of living my life by divine guidance.

As soon as we started descending in altitude and heading south, she started feeling much better. We were traveling in a southeasterly direction across the state heading for I-10 where it crosses into New Mexico. We stopped in Arizona and parked for the night.

Continuing on the next morning, we decided to get as far as Las Cruces, New Mexico, and then decide if we were really going to go south into Texas or north toward Albuquerque. When we got to Las Cruces, we stopped at the rest area on the hill above town. We decided to spend the night and check out the city the next morning. The way the rest area is situated, we could look out across the valley and see all the lights of the city. It looked stunningly beautiful. When the moon started coming up, it appeared directly behind the "Pipe Organ Mountains" and was gorgeous. It was the most stunning view we had ever seen; these beautiful lights of the city and the moon behind the mountains…wow. We knew that we had found "the place". We just knew we were home. Were we in for a surprise. I don't know what it was we were expecting, but whatever it was, when the sun rose, it didn't come through. We took one look the next morning and decided to move on eastward.

- *Texas Bound* -

At this point we decided to head south into Texas because Jackie was feeling wonderful and took that to mean "Go to Texas", even though she was still not totally convinced we were supposed to go there. We chose to head toward San Antonio to see the Alamo and learn a little history.

All the way along this trip I was opening up more and more to the spiritual side of my life. I was in another growth period and I was feeling things that I had never experienced before. When we arrived in San Antonio, it felt very good. Psychically, spiritually and emotionally, it just felt good. We decided to stay in San Antonio for an extended period, but we really didn't know how long that would be. We found an RV park and paid for a week in advance as we were feeling like we might stay even longer.

After getting settled in we decided to explore the area, visit the Alamo and see the sights of San Antonio, Texas. Then, we were going to visit some metaphysical bookstores to see if there were any psychic, spiritual, channeling or meditation groups we could attend while we were in town.

Before going to the Alamo we decided to see a movie about the battle that took place there. I had studied the Alamo in school and had gotten into the study pretty deeply. The movie covered the history and detailed some very interesting facts that we hadn't known before. Jackie and I always took any opportunity for the kids to get a history lesson and we were pleasantly surprised to find that we also learned more about the area.

When we arrived at the Alamo, a feeling started building within me. A sensation like when you walk into a room where there is a party going on and everyone has turned to see who it is that just arrived. Except that no one was looking at us. I was not expecting the feelings that were bubbling up from deep within my soul. I got incredibly emotional; it was almost as if I could feel the presence of the men and women who had died there. It was like their spirits were trying to communicate with me as if they were still there watching over the place. I was really moved by what I saw, heard and felt. I later realized that what I had felt there in that historical place was, in fact, a form of spirit communication. I just wasn't ready for it yet.

Earlier in the day, Jackie and I had searched the yellow pages to locate the local metaphysical bookstores. We needed some new material to read and thought that we might be able to get the companion tapes to Sanaya Roman's book, *Opening to Channel*. We found only three metaphysical bookstores that were open after 6:00 PM in the entire town. We decided that after we left the Alamo, we would visit them all and see what they had to offer.

The first bookstore was about to close when we got there. We had about five minutes to quickly look around. The energy felt kind of strange, as if we weren't supposed to be there. Since we were on a quest to find the "right" place for us, we were very tuned into our "feelings" and following them to a "T", we moved on to store number two.

When we arrived at the second store, they had some kind of meeting about UFO's and abduction survivors coming up in a couple days. They also had something going on about "Risen Masters" or something like that but neither was exactly what we were looking for. We bought a few books, but we still didn't find the tapes we desired so we decided to continue to the next store.

Up to this time, neither Jackie nor I had any idea what it was we were moving toward. We both had the feeling that we were not supposed to be in Seattle. All along I felt as though we were supposed to be in Texas. I had no idea why, I just knew that Texas was important. At the same time Jackie kept saying "I don't want to stay in Texas, I have no desire to be in Texas at all. I really want to go to New Mexico, to Santa Fe."

The next store was to be our final stop for the night. It was about 8:00 in the evening. As we entered the store, I felt a comfortable feeling coming over me. I moved from the entrance toward the closest table to me. On it were six or eight stacks of books laid out in two rows with three or four books in each stack. I quickly looked over the stack and one of the books seemed to jump out at me. It was titled, *Motherless Daughters*. I pointed it out to Jackie and she said, "I'll think about it," and went off to look at other items in the store. I moved on looking for the tapes that I desired. I found the book, *Opening To Channel* by Sonaya Roman, but no tapes.

Then Jackie looked in the back of the book and said, "There is an order form right here in the back of the book and a number to call to order them," so we decided to call in an order the next day. We bought a few more items including another very interesting looking book called *The Psychic Pathway* by Sonia Choquette.

When we got into the car, I said to Jackie, "Did you want that book, *Motherless Daughters?*"

She thought for a second, then said, "Yeah, but you have to go in and buy it for me. I don't want to get out and go back in."

I said "Sure, I'd be glad to."

I got out of the car and started in the door of the bookstore. As I opened the door, the lady behind the counter was looking right at me. Our eyes locked and without another word, she said to me, "I recommend that book right over there." She pointed to the table that held the book, *Motherless Daughters*.

"Amazing. I was just coming back in to buy that book," I said as I reached down to pick it up.

Then she said something surprising, "No, not that book, the one in front of it."

I looked down at the table and saw a little unobtrusive white book with the picture of a man standing in front of a lake. The title was *Conversations With God, an uncommon dialogue, Book 1*. The author was Neale Donald Walsch.

"Interesting title," I thought and then I said, "Looks like an interesting book. I'll take it, too." I paid for the books and left the store. I was unaware that I was about to move into the next awesome part of my life, my total awakening!

Chapter Three

The Awakening

- Changing Directions -

Conversations With God was the single most important book that I had ever purchased up to that moment. This book was the key for me to change the direction of my entire life. The information in that book caused me to understand what my life is to be about. It heralded a time in my life when I took a look back at almost everything that I had ever been or done and made a judgment as to whether I wanted it to continue in this manner any longer. It made me look at all my accomplishments, or lack thereof, and see how my life was going and what I wanted to do or not do about it. In essence, it "changed my life."

After purchasing the books I went back out to the car to my waiting family. Jackie said in a kind of whining, droning voice, "Now what did you buy?"

"You're not going to believe this," I said. I then related the story about what happened in the bookstore.

"That's interesting," Jackie said. "Must be a sign!" she proclaimed, with a bit of sarcastic laughter, and we all laughed and agreed. As we headed back to the motorhome, I had no idea how prophetic those words would become.

When we arrived at the motorhome the kids wanted to watch a "Star Wars" tape. As we were watching the video, I noticed that Jackie had picked up the *Conversations With God* (CWG) book and was reading it.

I said, "How is that book?"

"Cool," she replied with a smile. "It is really interesting, but I will tell you more later."

"Great," I said, "I want to hear all about it when 'Star Wars' is over."

After the tape was over, we were putting things away and Jackie seemed mesmerized with that little white book. She appeared to be spellbound, as though she were in a trance.

"Jack, are you still with us?" I asked. "How is my book?" Then as though answering myself I said, "That must be a great book. I think I'll enjoy reading it."

Then Jackie piped up and chuckling said, "*My* book is great."

"Oh?" I laughingly questioned. "Your book? Since when did it become your book?"

"Since I started reading it tonight," she laughed and stated matter-of-factly.

I felt something come over me then. It was almost a jealousy of sorts, but I was wishing that I had been reading the book instead of watching the movie with my kids. I felt like I was missing something. That is probably why I awoke at 5:30 AM the next morning thinking about this book. I had to read it right then and it couldn't wait. It was a "burning desire" that I had to extinguish. So I got out of bed and picked up the book that would change the path of my life and give me the insight and tools I needed to proceed with the next part of my journey.

As I read the author's account of his conversation with God, I began to feel a kind of connection with him. I found myself saying, "I knew that. I knew that. I felt that. Yeah, I can relate to that." Most of the book brought about a feeling of knowing, but a lot of it brought on the feeling of relief. Relief in the form of really "knowing" that there was no right or wrong. That life had a definite and different path for each and every one of us, and the path that we choose was chosen by us before we ever got here. I also learned that we chose it as individuals, for us as individuals, but at the same time very much intertwining with each other's path. There was a lot of information to digest, and it would take me some time to finish it. I was still reading at about 9:00 AM when I heard a rustling in the bunk above the cab, where Jackie and I slept.

Jackie was looking down at me from the bunk with a grin on her face. She said still smiling broadly, "How do you like my book?"

"I love *my* book," I laughingly retorted. We went on joking for about ten minutes about whose book it was until I said, "O.K. that's it, we have to go and buy another book for you Jack, 'cause this is my book."

"Oh alright," she said sarcastically, "you can have my book if you buy me another one." At which point the kids woke up and Joel, in a serious but joking manner said, "But Dad, that was my book so you have to buy me another one too!" Then Leo, my younger son, and Andrea both voiced their desire to have a book so when we went back to the bookstore, I bought four more copies, one for each of us to read. As it turned out, the book made such an impact on us that we eventually bought about 45 books over the next five or six months and gave them to friends and acquaintances.

After reading the statements in CWG that I took as truths, I felt that everything in my path was pointing to us continuing on our journey. That journey also pointed to us staying in San Antonio for a while longer. After I had looked extensively for computer jobs, I even went out and applied for a manager's job at a local automotive repair shop.

That afternoon we all went to the office in the RV Park and decided to see if we could get a month-to-month space. The people were so nice and helpful that we really felt we were supposed to be there. While we were standing in the office talking to them about the only space that was open on a month-to-month basis, the lady behind the counter noticed that we had three kids.

She said, "Are there five of you?"

"Yes," I answered, "why?"

"Well, we only allow four people to a spot, so I am sorry but we can't rent a month-to-month RV space to you."

"You're kidding," I said while laughing nervously, "only four to a site?"

"Really," she continued kind of sheepishly, "I am sorry, but those are the rules of the park."

Now normally, I would have put up some kind of argument, gotten angry and raised a ruckus, but I immediately had an overwhelming feeling that I had just been given a sign from the other side.

I very calmly said, "I understand completely." Then I turned and asked my family to come with me and leave to go back to the motorhome.

When we got to the car, we sat quietly in it for a few minutes kind of reassessing the situation. I turned to them and just said, "Let's go back to the motorhome and talk about this. We have a decision to make."

That was in December of 1995, about ten days before Christmas Day. We had driven around San Antonio the day after finding the book, and noticed all the beautiful lights and Christmas decorations, and were feeling all alone and out of place.

I was reading and understanding that to be free you only had to "be", and to "be" was a state of mind, body and soul coming together. We felt that our minds, bodies and souls needed to be around family to be able to reach that state of be-ing. We also felt lost and the kids missed their cousins, so we took a vote and decided to head back to Seattle.

The one point that I didn't really see until much later was that this trip was specifically for the purpose of us finding and reading *Conversations With God*. That was why I had seen us taking the route through Texas even though Jackie was adamant about going through Santa Fe, New Mexico. This fact is true for everyone: we all have a specific path to follow. If we would just get out of our own way and quit trying to *make it happen* and just *let it happen*, life will become much easier to live. We can begin living instead of just existing.

- Returning Home -

We had a few days to get home before Christmas and we were all pretty much ready to go back to Seattle and see everyone we had left. For some unknown reason, inside, I knew that this was the right decision. It was exactly what we were supposed to do; the next process to go through. Coming back home was a major turning point in my life and during the trip everyone was reading and remembering. The kids remembering what they had left behind, Jackie and I remembering "who we really are."

On the trip home there was one incident that showed just how much the kids were getting from the CWG book.

They were all saying how great it was going to be to get back in their old schools. I have to go backward a little to put this into perspective.

When we were living in my mother-in-law's home before it sold, the kids were in the Seattle School District, in schools determined by where we lived. Once the house sold and we moved into a motorhome, we just kept taking them to their respective bus stops and they continued in school for about a month that way. So when we were on our way back, being innocent children, they just assumed that we would be able to do the same.

Well, we had been gone for quite some time and I had some doubts creeping in about them getting back in their schools. I didn't think Andrea would have a problem getting back into her school, but both Joel and Leo were in special programs that required applications for admittance.

I told Leo about how hard it might be to get back into his school because he was in the "gifted" program. He just looked up at me and said, "But Dad, in *Conversations With God* it says that you only have to have the 'faith of a mustard seed', and I have a lot more than that!" I just sat there looking into these big beautiful innocent blue eyes and was given a gift of faith by my son. Thank you for that, Leo.

Even so, being the adult, I felt it was my responsibility to set him straight. Let him know what the world was about. But I couldn't. I just said, "Well I hope you are right, but I really don't feel like it is going to happen."

He just looked at me with that determination that Leo can get and said bluntly, "Well, I have the faith of a mustard seed that I will be back in my school and I know that I will be."

Then he smiled as Joel and Andrea both piped in at

almost the same instant, "Me too, Dad." I was overwhelmed by their strength.

When we arrived in the Seattle area, we went to Jackie's sister's house and parked the motorhome in her driveway until we figured out where the kids would go to school. We had been gone about six weeks and it was Christmas vacation, so we had some time before we had to make a final decision about school. Christmas was fun and we had a little tree in the motorhome with presents around it. All was perfect then.

- *Starting Over* -

We were home and now I had to figure out what to do for a living. It was easy; I just put an ad in the paper and I was back in the computer repair business. The business was rolling in. As they knew would happen, the kids did get back into their respective schools, and life was moving forward. I felt I was too, and it really felt good to be back home.

We got a month-to-month rental space at a local RV park and I was running my computer repair/consulting business from our motorhome. I would receive phone calls there and then go to homes and offices to do whatever type of computer work that needed to be done. I was an excellent computer technician and had been for over eight years. I felt I could provide the things like a good income, a house, a new car; all the material things that I thought would make me feel better about who I was being and what I was doing.

It just wasn't enough and I was coming to the realization that there was something much more important coming my way than any "job" that I was doing, or had ever done before. I had been dealing with self-worth issues in every aspect of my life and now I could see that this issue was coming to a head.

The beginning of the end of my relationship with Jackie started when we bought a laptop computer. It was a great machine and I felt it would be a tremendous help in my business. All my desktop computers were in storage, and I convinced Jackie that we should buy it.

She reluctantly agreed and said, "OK, but only if you teach me how to use it."

"You got a deal," I replied. The next day I bought it and brought it home.

- Psychic Explosion -

From that point on, my life took a drastic and somewhat chaotic turn of direction. The first thing that started to change was my use of the computer. I began to use it to highlight my psychic abilities that had been dwelling under the surface. I hadn't had a place to exercise my psychic muscles. I felt that since I had just finished reading the book, *The Psychic Pathway*, and was shown how to "play" psychic, I needed someplace to do just that.

I had heard from one of my friends that America Online (AOL) had some interesting metaphysical chat rooms and that people even gave free psychic readings online. I thought, "That's an interesting idea." I could do that and "play" psychic as Sonia taught in her book and maybe my own psychic ability would get stronger.

I keep referring to "playing psychic" so I feel I need to explain. In Sonia Choquette's book, *The Psychic Pathway*, she explains that when you "play" psychic, the ego doesn't have time for games so it goes away and is not involved. This allows the psychic ability to come forth and grow stronger because there is no ego involved. I know, it sounds very strange but let me tell you, it worked for me.

When I logged on to AOL for the first time, I didn't know anything about online services or chat rooms. I knew about the Internet and the research that could be done there because of my involvement with it at my former job in a senior high school. So when I got online and found all these people there chatting (typing) in areas they called rooms, it struck a chord with me.

"This is cool!" I thought. After spending a little while getting familiar with the rooms, I decided to open a room and go for it. The room I opened was called "FREE PSYCHIC READING". This was the next greatest event in my life. All the psychic stuff before this had been with people I knew or at least was acquainted with, but now in this room I was "playing" psychic with people I didn't even know. I just felt that it was the right time. I know my guides were saying, "Go for it. Do it. It is time."

So there I was in a room all alone, waiting for someone to come and ask me some questions. To allow me "play" psychic and have some fun and maybe even help someone. I was excited beyond belief. Very calm but at the same time scared silly. The **D-o-u-b-t** was creeping in because I just wasn't sure of my ability yet.

When the first person came in and asked a question, I didn't have any idea what was going to happen. So I just waited, greeted the person with a "hello" and a "welcome", and sat back to wait for a question.

The words appeared on the screen as if screaming at me, "ARE YOU THE PSYCHIC?"

Now I had to answer. I had no choice. There was no one else in here but me, and this other name on the screen. "Yes," I typed very apprehensively.

I had to remind myself, "Dennis, remember, you are

just playing psychic tonight. So don't let that 'yes' go to your head. You must also remember, you aren't doing anything that isn't supposed to be done, or passing information that isn't supposed to be passed." I also started something else that night that carries on in the readings I do now. I silently said a prayer of thanksgiving to God for all the information that He/She would pass through me to all the people I would come in contact with during this session. I am just a channel for this information to travel through. I am a willing conduit of spirituality.

I will never forget that first night. I was sitting in front of my laptop as people started filling the room. First there was one, then two, then five, then twelve. Finally the room was filled to capacity with all kinds of questions being typed on the screen. I was answering questions as fast as I could. There were questions about money, jobs, careers, schooling, cats, lovers and relationships. They were coming up with every conceivable question, or so I thought, that could be asked. They were coming so fast that I didn't even have time to think about one before the next one was flashing on the screen. I answered each and every question that I saw with a love and heartfelt warmth of a true psychic and spiritual person. I really wanted to help each of those souls on the other side of that computer screen.

It was at the point of overload that I noticed this one person kept asking the same question, "When will I meet the love of my life? I am tired of waiting!"

I don't even remember the screen name, but I answered, "I see you meeting him within the next 90 days, and it will be wonderful." Then I went on to the next question thinking that I had answered it fully.

This person came back with, "What is this person's name?"

It was then that I saw the name "Bob" flash in front of my eyes, so I typed "Bob".

I went on to someone else but the person came back with, "Did you know that I am a man?"

I typed, "Oh, I am sorry, but that is the name that came up."

He said, "Oh, don't be sorry. I am gay."

That was a surprise, but I realized had I been taking myself seriously as a psychic, I would have probably asked him if he was male or female and edited myself. As it was, I learned a very good lesson there and then. I was learning to trust, but the total trust was to be some time in coming.

There were others like that during that first night, but the biggest and best part of the night was when someone asked, "Do you see any major things for me in my future?"

To protect this person's identity, I will refer to him/her as "SN123". The first vision that came was the picture of a hospital and the words "major visit" emblazoned over it. So I said, "I see a major hospital stay for you." I didn't even realize the enormity of what I had just said. It was as if the words just shot out of my fingers and onto the screen. I thought, "Oh my God, what did I type?"

SN123 immediately typed back, "Exactly what kind of major hospital stay?"

That is when I really had to trust because the next thing that came through was "sex change operation."

I turned to Jackie who had been watching all of this transpire and said, "I just got that this person is having a sex change operation. I don't know if I can say that!"

She said, "I wouldn't, but you need to do what you

need to do," yet this nervous laughter was coming out of her.

So I said, "Well, here goes nothing," as I typed the words, "I see you having a sex change operation."

Silence. There was no answer from **SN123** at all. Everyone else in the room was going nuts and asking all kinds of questions and I was feverishly typing, trying to answer each and every one. All the while little boxes would flash on the screen as I was typing but then as soon as I tapped a key, they would disappear. They would never be on the screen long enough for me to read and I didn't know what they were or how to get them to stay.

Then there was a message in the chat room from **SN123** that said, "Did you get my IM?"

I typed, "What is an IM?"

Almost everyone in the room replied and some gave me directions on how to retrieve an IM. For those of you who have never been in a chat room, an IM is an "Instant Message" between you and another user on the computer. The dialog is then private and no one else can see what is being typed.

Now that we had cleared up what an IM was and how to get it, I looked at mine. In the box was an IM from **SN123**. To my utter amazement it said, **"You are absolutely right."** I almost fell out of my chair.

"Whoa, amazing," Jackie said. "That is too cool."

I just sat there, repeating silently, "Thank you God, thank you for this gift." I went on to answer many more questions that night for **SN123** that provided me with proof that has helped me in learning to trust this gift that I have been blessed with. That night was a major turning point for me. It is something that has helped me along this path for a few years now and I feel it will continue for quite a few more.

- Neale and Co. -

It was sometime in February of 1996, right around my birthday, when I heard from a member of my meditation group that Neale Donald Walsch was going to be speaking at a small church in Anacortes, Washington. He would be there on Friday, February 22nd, and at another church, in Mount Vernon, on Saturday night. I had finished reading CWG and was looking for other people who had read it to maybe start a study group. We decided to go and take the kids with us because they had all expressed an interest in meeting the author.

I had already finished my first reading of CWG and we had signed up for a three-day retreat at Neale's Heartlight retreat facility in southern Oregon. It was called "The Awakening" and promised to be a very spiritually centered retreat. It was about a month away and we were excitedly looking forward to it. So to get a chance to meet Neale before the retreat and see just who he was, well, we just had to do it.

Anacortes, Washington is a small town nestled on the banks of Puget Sound and is a shipping port for the oil tankers that come down from Alaska with loads of crude oil. It is about a 50-mile drive to get to the church from where we lived, so we had about a two-hour trip just to drive up and back. We had fun driving and anticipating what he was going to be like. We expected him to tell us about how he wrote the book and maybe clarify some questions that we had. We were not disappointed in any way.

When Neale walked into the room, he was wearing a

loose fitting top and pants that were made of a white cotton material and Birkenstock sandals. He looked like a guru should look. In fact, and maybe that was just my perception of my expectations, but I swear, to me, he looked like Jesus Christ with glasses. By that I mean he had the quality of a man who was connected and he was someone that "knew" something that I didn't. This was someone from whom I could learn. I know now that it was a "recognition" of him. I knew this man who walked into the room, but I couldn't figure out where from or how I knew him. I just knew him!

As he began to speak, there was a "softness" in his voice, a caring for the souls who had come to hear what he had to say. I turned to look at my kids and was amazed at what I saw. This man mesmerized them, as he did me, with his quiet, loving tone. They looked like they were watching a Saturday morning cartoon, totally tuned into what was being sent to them via Neale. My son Leo had a cough and Neale offered him some of the water in his cup. I expected Leo to turn him down because Leo normally won't even drink out of a cup that his mother or I had used. To my amazement and delight, he accepted the water without even the slightest hesitation.

The event was a very interesting and informative meeting that left us with the feeling that we wanted to hear more, to connect with this man even more closely. After the talk we all had the opportunity to chat a little with him and to have him autograph our books. We purchased tickets to the next night's engagement because the connection was so strong. We enjoyed the second talk just as much and looked forward to the retreat coming up in March.

On the drive home that night I knew my life had changed. It had changed even more than it had after reading the book. I had a new understanding of what was being said in the book and what it meant to me. We joked about how we were going to be more forgiving just as a car on the freeway cut us off. We talked about how we were going to accept ourselves and learn to love ourselves more. It was during the ride home that a new feeling came over me. A feeling of having a direction again. We were excited while anticipating all the good things that were coming; looking forward with delight and starting to do all those metaphysical things that we had enjoyed before.

- *The New House* -

It was in late February that the next turn in my path took hold. Up until this point we had still been kind of toying with the idea of leaving Seattle again. Then the house deal came up. It was a perfect deal for us. A down payment for the lease with an option to buy, and then payments on a real estate contract. The bad part was that the down payment was non-refundable, and the house was 15 miles from the kids' schools, but we were not worried because we just "knew" that everything would work out for us.

We moved into the house with an anticipation of returning to real life and not living in a motorhome anymore. Everything was working out pretty well so far. Now we were ready to proceed on with our lives. We decided to let the kids finish the school year at their Seattle schools, and every morning I would drive them to their respective bus stops.

Jackie was quickly learning to use the computer and was enjoying the Internet. Since we were now living in a house, I had my full sized computer set up so she could use the laptop for learning and exploring.

It was about this time that my sister Wendy told us about a service called Prodigy. It was an online service much like America Online, but it had a larger metaphysical selection. So we decided to try it. It was great fun and it was a good area for me because I could create a private room to give free private readings. I no longer had to be in the middle of a crowded chat room giving readings to everyone all at the same time.

Both Jackie and I were having a ball online. We enjoyed meeting new people and making new acquaintances. It was like a whole new world had opened up for us both, and our personal life seemed to be coming together, too. This went on for about two or three weeks before we went to the first retreat hosted by Neale Donald Walsch.

- The First Retreat -

This was the first of three retreats offered by Neale that I would attend in the next four months. It was to be another major turning point in this part of my life. The retreat, held at a new facility named Heartlight, was entitled "The Awakening". It was an interesting title, but would not seem appropriately named until we were leaving.

Jackie and I flew down to Medford Oregon, where the retreat was to be held, on two of the smallest planes we had ever flown on. It was interesting yet kind of scary, too. A woman named Rita, one of the staff members, met us at the airport. She was also the person responsible for booking Neale for events. She was very interesting and we enjoyed spending time with her.

On the way to Heartlight we chitchatted about many things including music, what Rita did for a living, and how we came to find the book. As we were driving up into the mountains toward the retreat site, the feeling of calm excitement was coming over me. Along the way there was some kind of store and up on top of a very tall flagpole was a light in the shape of a heart! It was a real heart light! I thought, "How appropriate, here is a heart light as we are heading toward the retreat site called 'Heartlight'. I have to remember to tell Neale about this."

I said to Rita, "Look, a heart light up in the air! It must be a sign!"

She laughed and said, "Wow, I have never seen that, I wonder why they have that light up? Yeah, it must be a sign of good fortune or something."

It was only a few more miles up the road to the retreat site but it seemed like 50. We were very tired as it had been a long trip from home. I was also anxious to get there and see what this place was like, and I was looking forward to seeing Neale and Nancy again. It had been less than a month since we had first met them in Anacortes, Washington, but I felt like we were on our way to visit old friends. I had spoken to another person on Neale's staff, Will Richardson, many times on the phone about the retreat. I had no idea what he looked like, so I was also anxious to meet him. I just had a very strong feeling that these people were about to have an intense and extreme effect on my personal life, as I knew it then, and I wanted to get started, right now!

When we got there, it was dark and very hard to tell what the place was like. The first thing I noticed was that there were two buildings that looked sort of like a ski chalet. The main building had the kitchen, and a meeting room that also served as the dining area. Neale and Nancy's private residence and office area were on the main floor with the kitchen and dining area.

Will had gone into town to pick up someone who had arrived at the airport after us. Neale and Nancy were there and they got up and greeted us with warm deep hugs and they really seemed genuinely happy to see us. It felt so wonderful to connect with them again.

When Will got back he showed us to our sleeping areas, which were dormitory style bunking with the women upstairs and the men downstairs. I fell asleep, eagerly anticipating the weekend's events.

- The Comet -

It was a beautiful spring-like morning. The sun was shining, the birds were chirping in the trees, and it felt like we really were far up in the woods and away from civilization. It was crisp and clear and there was an air of anticipation running through the people. I could feel the energy of the people and it felt good.

During the next two days and nights we experienced the awakening that was promised and much more. One light moment came during Saturday night. The entire group was outside watching the much publicized comet when a shooting star went streaking across the sky, crossing the tail of the comet.

As it did Will commented, to the amusement of everyone there, "And now a word from our sponsor!"

It really fit the feelings of connection we were all having at that moment. It was one of the beautiful moments of the retreat and it was like a sign to us all that what we were doing was being blessed by God Herself.

Because of the personal nature of "The Awakening", I am not at liberty to give any details about the events that transpired there, other than my own. I am happy to say that I went away from that retreat with a new understanding of who and what it is that I am. I was allowed the opportunity to move forward on my path and I accepted it. It was another key turning point for me. It was three days of intense growth, intense soul searching, and questioning of life itself.

This was the point where life as I knew it changed. I went away, knowing that my life was never going to be the same again. I was filled with a confirmation that all of the thoughts that I had about life were true. I was "awakened" to myself, to "who I really am". Now it was time to go home and put it all into practice. To begin to live my life as it was shown to me during this retreat. I had declared who and what I am and now I had to "be" it.

Chapter Four

The Onion Peeling

- *Computer Friends* -

Now that the retreat was over and we were back home, we could start moving forward with our lives. With our new understanding, we could begin focusing on establishing ourselves in a new community. I had new ideas on which direction to take my business, and I had begun doing readings online almost every night. Jackie was also getting online and beginning to help people in her own way. She was tapping into an area of healing and using it for the good of many other people. Life was proceeding in a growth oriented and loving way.

It was the middle of March 1996 when we returned from the retreat. During the course of the next two to three weeks, I did a lot of growing because of the psychic readings that I was doing online. We were spending a lot of time logging on and chatting with people. It was becoming a nightly ritual that after the kids would go to bed, between 9:00 and 9:30 PM, we would log onto our computers. I used my desktop computer and Jackie used the laptop, chatting, doing readings and generally making new friends. It was during one of these sessions that, unknown to me, Jackie was approached by a man who started giving her a psychic reading.

That was April 12th, 1996. Two days later we were driving along checking out garage sales when I got really hungry. I stopped at a little convenience store and bought a couple of hot dogs for us to eat. I came back to the car and while we were eating, Jackie kept talking about the online people she was meeting. She talked about how cool it was that she was finding out and becoming "who she really is" and really opening up. I could feel that she was working up to something very important, but I didn't know what it was. I could just sense that something big was about to be said.

She continued talking about the people online then she said, "I met someone in a chat room that really blew me away."

"Oh?" I asked, "What do you mean by that?"

"Well, this guy in the room said to me, 'You have 3 kids, you are female, you are 43 years old and divorced.'"

She then said, "I told him that he was right except for the divorced part, and that I have been happily married for 22 years." Then she continued, "That was pretty wild but it was the connection I felt toward him that surprised me. At first I thought he was just a pervert trying to make time, but then I started feeling a real connection that was weird."

"Wow," I said, "What is his name?"

"His screen name is BROKEN EAGLE, but his real name is Jeff."

"So, what is it that really blew you away?" I questioned.

"Well," she cautiously replied, "you know how I have declared that I am 'Love'? Well, I love him!"

At that moment you could have knocked me over with a feather. Talk about being "blown away"!

"Wha, wha, what do you mean, you love him?" I beseeched her. "How can you love someone across a phone line?" My voice was rising. "What do you mean you *love* him?" I said, now half screaming. "You're married to me."

"Wait a minute, Dennis," Jackie said. "It's not like that.

I love everyone; I am love." She continued. "It's like we learned at the retreat. I'm just declaring who I am and I am love!"

Even though she was saying that what she was feeling was a declaration of her awakening, I was psychically feeling and seeing something much deeper.

Then she looked at me with a very strange look and said, "Dennis, I hope you can understand this and will support me in my awakening."

At that instant I saw it all. I saw everything that was going to happen in the next few months. I feel I was given an instant view of what was to lie ahead for me and my wife in the coming months. I couldn't handle it. At that moment, I began what was to be the most intensive onion peeling of my life. I was embarking upon a journey of self-discovery. I started working through all the layers of who and what I perceived I was or had been for the majority of my life.

After we went home, I decided to find out who and what this "Broken Eagle" was all about. I felt he was the ruination of my life. I felt he had come between my wife and me. He was tearing apart everything that I knew. So I decided to confront this evilness head-on. I got online and began a conversation with him.

I logged on that night with a quest in mind. I was going to get this guy to back off and tell him in no uncertain terms that I was not going to stand for him coming between my wife and me.

As my computer was connecting I thought about how I would approach this guy. He obviously was a wolf, just waiting in the wings for any unsuspecting woman who might be just a little bit needy or weak. I didn't see my wife as either of those, so I couldn't figure it out. Then I decided that he couldn't be any more than a low life jerk. I would just go online and overpower him with my energy.

This was my human side coming to the forefront. My spiritual side was quietly scolding me saying, "Wait a minute Dennis, you know it is supposed to be this way. You know your life is now in a changing time. You know it is perfect and everything will work out perfectly."

Well, was I ever surprised! Not only was the guy a very nice man, but he and I started conversing online and I even grew to like him. I still had this feeling in the back of my head that he was someone important that would have a negative impact in my life and I wasn't wrong. Although the negative impact was not a truth in the spiritual world, it was in the human world in which I lived.

Psychically, I was becoming very sensitized to my third eye and my sixth sense. I was being given glimpses of future events. I saw that this man and his involvement with Jackie were going to emotionally tear me apart. I saw that I would be getting a divorce. I was really focused on Jeff and Jackie and I saw them being together, but what I wasn't being given at that time was the fact that they would not choose to be together in the future. In fact, I was being pushed by the Universe to move on with my life and was unknowingly being prepared to meet my twin soul.

I started the terrible shedding of my past. I felt like a snake that was shedding layer after layer of skin. I felt at the same time like an onion. As I peeled off a layer I would hurt. I would cry and feel the pain of losing, and then the next layer would come off. Then I would go through the same process over again.

All this time Jackie was saying, "No, Dennis, he is just a friend and that is all. I love you and we are together."

At the same time she was saying that in my psychic eye I was being given visions of Jackie and Jeff together and it would tear me apart. I could see that she was falling deeper and deeper in dependence on his input. He was a "key" for her, but at the time she couldn't see it. She really was falling in love with him just from his connection over the computer. I know that people can feel energy this way because I had been doing readings online just that way. I was sensitized to it and knew that when a connection is made, it is for a reason.

- The Second Retreat -

During the next month it became more apparent that life was changing rapidly. I was really feeling crazy. I thought that I was losing my mind and really couldn't go on without some kind of help. I knew that the normal counselor would not help me in this situation. What I needed was some "soul" counseling.

That's when it hit me: Neale was having a retreat coming up soon in April and maybe I could go to that. I could go there and make a stronger connection with Neale, Nancy, Will and Rita. I really felt close to those people and just maybe I could help CWG to move forward in my own way, and at the same time, try to understand what was happening in my life.

I called Neale and asked what I could do for them at the retreat. I didn't have the money to pay for the weekend, but I offered to work in the kitchen and run the food crew if I could come to the retreat. I told him my experience as a cook in the U.S. Coast Guard qualified me for kitchen work. He agreed and said that he would also try to come up with something that I could do in conjunction with the foundation, ReCreation. I was ecstatically happy about that. I really needed to get centered on a spiritual path, and this was the perfect place.

As it worked out, both Jackie and I were able to go to the retreat. This time instead of flying down to Medford from Seattle, we rented a Lincoln Town Car since our own car would not be able to make the trip, and drove the 700 miles.

The trip was fun, but also very painful for me. All I could think about was how my wife was in love with another man and I was unable to convince her otherwise.

At one point, I asked her, "Are we going to make it? Are we going to get a divorce?"

She replied, "I don't know what is going to happen in the future, but we are together and I know I love you now."

I know she was saying it to console me, but there was no life in her words anymore. I knew it was just a matter of time. It was just around the bend and I was scared to death. I was totally afraid of the unknown. I didn't know what I was going to do. I just knew that I had to do something and the retreat with Neale seemed to be the perfect thing to do.

During the trip we stopped in at a mall in Vancouver, Washington. Jackie had said that she wanted to get a Walkman type tape player for the retreat. It was so that she could listen to her meditation music at night before going to sleep. We had also purchased some tapes to listen to on the way. I had a weird feeling about this. Psychically, I saw a picture of her listening to music and thinking of Jeff. There was that churning in my stomach again. I hated that feeling.

As we drove on, we listened to a Bette Middler CD. When the song "Wind Beneath My Wings" came on I became choked up and started to cry. I didn't know why I was reacting this way. I figured I was just too emotional and that every sad or emotion grabbing song would affect me that way. As it was, Jackie later confided that she had gone in specifically to purchase that Bette Middler CD with the song "Wind Beneath My Wings" on it. Apparently Jeff had said that this particular song reminded him of her and that it was a special song for them. I had been correct in my feelings, but I was still doubting my own psychic ability then. For the longest time after that, I couldn't stand to hear that song. The strange thing is, for Alice that song has an entirely different feeling and is quite special for her.

When we arrived at Heartlight, it was like coming home. I felt so at peace there. It was different than before because I felt like the alumnus coming back. This was the third retreat Neale had offered after publishing CWG and I was happy to be here. It also felt different this time because I was coming to do some intensive processing. I had no idea how intensive this processing would be, but during the retreat I got in touch with deeply buried feelings that I had to confront.

Jackie and I had agreed to be the kitchen personnel, so we had to be in the kitchen before every meal to get everything ready. This put us in the fortunate position of being able to get to know each of the retreat participants very well, on a personal level, because everyone took a turn in the kitchen with us. It was nice, being able to make a bit of a different connection with them all. Because of that connection, when my feelings of needing to process came to the surface, I was not afraid to get up in front everyone and go through it. I felt very comfortable bearing my soul in front of these people. I felt safe.

On the first morning of the retreat I could feel my deep fears coming to the surface. I didn't know what was going to happen while we were here but I was ready for anything. When we came into the room to start the meeting, there in the middle of the room was a mattress that is always present for use in what is known as "Gestalt Therapy". It was a safe place to deal with anger or anything else that came up.

The first feeling that came through after seeing it was a growing anxiety. I knew I was going to be "at the mattress" very soon because the subjects that Neale was discussing were hitting me like a ton of bricks. I felt like there was a huge weight on my shoulders and I couldn't go on without dealing with it.

During each of his retreats, Neale invites people to have a dialogue with him or come forward and sit on the mattress as he helps them to confront the situations that may be stopping them from being who they really are.

He also had a short length of rubber hose and a stack of six or seven thick phone books in case what is being dealt with is anger. When I saw those phone books and the hose, I really felt the pull to go up and release some of the deep-seated anger I had buried away for so long.

It was as if I were in a movie. I watched myself move forward to the mattress. I saw myself take the rubber hose in my hand. Then it erupted. All of the anger that had been buried away for my whole life came tumbling to the surface. I exploded with emotion and began pounding on the phone books with such ferocity that it scared me. I didn't realize that I had so much anger buried away. I kept pounding and pounding at those phone books. Pages and bits of paper were flying around me as I would strike the processed trees with the length of hose. Neale was tossing the books to me like steaks to a hungry lion. Again and again, over and over, my arms would climb into the air and come slamming back down into the pages that were beginning to resemble pulp again. With each blow I could feel myself becoming lighter. I could feel the power erupting from deep within my soul.

And then it was over and I was completely drained. My body ached, my arms felt like limp ropes, my knuckles were hurting and when I looked at them, I saw blood. I had struck the phone books so hard, my hands had scraped on the mattress and ripped the skin off. I hadn't even noticed it until afterward.

The feeling that overcame me then was one of relief. I felt very calm and centered as though nothing could get to me or hurt me. Nothing could cause me pain from here on. I was hoping that this feeling would carry over into my life after I left the retreat. This is what I needed. It was a cleansing of sorts, but it was only a beginning.

Before coming to the retreat Jackie and I had arranged with Neale that we would stay over Sunday night, and on Monday discuss a few ideas he had on what we could do in conjunction with ReCreation. During the Monday meeting the discussion of a divorce came up.

"What if you were to get a divorce? Could you work together?" Neale had asked.

He wanted to be sure that we could and would work together on the concept even if we were not together in a marriage. I should have known then that my married days were numbered, because at an earlier time Neale shared with me that he had been a practicing psychic for over 20 years. This was just another sign of things to come.

Unfortunately, the human feeling of not wanting to fail at anything blinded me and I was not able to think clearly about what I was agreeing to. If I had been able to see the signs I would have known that some incredible changes were coming for me. I now had to go home and finish the process of the onion peeling.

On the drive home, while talking with Jackie, I could feel the life draining out of me. I felt like everything was turning upside down and I needed to find out where I was headed and what I was going to do. We hadn't even gotten 25 miles from Heartlight when it hit me: Neale was going to be facilitating a five day intensive retreat in Baltimore in June. I knew at that moment I had to be there, I didn't really know why, but I felt it was going to have a profound effect on my life. I thought that the effect was going to be on my spiritual growth and I was really trying to get out of the human and more into the spiritual side of this life.

We had been talking about our life together and where it was headed. Jackie had not been negative about it, she just had this nonchalant, "don't really care, I know it will work out perfectly" attitude. I, on the other hand, in my own way, was asking for a commitment that she was unable to give. I took that as a negative, when in fact she was being very positive about her life. She really didn't know what was coming up next for her and was being very honest about it. I felt my life slipping away.

- The Real Work Begins -

When we arrived home, what I call "The Onion Peeling" really began in earnest. I began to sink into this feeling of total despair; my life as I knew it was ending, quickly. I began to feel a hatred for this man who apparently had a soul connection with my wife. I also had feelings of liking the guy and it was very confusing.

The only place I felt connected was when I was on the computer giving psychic readings and helping people. It got me out of this world and into another place of love and comfort. It is hard to explain, but I know that everything was happening for a reason.

I began to use *Conversations With God* as a guidebook. When I would get into a tough situation, I would open it and right there would be the answer to the problems I was going through at that minute. It was uncanny. I knew there was a higher power at work here and I was beginning to realize that an unseen force was guiding my life. Someone or something was leading me on a path that was becoming increasingly harder to deny.

The moment that I knew something had to change was when I got to the bottom of the barrel, so to speak. It was one of the challenging moments of my life. It is actually a very low point in my life that is embarrassing to talk about. I also know that it was perfect in every way and I am telling it now to show how low and depressed I had gotten. I had been online doing some readings and as had become the nightly ritual, Jackie was online talking exclusively to Jeff. I had been trying to ignore the situation but it had become too much. My tolerance had reached the point of no return. I blew up and started yelling and just going off the deep end. I felt like I had lost my mind; I had gotten to the bottom. I had peeled off the final layer and now it felt like raw nerves were showing. I couldn't take anymore and without thinking, I went and got out my pistol. It was a .357 Magnum. I took it into the kitchen dining room area where Jackie was sitting. I don't really remember all the events in the sequence, but the main part I remember is sitting there with the gun pressed against my temple. It was as though I were an onlooker watching the events unfold in front of me. I couldn't believe what was happening and yet I couldn't stop it.

I heard myself saying, "Jack, if you don't stop this relationship I might as well just pull the trigger and get it over with because you are tearing me apart. I can't stand the unsure feelings of it all. Right now I feel so empty."

I continued with, "Not knowing what is going to happen one day to the next, and watching you being online with this guy, knowing that you are having an emotional affair with him, I might as well shoot myself in the head."

She looked at me with disbelief and very calmly said, "Dennis, I really don't want you to do that but if you must, I can't do anything to stop you. I have to allow you to be who you really are."

She then continued, " But remember that I love you, always have and always will, no matter what happens."

It was at that moment that it all became very clear, at least in the way that I was looking at it. This relationship was dying. It was dying a slow torturous death and the events of the following few weeks would prove that.

As I slowly took the gun down from my temple I simply said, "I know now why I am going to Baltimore. It is to decide whether to continue on in this marriage or not."

I then said to her, "I also feel that it is a time for you to decide what you want out of this life. Whether you want this relationship or not." She agreed and I left the room to go to my computer and see if I could connect with anyone. Maybe a couple of readings; by helping someone else it would help me, too.

When I got online there were a lot of people that I knew chatting in the room. It occurred to me that maybe I should check there and see if anyone that I had connected with lived in Baltimore. I sent out a note telling my online friends that I would be in Baltimore and that I would love to connect with them if it were possible. I actually put it out in the room and was amazed at the responses I got. There were a lot of people who said they would like to get together and meet.

Out of all the people, I connected best with a woman

named Lori. She lived in Baltimore and said she and her boyfriend Greg would love to get together when I was there. They were willing to host a gathering at their home and sent out online invitations.

Pretty soon we had about 10 people who said they would like to meet. We finally had four or five people that would be able to get together that week I'd be there. I was feeling much better then and went to bed looking forward to meeting my online friends in Baltimore.

- Jackie's Dilemma -

It was Friday night, June 7th, and I was getting ready to go to the Baltimore retreat. Jackie was going through her regular ritual of getting online and going into a private room with Jeff. I was also online in a metaphysical room chatting with a few people about life. While there, I saw that Jackie was off in a room chatting with Jeff and I began going through my "stuff". I was feeling like I wanted to reach out and tear out this guy's heart and stomp on it, but I suppressed the urge. At the same time I was thinking that, I saw Jackie get off line. I was down in the basement and I could hear her walking down the hall toward the bedroom. I wondered why she had left. I decided to go upstairs and check on her.

When I went upstairs I found her in our bedroom with the lights off. I asked if everything was ok and she answered, "It doesn't matter. You really don't want to know."

I said, "Yes I do, come on Jack, we may not be getting along but I still care about you."

I meant that from my heart. I always have and always will love her in a very special way. At that moment I was very concerned about her because she sounded like she had been crying.

I repeated, "What's wrong?"

She said apprehensively, "Are you sure you want to know?"

I said very quickly, "Yes, please tell me what's going on. I'm concerned about you. I'm also concerned about us."

Then she said, "You know you are going to be gone all week and you are staying the weekend with Lori and Greg?"

"Yes, why?"

"Well," she tearfully said, " I just talked to Jeff and I am upset."

"Why, what is going on?" I was getting a little angry that she had actually talked to him over the phone. "You seem to be very upset. What did he say to you?"

"Yes, I am very upset," she exclaimed, tears welling up in her eyes. Then she started crying harder than I had ever seen her cry before. She was beside herself and could hardly talk. I was really concerned now.

I asked her again, "What has upset you this much? What could have happened to cause this?" I was at a loss. I couldn't understand what was going on until she finally told me what it was.

She then said, "I booked a flight to Utah to go and see him, and he told me no! He told me not to come. He said, 'You are a married lady and it's not right. I don't want you here.'" Then she broke down and wept profusely, bawling and just completely losing control.

I was now in a rage and screamed at her, "What do you mean you booked a flight to Utah? When? When were you going to go? While I am in Baltimore at Neale's retreat?" I was so mad that I couldn't see straight.

"See, I knew you wouldn't understand."

I knew that I had gone to another world because the one I used to live in just caved in around me. I was totally devastated. I didn't know what else to do, so I went downstairs and went online to see if I could find a caring soul to talk to. I was alone in this situation and I didn't have any idea what to do. I soon went to bed and tried to sleep, but I stayed awake most of the night thinking.

- Energy Lady -

When I got up in the morning I was just as upset as I had been the night before. I was feeling so bad, I thought about what a friend of mine used to say when he was down. He would say, "I am so low I could walk under a snake's belly with a top hat on!" That is just about how I felt that morning. It felt as though my life was totally screwed. I ventured onto the computer to see if anyone was online to chat with. I saw my friend that I was going to spend some time with in Baltimore. I had readily accepted Lori's invitation to stay with her and Greg, and was looking forward to connecting with some real spiritual people off line and in person.

Lori is an energy worker. This means that she is able to manipulate energy and use it in a healing manner for anyone that needs it. When I saw her, she had come into the room and had immediately perceived my low energy.

She said, "Wow, Dennis, your energy feels very low. Would you let me help?"

I typed, "If you think you can help this situation, go for it."

She replied on the screen, "Ok, now what I want you to do is this. Close your eyes, put your feet flat on the floor and visualize a rose opening on your chest. When you have done that, type 'ok' and then prepare to receive energy from me. Ok?"

I replied that I would. Then when I was ready, I typed "OK" on the screen and stayed with the visualization. What happened next took me completely by surprise. I started vibrating. I could feel a warm feeling coming up through my feet and continuing through my body up to the top of my head. It was absolutely invigorating. This went on for about fifteen minutes. After she was done, I felt wonderful. I was almost in a state of being high without drugs. That feeling stayed with me for the rest of the day.

That day was Saturday and it went on pretty much without incident until late in the night when the online thing started again. Jackie was talking to Jeff and I was thinking about her actually booking a flight to Utah. Even though Jeff had turned her down, it was really having an ugly effect on me. I really didn't know where to go or what to do. I felt totally alone in the world. I had nowhere to turn and no one to turn to. I was completely devastated and unable to comprehend how someone to whom I had been married and lived with for so long could do that. I finally went off to bed feeling totally dejected and beat up.

Sunday morning came and I woke up early. I again went downstairs and went online to see if anyone was around to talk to. Lori was there again and immediately hailed me with an IM and asked how I was doing. When I related to her how I had been feeling, she quickly said, "Looks like you could use some more energy work."

"That's for sure, and I could use it right now if you're not busy."

She typed, "I came on because I felt you would be here and would be needing some energy work done. So here I am. You know the process so close your eyes and sit back."

She proceeded to send me energy and I again started vibrating. It was incredible, and I felt rejuvenated again.

The connection that I had made with Lori was a very important one for me. I was to find out just how important in the following few days. Actually, events would transpire on the next day that would change the very way that I looked at life. I didn't know it then, but she would be a significant key in my connection to my twin soul. This was Sunday and at 10:00 PM I would be flying to Baltimore to begin a 5-day intensive retreat with Neale Donald Walsh. The rest of my day was spent getting ready to leave.

Chapter Five

Baltimore to Annapolis

- Lori and Greg -

It was Sunday night and I was flying toward what, I didn't know. I just knew I had to be there to meet some online friends and attend a retreat. The retreat was my third with Neale and promised to be very enlightening. I was flying the "red-eye" from Seattle to Baltimore, which leaves very late and arrives very early in the morning. Sometimes you can get some sleep, at least a little, and after the weekend I had just had, well, I needed some sleep. So I ate the little snack the airline gives you, read a little, then stretched out on the middle row of seats to grab some shut-eye. As luck would have it, no one had chosen to sit in my row and I was able to stretch out and sleep. After about three hours, I couldn't take the seat belt in my back and the uncomfortable way I had to lay, so I sat back up and continued re-reading *"Conversations With God"*. I read until we were getting ready to land. "So much for getting some rest," I muttered to no one in particular.

On arrival, my cyber friends, Lori and Greg, met me at the gate. They were smiling, cheerful, and very friendly. As we all hugged, I felt an instant connection with them both.

Lori said, "Hi Dennis. Welcome to Baltimore."

"Welcome," Greg repeated.

As we were waiting for my luggage I told them all about my trip from Seattle, and how I hadn't slept in the last three days except for the three hours on the flight. It was now early Monday morning, Eastern time. We chitchatted about all sorts of things until I got my luggage. After we got to the car and started toward their house, I talked about my marriage and how it was going down the tubes. About how I had blamed it all on the online "friend" that my wife had met and how I was coming to the conclusion that it was supposed to be this way but I just didn't know why. I continued to vent about my life until we arrived at their house.

At which time Lori said, "Dennis, I think that we are going to have to do some energy work on you very soon."

She told me that I had to learn how to let go of many things in my life. I didn't understand what it was she meant until much later. I had been opening up to all kinds of energy and doing psychic readings online so I felt that this was a time for me to listen and learn.

We must have covered a decade in the twenty-minute ride to Lori and Greg's place. They were genuine and what I would consider very nice people. I just felt this was going to be a great day. What I didn't realize was just how "great" of a day it was going to be.

When we got to Lori and Greg's, I was beat. It had been a long, long night and morning and I felt like I needed some rest. I was to check in at the retreat by 6:00 PM, and since it was only 9:00 AM, I had the rest of the day to explore.

I told Lori how tired I was but that I didn't want to sleep. I wanted to just visit and enjoy their company.

She said, "Well, let me do a little energy work on you. Sit down and we'll start."

I got some water to drink and sat down expecting as wonderful of an experience as I had received through the computer while in Seattle. I was not to be disappointed.

She put on some incredible music by the group Enigma. The song she played was "Return To Innocence", and I closed my eyes. As the music came on and the volume went up, an incredible feeling was beginning to escalate. It is hard to describe, but what came over me was an intense feeling of filling up. My very soul began to feel as if it was being fed energy. I was growing stronger by the second. I felt incredible bursts of energy, pulsing and vibrating my whole body. I felt my vibrational level increase ten-fold, then a hundred-fold. My skin was alive and pulsating. Absolutely everything about me was on the alert. I was increasingly aware that my strength was growing and I was feeling as if all my guides and helpers that show me signs were feeding me energy. What an intense and focused feeling I was now experiencing. I was wide awake and anticipating something that was going to change my life but I had no idea what that would be, or how it would manifest.

I looked over at Greg, who was sitting on the small couch under the front windows, and he just smiled and said, "I'll bet you feel great now don't you?"

I could only reply, "Wow! What an incredible sensation." I was still buzzing and vibrating and I would stay that way the rest of the day.

- Remembering Annapolis -

Lori suddenly burst out with, "I have to take you to Annapolis! I don't have any idea why, but I was told to take you to Annapolis."

Having just experienced what I had in the energy work, and "knowing" that I was supposed to be with these people, I said with a somewhat anticipatory grin, "Cool, let's go!"

"Unfortunately," Lori said, "my car doesn't have any air conditioning and it is really hot and humid today."

Just about that moment, Lori's ex-husband, Tony, called on the phone. Now Lori and Tony have an interesting relationship. It is very friendly and loving, and I was surprised by the way they communicated with each other. It was nicely refreshing to see these two people relate the way they did. I feel as though the two of them still love each other very much, but just can't live with each other. I believe that this was a preview to what my relationship with Jackie would in time become. Taking the opportunity that was presented when Tony called, Lori set it up so that we could use his car for the trip to Annapolis.

When she was done talking to him on the phone Lori turned and smiling a big grin said, "Tony is going to bring his car over and trade with me for the day. His car is fairly new and has air conditioning so that means we will be able to go to Annapolis after all. He is such a sweet guy."

In a short while Tony arrived with a smile and a joke. After introductions, a short visit and exchange of car keys, we were on our way.

Annapolis is a very well known city in Maryland and is rich in historical events of the early years of the United States. It is home to the United States Naval Academy, but what is more important for me, it was a turning point in my spiritual quest. I was to have an experience this day that will stay with me forever.

As we headed toward Annapolis, Greg drove, I sat in the passenger seat and Lori sat in the back seat. I felt an energy, almost a spiritual rebirth overcoming me and I confided in Greg and Lori that I was feeling strange. I had the feeling that I had been here before; almost like I was going home.

From the backseat Lori said, "Just go with it, close your eyes and feel the feelings. Let it flow through you, and you guide us; tell us where you would like to go. Relax and let the energy pulse through your soul."

I closed my eyes and Greg turned up the music. He had again put on the Enigma song "The Return to Innocence" and I began feeling the energy course through me. I realized that Lori was in the back seat doing her magic again, manipulating the energy and increasing it to a fever pitch. I was vibrating again! I started seeing visions in my head of an old street, a house, all kinds of different things. I was getting a preview of another life. I felt I was about to go through another step in my evolution right here in their car.

Lori broke into my visions and said, "Now Dennis, tell Greg where to go, tell him where to turn. Go with it".

I said, "Ok," not knowing what was coming, and went with the feelings I was having.

We were coming into a traffic circle in the middle of town. "Go around the circle and make a right turn just past that building, and go down that street," I said to Greg while pointing toward the building and street I meant.

"Wow," Lori said, "that is the 'Reynolds House,' one of the places I wanted to take you to see. It has a fascinating history. Supposedly, during the 1700's, travelers who came to the house to stay but couldn't pay for their lodging were allowed to paint or draw a picture on the mantle. This was payment for their lodging and meals. The owners have been offered a large sum of money for the mantle by the Smithsonian Institution, but turned it down because they wanted to keep it intact."

As Greg turned the corner, I was focused on the vision I was having about where we were going and I really didn't pay much attention to what Lori had just said. Except for a slight feeling of recognition, it didn't register. I was to learn later that this place known as the "Reynolds House" was a very important piece in my journey.

We proceeded down the street and I was feeling incredible sensations of remembrance. I "knew" this place. I exclaimed, "Turn left here, Greg," but it was too late, he had passed the street. We went on down the street and turned around, all the while my body was vibrating and I was feeling things I didn't understand, and wouldn't until later.

After coming back we turned right onto the street I had pointed out before. As we proceeded along, crossing another street, I was overcome with the need to stop, so I shouted, "Stop! Right here, I lived and died right here in that house!"

I sat dumbfounded, not knowing what was coming next, but feeling like I should be worried about what these people were thinking of what I just said. At the same time I knew that I was in safe company and I was feeling very relaxed about what had just occurred.

It seemed as if we sat there for hours, just looking at the house and taking in the feelings that were coming, but I'm sure it was only minutes.

Then Lori said, "Dennis, when? What year was it?"

"It feels like about seventeen..." The words hung in the air and at almost the exact instant I was saying "thirty", I heard Lori say the same exact number.

It was uncanny but we were completely connected, like twin travelers in time. It was wonderful. Here was someone who was on this plane as a guide for others and me. I realized in that same moment that Lori was here as my teacher to bring me to a place where I had never been before. She had been given knowledge and power to use for the good of the world, and I was blessed with her and Greg's loving presence.

I was overcome with emotion and started to weep. I was in touch with a place within me that I had not been in touch with for a long, long time. I was beginning to find myself, and in the days that were to follow, to love "ME", for the loving, kind and caring man that I really am.

This was a threshold, I thought. This is the "thing" I felt was going to happen when we started our trip here, but I was mistaken. It was not the total thing, it was only the beginning, and the best was yet to come! We continued on down the street because a car had come up behind us.

As we pulled away from the house, the feeling of discovery was overwhelming me. I felt as if I had touched a nerve within me that was the key to a door that was opening, a door that would never be closed again. I was beginning to feel as if the journey to Baltimore was not about the retreat, but about self-discovery, my continuing awakening to Spirit and the job that lay ahead for me.

We drove to the end of the street and as we stopped at the corner, I noticed the signpost had an inscription on it. It said the street name, and under it were the words, "Established 1696." The street had been established in the 17th century, so my feeling of being here in 1730 was even more plausible. I had been given a glimpse of a past life that I had lived in this town. I wanted more, but we were heading to the docks for some lunch. Lori and Greg wanted me to taste the famous Maryland crabs.

- Crabs and Crystals -

Greg had been going on all day about eating some of Maryland's specialty, the Blue Crabs in some kind of marinade that was very spicy. I was familiar with "Dungeoness" crabs from the west coast that are always boiled and served with melted butter. They are delicious. Because of my love for the Dungeoness crabmeat, I was anticipating a great new taste, spicy "Blue" crabs from Maryland. We found a parking place in a local parking garage and made the three or four block hike to the restaurant where they wanted to eat. Unfortunately they were sold out, so my introduction to the famous Maryland crabs would have to wait. We did have a delicious sandwich and some clams there and then headed back to the car, but I was disappointed.

So Greg said, "There is a place right near our house that we can go to that I know will have plenty. When you are done with your retreat on Friday, we'll go there."

We were walking up the street chatting and window-shopping when Lori suddenly blurted out while pointing at a shop across the street, "Dennis, I have to take you to that shop over there. I am being told we are to go in there to shop for a crystal."

I said "Lori, why do I need a crystal?"

"Because they are incredible centers of energy once you connect with them," she replied. "But, first you must cleanse it with sea water. Then you connect with the crystal and energize it with your own energy. If you ever feel drained or a need for an energy boost you can connect with your crystal and it will help you focus."

My feeling at this moment was one of amazement and wonder. "How could a crystal receive and hold a charge of energy?" I thought. A bigger question I had was, "After receiving and holding this charge, how does it give it back?" It was really baffling me. "But, what the heck?" I thought. "I have had some pretty interesting experiences so far." So we went into the store.

The inside of the store was very interesting. They had some metaphysical items, but mostly there were exotic things. There were compact discs of animal sounds with music, different kinds of rocks and stones, children's toys, clothes, knick-knacks and a drawer full of about fifty to seventy-five different sized crystals. There were big ones, medium ones and many small ones. I was dumbfounded. I had no idea of how to choose a crystal.

I turned to Lori, who was looking at some other beautiful stones and said, "How do I choose the right one for me?"

She chuckled slightly and said to me, "You must pick it up and feel it. You have to feel its energy. When you find the right one for you, you will just know."

With that I began picking up each one of the many crystals, trying to feel its energy. I was getting rather frustrated about not "feeling" the energy of these raw crystals when something hit me. I had just picked up a crystal that "felt good." It fit perfectly in my hand, but what was strange was, this crystal seemed to be pulsating. I set it down and picked up another. I felt a little bit of a pulsing. I began picking up the ones I had already felt when I realized I had suddenly become aware of the energy pulsing from these "clear rocks". Now you might think that I was feeling great about becoming aware of this energy, but I wasn't. Now I was faced with the task of choosing one of these pulsating rocks and feeling it as my own. The fact that I felt the energy of each one of them now made it even more difficult to choose. That's when it hit me. I thought, "The crystal that I picked up just before I started feeling all of them pulse must have something to do with it!" I had wandered around the store while thinking this over so I went back over to the "crystal drawer". I opened it up and picked up the crystal that had started it all and was really surprised when I felt the energy of this one. It had become very strong. When I held it in my left hand, it felt as if there were some hidden electrical wiring connecting me to this "rock". There was energy flowing into me and I was becoming energized. Suddenly, I thought, "here it is". This is the crystal that I am supposed to have.

"Cool," I blurted out.

Lori and Greg looked at me and Lori said, "I see you just found the right one." She then chuckled, "I told you that you would just know. That is the one that is for you."

She smiled and we left after I paid for the crystal. This was another of those key moments one never forgets. This crystal was to play a very significant part in my awakening.

- Reynolds House -

We were back in the car driving up the main street from the docks and toward the "circle" when Lori said excitedly, "Oh we have to go into the 'Reynolds House' before we leave. I need to show you the fireplace mantle I was telling you about."

We drove around the circle a couple times but couldn't find a place to park. Lori told Greg to drive around until we were done and not worry about a place to park. When we came out, he could pick us up. He said "Ok, you go ahead," and Lori and I got out in front of the "Reynolds House" restaurant. I had no idea why she wanted to show me this place and I don't think Lori did either. She just knew that I was supposed to visit here.

We went up on the front steps, but the restaurant was not open for business. Lori said, "That's OK, I guess we were just not supposed to see it today. Let's go see if we can go in the pub downstairs." So, we went around the corner and down a few steps and into a side door that was open.

As we walked in, I got an overwhelming sense that I

had been here before. It was so intense, that it took my breath away.

I said, "Wait a sec Lori, I'm feeling light headed. I recognize this place."

There was a man standing behind the bar, and he looked at me with a kind of "what is wrong with you" look. He mumbled something about not being open, and that he didn't work there. Lori nodded her head and smiled and they had a quick conversation about something of which I have no idea, I was lost in a remembering. A remembering of what this place looked like. I could see stools with men in long dark coats, men with long handlebar mustaches and some with beards. There were old muskets, like the ones I saw in the Davy Crockett movie when I was a young child. Mostly there was a din of noise; men drinking and laughing from pewter beer steins and pitchers.

"Are you OK?" I heard through the noise. Lori was looking at me with that knowing look. "Oh, I see, you weren't even here," she chuckled. "Where were you?"

I came back to the present with a start and said, "I was right here, remembering what this place looked like before. I even know what it looks like in the next room."

I described the room to Lori as it was laid out in my vision. As we walked into the next room, it looked the same as to the placement of the large oversized fireplace and of the windows. Of course the tables were different, and there was a dartboard on the wall opposite the windows, but the basic layout was exactly the same as in my vision. Lori wandered over by the fireplace and then by the dartboard. I was pulled toward the windows.

Because this was a basement, the windows were located up high on the red brick and mortar wall. I was looking at the bricks and noticing how fresh they looked considering this was such an old building. How old at the time I had no idea, but Lori had mentioned when we came in that it was established in the early 1700's. I stretched out my right arm and leaned with my right side toward the wall. As my hand touched the brick, I was hit with a jolt of energy and I felt a pulling on my right shoulder. I thought, "Whoa, this is very weird because it wasn't Lori touching my shoulder; she was on the other side of the room. It must mean something for me," so I moved back to where I was in line with one of the windows and leaned toward the wall, and something told me to look up. As I did, my hand again touched the wall and a three-inch piece of the almost 300-year-old mortar came off in my hand.

I must have let out some sound or uttered something, because Lori came over and said, "What's wrong?"

"Nothing, except that this mortar fell off the wall and into my hand."

I started to push it back into the indentation it had made in the wall and Lori excitedly said, "No! Don't! It fell off in your hand so it was meant for you. Keep it. Put it in your pocket for later."

I did and we left, hoping Greg was waiting for us so we didn't have too far to walk. We were in luck; he was driving up as we stepped onto the sidewalk. We were both excited about what had happened and we were very animated while telling Greg all about it. I don't think Lori was aware of all the visions that I had experienced while we were there but I was totally blown away.

- The Bricklayer -

As we were driving back toward Baltimore, Greg put on the Enigma CD and I started that vibrating thing again.

Lori was doing energy work again and I was getting in contact with the life I had in Annapolis. After about fifteen minutes I turned down the volume. I was suddenly feeling overwhelmed with the events of the day so far.

"Lori, why did you say that I should keep that mortar that fell off in my hand?"

"Take it out. Hold it in your left hand and feel the vibrations."

I had no idea what was in store for me, but I trusted her completely, and I did as she requested with great enthusiastic anticipation. As I closed my eyes, I felt the vibrations of the mortar coming up my arm. It felt like little pinpricks, like when your foot has fallen asleep and the feeling is coming back into it. A warm feeling was overcoming my body and I just let it flow.

All of a sudden I had the vision of a man. I was standing behind and below him on the ground. He was up on scaffolding. He was a jovial man, with a happy-go-lucky attitude. Smiling and joking with his co-workers, he was laughing and chuckling, while spreading mortar and laying bricks. And then, he turned around and looked straight into my eyes and I knew at that moment. That bricklayer was me!

I was ecstatic! I had found another part of this life in Annapolis. I repeated all of this to Lori and Greg and they were as excited as I was. Then the **d-o-u-b-t** set in. Even after all of this, I still thought, "Wow, this is just too much. Is all this real? I could use some kind of sign that says I am OK and I am not crazy or hallucinating." So I said to God, "If all of this is true, please just give me one more sign that says I am OK."

I thought about why I was here in Baltimore. I was

here for a retreat to continue in my awakening to discover "who I really am". I was learning how to love me for me! Yeah, this is what it is all about. Learning how to love myself and accept myself and know that I am OK. I had to understand that everything that was happening was supposed to and was perfect.

Just then I was brought back from my thoughts with a human realization. The traffic was horrible. It was moving so slowly I knew that there must be a wreck up ahead. We crept along for about thirty to thirty-five minutes.

- The Crystal Speaks -

About this time, Lori said to me, "Dennis, let me see your crystal. I would like to take a closer look at it before you cleanse and recharge it with your energy."

"OK," I said, "here you go", and I handed it back to her.

"Wow, just look at the way it shines and reflects the sunlight." Lori stated matter-of-factly, "This is a really cool crystal. And look at the great lines in it." She cooed over it for a few more minutes and then handed it back.

The sun was shining very brightly into the front of the car and onto my legs. I held the crystal in the sunlight and watched the silvery slivers of light dance on the dashboard. Then, to my surprise, I noticed something in the light. It seemed to be letters. I took a closer look, and sure enough, there it was, three letters as clear as the letters on this page. It spelled out **L-U-V**! Wow! I was astonished with what I was seeing. I sat for a second, and took the crystal out of the light. When I put it back, the letters were still there.

I exclaimed, "Lori, Greg, look at this! Tell me what you see." Lori moved forward from the backseat and Greg leaned over from the driver's side and they both said at almost the same time, "Love."

"Spell it," I said.

"**L-U-V**" Lori spelled.

"Do you see the same thing, Greg?" I asked.

He said, "Yeah, wow, that's great. How did you do that?"

"It's natural as far as I know."

I then proceeded to turn the crystal in the sunlight to see if there was anything else, but not really expecting anything. There, on the opposite side was another stunning sight. In another beam that shown onto the dashboard was another letter. It was a capital "**U**". As I slowly rotated the crystal it all became clear. I read **U, LUV, U**; this was my message from God. He/She was telling me to love myself. I sat there and tears started to flow. I had my message. I really did have a life here in Annapolis. What a day, and it wasn't even half over!

I had to be at the monastery by 6:00 PM and it was then about 3:00 PM. Having three hours to get there I wasn't too worried, except this traffic was moving so slowly. As we approached the wreck that was causing the slowdown, I saw a man standing over what appeared to be a body under a sheet. It seemed so strange to have this person not in a uniform, standing over this covered form. He was just standing there, staring downward.

I questioned out loud, "I wonder what that man is doing standing there?"

Greg looked at me with a questioning look and asked, "What man?"

Before I could answered Lori piped up with, "The one standing by that sheet over the body on the ground."

I then asked, "Don't you see him, Greg?"

He just answered with the same question, "What man?"

Lori and I came to the same conclusion at almost the same moment. He was the driver of that car who had just died and had left his body. He was looking at himself, probably wondering what was going on. For reasons unknown to me then, Lori and I were allowed to see him, but Greg wasn't.

As we passed the wreck, we looked back and he was gone. We were given, for only a moment, a short glimpse of life after death. For me it was only a preview of things to come and was so spiritually moving that in that one moment, my whole belief in life after death was confirmed. These were such profound signs they could not be denied. I just sat back and carefully thought about the day's events and what it all meant.

It was on to the retreat and the next step in my process.

Alice

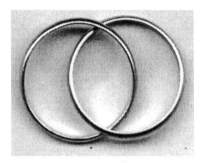

Chapter Six

Getting Ready

- *Meeting Hans: The First Reading* -

It was August of 1994. Sandra had died a little more than two years before, on May 7th, 1992. Sandra's death, coming so soon after Sherril died in June of 1989, had greatly affected me, and I knew that I was not coping well from the loss of my two dearest friends.

Sherril had been my best friend from the time we first met in elementary school. Sandra had been my best friend during my adult years. There were so many times when I wanted to pick up a telephone to talk to Sherril or Sandra and I knew that I could not.

Then, synchronicity in motion, I ran into Vicki, a friend I hadn't seen in months. She raved about a channeler she had just been to see, and said that he was fabulous.

I called immediately and made an appointment for a channeling/psychic session with Hans Christian King. Hans is a medium who lives in South Florida and travels extensively throughout the world. Of course, since it was important that I meet with him, he was in town and available when I called.

August 26th, 1994 was a day that was to change the course of my life forever. I stepped off the elevator and onto the second floor at the building where the Miami Institute of Expanding Light (MIEL) was housed. Little did I know then that I was to spend a good part of the next two years of my life going through the doors of MIEL.

I was there for my 3:00 PM appointment to see Hans and was met by his assistant, Aaron Hunt, a six foot two, twenty-three year old darling of a bear of a boy.

When I had called to make the appointment, Aaron told me I could bring photos, writings, or other items to the reading. Although I had been to psychics and astrologers many times during the previous 20+ years, I had never been to a channeler or medium such as Hans. When I learned that Hans could "speak to the dead" I deeply wanted to be in touch with Sherril and Sandra.

Hans Christian King, another six foot two older version of an adorable bear of a man, came into the waiting area where I had been chatting with Aaron. Hans and I then went into a private room where he explained to me what channeling was about. Hans was soft-spoken and gentle in his manner and I immediately trusted him with my deepest and most sacred thoughts.

I was amazed at what came through in the hour we were together. Hans first took some time to explain to me what he was about to do in the session, so that I would be comfortable with whatever was going to happen. I told him that I trusted him completely, and felt no fear, just eager anticipation.

He began by telling me that I had my own intuitive abilities, and that I had not yet tapped into them, but they would be made available to me if I would just slow down and listen. Getting me to slow down would take some doing, and I could certainly use the help of the spirit world! He also told me that I had not yet found what I had come into this life to do.

Hans continued, "You're in maintenance now, sort of maintaining your life. I have a sense of you somehow being more 'out there'. I have a feeling of your soul wanting to do something."

He then questioned with, "Do you ever feel that way?"

"I need to know what my purpose is," I said.

I knew that my life's purpose had to be more than just being a divorce attorney. But somehow I knew that the knowledge and experience of being an attorney would lead me to the right path.

- The Channeling Begins -

Hans told me that there were a lot of people coming into the room. Only he could see and hear them, through the eyes and voices of his guide. He told me many people had come into the room, some bearing flowers, and all were smiling and talking at once. He was audio taping the session, so I did not have to take notes, and I was able to focus totally on the experience as it was happening. It had been quite some time since my friends and I had communicated, and it was important for them to get through to me now that I had found a source for us to be in touch. What happened next literally blew me away and I became an instant believer in the afterworld and the other side.

- Sandra -

Hans appeared to have a pained look on his face and placed his right hand on his right upper outer thigh and said, "Someone must have had a difficulty with a leg or a hip. Who was that?"

My mouth flew open and I whispered "Sandra."

Hans continued, "Yes, she's here and she wants to bring a lot of love to you. I don't know who she was to you, but she's bringing lots of flowers to this room."

Then he asked, "How did she die?"

"Bone cancer." I replied. The part of his leg that he touched was the exact location where Sandra's tumor was first discovered.

He then stated, "She's telling you to buck up. 'Buck up, you're not alone.' In other words, cheer up, it's not dark, you're just in a phase-out period. It's what I call a void."

He had to tell Sandra to slow down because she was talking so fast and waving her arms to get his attention. I smiled because I knew that it was Sandra, talking non-stop and being so animated.

Hans continued, "She wants to tell you how excited she is to see you and to speak with you." I showed Hans a photo of Sandra, and he said he wanted to increase the energy by studying the photo of us together.

"She's going to act as a guidance for you," he said and then asked, "if that's all right?"

Then he continued with, "She's going to learn to do it, and you'll learn to receive. Together, you're going to act as a team."

Then, Hans laughed and said, "Motor-mouth will probably continue to always give you advice. I just want you to know that she's there for you."

I laughed too and said that she had always acted as my guidance when she was here. For years I would go to her and her husband, Michael, for advice in my personal life. I didn't always follow their advice, but I always asked and discussed things with them. I was thrilled to hear that she was still there for me.

Then he asked how old Sandra had been when she died,

and I said she was 43 years old. He said she was now 28 or 29, and that when people pass over, they usually select an age that they enjoyed, and for some unknown reason, spirits generally choose 28 to 30 as their ideal age. When I met Sandra, she had just turned 34, so I never knew her as a 28-year-old.

Somehow, I just knew that Hans was actually seeing and hearing Sandra, and I felt warm and wonderful. What happened next was further confirmation of Sandra's presence.

Hans continued, "She wants you to start writing in your journal again."

Sandra was one of the few people who knew that I kept a journal and in fact, the last time I had made an entry into my journal was when Sandra was in a coma in her hospital bed. It was while I was sitting on the floor in her hospital room during the 36 hours before she died.

He said, "She says that if you begin writing in your journal, you'll see that after a little time, you could do some automatic writing that could come through her. You will see a message in the writing."

Hans then told me to write her a long letter, just filling her in on the news and everything that had happened since we had last "spoken". I did just that, and the next month when I met with Hans again I was made aware that Sandra had received my message.

- *The Skeptic* -

I had confided in Sandra's husband that I was going to have the reading and because Michael was a skeptic, he had asked me to get him some proof that Sandra was really coming through. So, at his request, I asked Hans to ask

Sandra what nickname she used to call Michael. Her response was so typical of Sandra's personality, I was certain that she really was there with us in the room.

"Can I ask you what nickname you used to call Michael?" Hans asked.

He then repeated what he was hearing her tell him. "She says, 'It is not up to me to prove that there is life after death. It is for Michael to believe.'"

What happened next did not make any sense to me until after I had played the tape for Michael. It then made perfect sense and also gave him some inkling that Sandra was really communicating with us both.

Hans said that Sandra was showing him a baby, and asked me if I had ever had an abortion or miscarriage. I responded that I had never had an abortion, and although it was possible that I had a miscarriage when I was married to Peter, it was so early in the term, a pregnancy had never been confirmed. I was four weeks late, and had been trying to get pregnant in 1981. A psychic told me then that I was pregnant (it was before the pregnancy test kits were on the market), and I believed that I was. However, we went out on a motor boat one Sunday, hit some severe waves, and that night, I began my period.

Hans then stated, "there's a child here that she knows about, she's carrying a child, a little girl. They don't bring them forward unless they belong around you somehow."

Sandra and Michael had deliberately chosen to not have children. They were the first couple I had known who had made such a decision, and other than the fact that this was their personal choice, I had never discussed the issue in much detail with them. Sandra had her tubes tied, and in fact, she referred me to her gynecologist when the time came for me to have the procedure performed. My decision was for medical reasons.

When I shared the tape of the reading with Michael, he in turn shared some very personal information with me. Sandra had been pregnant earlier in their marriage. That was in 1979 and she would have been around the age that Hans saw her. She and Michael knew they would not be ideal parents, so Sandra had an abortion. We both knew that this was the child Sandra had carried in her arms during my reading. In fact, she did it again in my second reading the next month, which confirmed that the child belonged with her. This was Sandra's way of showing their daughter to Michael, and her way of telling him that she was able to communicate if he would only listen.

The reading continued, as other people wanted their presence known to me. My paternal grandfather, whom I had called "Zadie", a Yiddish term for grandfather, came through. He said that he was going to be giving me guidance as I raised my vibrational level to be able to hear what he was saying. I have always known that Zadie was with me, and it was especially nice to hear that my intuition was correct. My very first attempt at journal writing in 1983 was actually an automatic writing that brought forth a distinct message from my grandfather who had passed over in 1970.

- Sherril -

Then, Hans asked if I knew anyone else with the initial "S". I certainly did, and I was eager to speak with Sherril who had died in 1989 at age 39. Sherril had been my first best friend, and we were inseparable from the time we met in 5th grade. We remained best friends from then on, and were sorority sisters in high school. I moved into her house for six weeks when we were pledges in the ninth grade. My sister Linda was then president of our sorority, Tri Beta, and made it insufferable for me to live at home. Sherril's younger brother and sister fondly remember the time, and still refer to me as their "other older sister."

Sherril served as my maid of honor in 1970 when I got married the first time. She was the natural choice to be my son's godmother when Justin was born in 1974. Ever the comforting friend, she stayed with me in Knoxville for a couple weeks when I was going through my divorce two years later. She made a special trip to Miami from Washington D.C. to be at my second wedding in 1980. Years later she made another trip to Miami, with her son Sammy, to attend Justin's bar mitzvah.

That was the last time I saw Sherril healthy. It was March of 1988 and she was then pregnant with her second son, Josh. Two months later she was diagnosed with breast cancer.

Josh was delivered early by caesarian so that Sherril could begin the chemotherapy treatments in May, 1988. I last spoke with her one year later on the morning she went into the surgery from which she would never awaken.

The cancer had spread to her brain and she was scheduled for brain surgery. Her brother telephoned me just as I was literally walking out the door to attend the Florida Bar conference for four days in Orlando. If I had missed his call, I never would have known Sherril was in the hospital and I would not have been able to speak with her before she died.

"Just routine," she told me when I called her the next morning, about two hours before she would go into the operating room. She bravely said, "You survived your brain surgery, and so will I." The major difference was that her condition was malignant, and we both knew it.

My own episode happened a few months after graduation from law school. It was November of 1986, and a grand mal seizure had been my only clue that something might be wrong. I had just gone through three years of law school without even a headache, so I was quite surprised to discover that I had a brain tumor the size of a walnut. I was extremely fortunate to have had superb doctors and a benign meningioma. My recovery was a complete success without any side effects or reoccurrence.

Before being able to be in touch with Sherril through Hans, I had not forgiven myself for not knowing how sick she was, and for not being able to say good-bye. I have missed Sherril's friendship tremendously, and think of her constantly. It is especially difficult whenever I see or hear of people getting together with their childhood friends. Sherril had truly been my sister, and I will always treasure her friendship for the 29 years we had.

The night before Sandra went into a coma, she said to me, "You're saying good-bye to Sherril, too, aren't you?" I told her that was true, and that Sherril was waiting for her and would show her around Heaven when she arrived.

At that first reading, I showed Hans a picture of Sherril. He said, "She says to tell you that you're not going to be alone. Your life comes in the second half."

That was good to know, because so far, life had been just mere existence, and I was hopeful that there would be more purpose. I was being told that up to that point, my life had been mere preparation for what was to come.

- *Twin Soul Preview* -

This first reading brought through other information as well. "They're saying that you're not alone. Your life is about to change." He asked me what I did for a living, and I replied that I was a lawyer.

"Is that what you wish to do?" he asked solemnly.

"It's a living," I jokingly responded. Together we shared a laugh, but we both knew this was quite serious information coming through.

Even then, Spirit was sending me subtle messages that there was more to my life than just being a lawyer, but I was slow on the uptake. The messages are no longer subtle.

Hans then said, "Somehow I feel that you're being called to a higher purpose, and I feel that you know that, too. I want to say that during the next four or five years I feel that you'll be quite surprised. I see your life changing upwards of 180 degrees. Your soul wants to make a difference and wants to have enough time to be able to do that. That means you'll have a long life span. Your energy changes around October or November. I see you increasing your sensitivity, your intuitive side, and that you will be using this in your work. I don't know how you're going to do that," he laughed, referring to the fact that law and sensitivity don't often mix. "I see more of a blend coming around your work than what you've seen before."

He continued on, not needing or wanting any more information from me. "In the area of relationships, I feel that they've been a bit of a roller coaster ride for you up to this time in your life, and it's been a bumpy ride. I feel that the person coming into your life is already on the way. You haven't met him yet. You will be joining up a little bit down the road, and it's going to be an instant recognition. Your souls will just know each other, and that's it. It will be like, 'It's nice to see you again; where've you been? Where's the wedding chapel?' That's how it's going to feel. There won't be a lot of testing or the trust issues that are part of a normal relationship. This is an instant recognition, so be prepared for that."

My face showed my pleasure at hearing that I would soon meet my soul mate. At that time I didn't even know the term "twin soul".

He told me that I needed to take my time and be cautious, because I was still dealing with my self-worth issues that I had been born with. "You didn't come into this life to walk alone, so please do not worry."

Hans said that both Sandra and Sherril were in the room with us. He said both of them were laughing and dancing, saying that they would dance at my wedding. He confirmed that my soul mate was on this plane and that I was fortunate to know that we would one day meet.

Hans lamented, "Do you know how many times I have to tell people that their soul mate is not on this plane?"

He continued with, "You are one of the lucky ones, but it will be a while, because your soul mate is waiting for you to get ready. Just hang on and know that someone is coming."

Hans then left the issue of relationship and told me that he saw me being "in service". As a new student of metaphysics, I didn't even know what that meant. "Your spirit and your loved ones and guides on the other side are aware of your journey and of your destiny. Now it begins to change."

His guides then told him to tell me, "Don't be surprised if you're called upon to do some unusual things that may stretch you just a little bit, they will be all right."

He then asked, "Have you noticed that with your work, you're becoming more enlightened and more spiritual?"

I nodded in the affirmative and he continued, "There's a direction that the Spirit is trying to make available to the public, and you're that directional change."

Hans told me that several of my guides had come into the room to present themselves to me through him. One was an older Chinese man, elegantly dressed in white robes who appeared to be a master teacher. Another was a tall Native American Indian, who stood by silently and watched over me. He said he saw an elderly rabbi on one side of the room, and a Buddha on the other. Each was a part of my past life history, and both were spiritual guides for me now.

The rest of the reading included information about my son, his estranged father, and my various relationships. Hans said that he saw me writing a book, and I laughed because I knew that I had nothing to write about.

Hans said, "You're going to do a lot of spiritual work in the future, my dear. You're going to be well known."

Chapter Seven

The Pathway Opens

- *The Second Reading* -

I went back to see Hans a month later, and continued to see him once a month for about six or seven months. I found that the benefit of one channeling session was better than four or five sessions with a therapist! Knowing that I could be in touch with Sandra and Sherril made it easier to accept the fact that they were physically gone, and I continued to be in touch with them through my journal writing. I also found that they were in touch with me through automatic writing which I have come to develop as my own form of communication with the other side and with my own guides.

Every bit of the information that I am including from my readings with Hans is documented on tape, and as difficult as it is for some people to believe, each and every word is true. Since I have come to know Dennis and learned how the information comes through to him, and how his channeled readings affect and often heal his clients, I have learned to understand and accept the process. I am deeply grateful for the details that were given to me through Hans in the early days of my spiritual path.

This was only the second time that I had seen Hans, and I did not expect him to remember me since he travels all over the world and meets with so many new people each month. He took no notes, and the only tape recording of the session was given to me. So I was quite surprised when the first thing he did was place his right hand on his right upper outer thigh and say, "There is someone here who had difficulty with mobility, or difficulty with the leg and hip.

She wants to say hello." I began to cry knowing that Sandra had again come to see me and speak with me through Hans.

The first thing he said after bringing Sandra into the room was, "She says congratulations, you have made it easier to communicate."

I told Hans that I had begun writing in my journal again, and after our last session I had written a long letter to both Sandra and Sherril. This was Sandra's way of telling me that she had indeed received my letter and was in return communicating with me through this marvelous man.

Hans was in direct contact with the spirit world once again, and as usual, Sandra was talking and running the show. Hans continued, "She says, 'You know, we could do some work together.'"

He blew me away again when he asked, "Dear, was there a child they lost back in the spirit world?"

I reminded Hans that Sandra had brought a baby to the first reading, and that I did not know then whose child it was. I told him what Michael had shared with me about Sandra's abortion, and he continued with a special message from Sandra. "She wants her husband to know that she has the child with her in the spirit world now. She's holding a child in her arms, and she wants you both to know that the child is just fine."

Hans then told me about a guide of mine who had come into the reading to give me information. He was the same elderly Chinese man who had come through in my first reading. Again, he was elegantly dressed, and appeared to Hans to be a master teacher. This was further confirmation for me that these people coming to me were here to give me specific messages.

Hans explained more. "He says his name is Master Ling,

and you may call him Ling. He wants to congratulate you on a journey well started. You're coming into what he calls your 'clarity' time. He says there's a bit of impatience brewing inside of you. But, he says that's a quality; don't be upset about it. It's a goodness wanting to accelerate and to expand. Don't fuss it because you really could be quite pleased with the outcome."

Hans then continued with, "He says the two of you have worked together before in the Hun Dynasty, where you brought a great deal of light to a difficult time. Your soul is back on the journey of enlightenment."

Ling went on to say, through Hans, that I was born into this life as a healer. "Don't forget to experiment with that fact this time." Hans explained to me that this meant that sometime down the road my guides would bring into my path some opportunities for me to witness this healing energy.

Then Hans continued to repeat what Ling was telling him, and he spoke in a slow and methodical manner. "'Alice', Ling says, 'you have risen to a new plateau. This will carry you for a little while yet. This will be a time for new discovery. Watch how Spirit works the wonders to behold. Please watch because you're going to be very pleased and very surprised, especially in 1995 as things start to unfold for you. Notice how your speech changes. You're going to be having more awareness in your speaking, more clarity in your 'lawyer-stuff.'"

Still quoting Ling, Hans told me, "'You have chosen a life filled with adventure. Most of your life comes in the second half more so than the first. You will be very busy in the second half. You will journey to the Orient once again, and you will understand more of what we have been speaking about.'"

- *More Channeled Advice* -

Hans then asked if we had talked last time about writing a book. I said that he had mentioned it, but I had no immediate plans or any topic. "Ling says you will be writing a book, and you will be quite pleased with the outcome." He told me it would be a book along the lines of spirituality and the growth process

At that time in my life, I had just stepped onto the metaphysical path, and was only beginning to learn what spiritualism was about. I was a novice, a student sampling every workshop that MIEL offered, and I was a long way from being an expert on any such topic. For Hans to say that I would be giving such information to others was beyond my belief, so what he said next was totally outside my realm of comprehension.

Hans continued to channel Ling's messages. "He's giving me some information to relay to you about clairvoyance, the ability to see. I'm being told that your ability to see will improve. This will come over a period of time."

Ling explained the process, and told me not to fight it, but to pay attention to the signs, and to be open to receive what messages were to be given to me. I was not able to follow his description or instructions at that time, but I have since come to understand and appreciate what was being transmitted to me through Hans.

Hans then introduced me, once again, to my Native American guide. "This person guides your soul through its lessons; you have known each other before, in another lifetime. He is a friend of yours, and he is saying, 'Thank you for being honest to your emotions. Thank you for being there for your truth. It is with great joy that we work with you. It has been a little difficult for us to get through to you. Your mind is a fine one, but it is constantly occupied.'"

Now, that was an understatement if ever I heard one! My mind chatter was always so intense it has been difficult for me to meditate or be regressed. Being a classic type "A" personality, my mind and energy level were always on high speed, and I didn't know how to relax or clear the head. This was one of my hopes, that in turning to the spiritual path and by spending more time at MIEL with other like minded people, I would learn how to relax and how to go within to hear my own higher self and soul.

Through Hans my guide continued, "We're working with you in redefining your energy so that you will be able to distinguish between your own thoughts and the messages we and Spirit are giving to you."

I asked what his name was, and Hans said, "He was called by the clouds. He calls himself Silver Cloud. You and he used to sit outside in the grass and among the flowers and watch the clouds overhead." I then told Hans that I still enjoyed looking at clouds and discovering shapes in them.

Hans smiled and continued, "Now, he says you should be surrounded by flowers."

Hans once again turned the focus back to Sandra, who often took the opportunity to speak with me through these readings. "I feel that your friend, Sandra, is someone who wants to work with you and help you as you move along this path."

I asked Hans if Sandra and I had been friends in past lives because we were such close friends in this lifetime. When Sandra and I met, it was as though we just picked up from a past remembrance of an existing friendship. We often marveled at our unique friendship, because we had very little in common. Yet, we never lacked for conversation or for things to do together. She and Michael were my closest and dearest friends who stood by me while I struggled through law school. They tolerated my shenanigans during my periods of various relationships. During my three years of law school, I was the third wheel in their life, and they included me for meals, football games, movies, and general daily contact. They were my family when Justin and I seemed to be alone at many times during those ten years of friendship.

When I was in private practice, and needed a place to rent, Michael generously offered me office space at a price I couldn't refuse. I will be forever grateful to him for that time which enabled me to build my law practice with minimal costs.

When Sandra became ill and after she died, Michael became the third wheel that we embraced into our social lives. When my then live-in relationship ended, Michael and I became confidantes, and I often joke that Michael is the brother I never wanted!

- *The Three Stooges* -

Hans told me that the answers to my questions were coming directly from Sandra. "She says, 'Yes, we were together in a past lifetime. We were good friends, and we worked well together in the past. I chose for my soul's direction a different set of circumstances than yours in this lifetime.' She says that she has learned that for her, 'there is no life and there is no death. There is simply love. And life and death are no more than an aspect.'"

Hans said he saw her holding up a prism, and that she was turning it in her hand. "'Life,' she says, 'is about all of these prisms. No one prism makes up the whole; they all make up the whole.'"

I knew that Sandra was in the room, because that sounded just like her. She was always philosophizing, and often spoke in metaphors. Hans could not have known that about her, and this was her way of letting me know she was there. One Christmas, she gave me a beautiful glass prism-like ball, and I pictured her standing there holding up that ball. She had given a similar ball to Dee Dee, as we often duplicated presents for the three of us. We were, of course, the Three Stooges, as Michael had dubbed us.

The reason was simple. Sandra, Dee Dee, and I met in 1982 while attending adult continuing education classes at Barry University in Miami Shores. We all became close friends and did everything together.

As for couples, it was always Sandra and Michael, Dee Dee and Jerry, and Alice and "whomever".

We had fabulous and spirited holiday celebrations together: Fourth of July, Halloween, Thanksgiving, and Christmas. Each holiday was lavish, and Dee Dee and Jerry's house was always decorated to the hilt. Halloween drew people from miles away just to see the outrageous adults who had created the crazy haunted house.

Even though each of us had careers and busy lives, we were always there when needed. Sandra and Dee Dee were at my side throughout my brain surgery ordeal and recovery period. In fact, they both stayed at the hospital with me the night before surgery just to keep me company so I wouldn't be nervous. It worked, because I was the first to fall comfortably asleep.

The stories are wild and wonderful and could be a complete chapter or an entire book just on the Three Stooges. Our antics became so natural, that whenever one of us did something worthy of becoming a "stooge story", it became known as "a stoogism" or "pulling a stooge". Usually, I was the one most often credited with creating a worthy stooge story, and Michael and Jerry are always eager to regale anyone with the tales.

One Christmas, Dee Dee gifted each of us with a Stooge doll of our own. Sandra, who was the oldest by 17 months, was considered to be the most sensible. Therefore she was designated to be Moe. I was six months older than Dee Dee and I got the Larry doll. By default, and because she had the most outrageous hair, Dee Dee became Curly. We began signing our gift cards "Stooge 1", 2, or 3, and we loved being the Three Stooges.

- Sandra's Message -

Since Sandra was the sensible one, I knew to pay attention to what she was saying when she held up the prism for Hans to describe to me in the reading. Hans said that when she held up the prism, he could see all its luster.

"Will you tell him I love him?" Sandra continued through Hans, wanting me to give a direct message to Michael. "It is not my job to prove life after death, it is for Michael to accept it. Can you say to him, 'can you prove it is not so?'"

I told Hans that Michael would only believe if I could bring back something concrete. He wanted proof in the form of the nickname or his grandmother's name, both of which I did not know.

Sandra continued to speak through Hans, and I was absolutely certain she was present. "No, he needs faith," she admonished. "That's what is lacking. It's not proof that is lacking, it's his faith that is lacking. How could I have shown him his child if it were not so? Michael has fear in belief."

- *Pookie* -

Out of the blue, Hans blurted out a question, "Who is Pokey?" I told him that I had no idea, but I wrote it down to save for later. It was also on the tape, so I would remember the name if it ever came up again.

This name did come up again, four years later, in a different pronunciation, and it came as a profound discovery and confirmation. It was Michael's birthday in 1998, and as always, the stooge couples planned to celebrate by having dinner. No matter how busy we get during the year, we have always taken the time to share our birthdays together: DeeDee and Jerry, Michael and now Jackie, and me and now Dennis.

Michael and his girlfriend, Jackie, had been together for a couple of years, and we had accepted her into our group. This was a significant accomplishment as well as high praise. Since Sandra's death, we'd harshly judged most of Michael's relationships, but as Michael's friends, we had given ourselves that power. It was total abuse, but often necessary.

Birthday celebrations for Michael were always a time of reflection, since Sandra had died on May 7th, 1992, and her internment was on May 11th, the day of Michael's birthday.

The night before we were to have dinner with the group to celebrate Michael's birthday in 1998, Dennis said to me, "I have to bake a birthday cake for Michael. What's his favorite cake?"

I accepted his statement without question and said, "Chocolate cake with chocolate icing." Michael is a major chocoholic, and it's always the best gift for him.

The next day, Dennis made the cake and we brought it

with us to the restaurant. In the two years we had been together, this was the first time Dennis had made a cake for anyone other than for his kids when they were with us in the summer. I acknowledged this as a nice gesture for him to do for my close friend, and thought nothing more of it.

While driving to the restaurant, Dennis asked me if I had ever heard the word "Pookie". I said that I had not, but I got a sudden strange feeling and knew that it meant something special.

At the restaurant, Michael sat at one end of the table, and Dennis sat to his immediate left. While the rest of us were chatting away, Dennis passed a piece of paper to Michael and asked him if he recognized the word he had written on it.

The color left Michael's face as he nodded his head and said, "Yes, it does. What else did she say?"

Michael knew when he read the word "pookie" that Dennis had been given a message from Sandra, and for the first time, he was ready to listen. Dennis explained to all of us that Sandra had come to him the night before and asked him to bake a cake for Michael's birthday. While he was making the cake, she came to him in the kitchen, and said, "Tell him it's from me, and tell him I said 'Pookie'. He'll understand."

Dee Dee and I both shed tears and shared our thoughts. We were so happy that Sandra had come through and we knew she had joined us for this special occasion, yet we missed her physical presence immensely.

Michael told us that "Pookie" was in fact one of the pet names Sandra had used for him, but in true skeptic fashion, he said it wasn't the main one.

It became clear to me that Sandra had attempted to get this message to Michael four years before during my reading with Hans, but the pronunciation came through differently, and Michael wasn't ready to listen then. It was also significant for Dennis to be the messenger of this important communication. Dennis was not only my twin soul, he was becoming a powerful channel for people who needed to connect with loved ones on the other side.

- Discovering Who I Am -

Hans then continued to tell me what was happening on my own path. "Alice, you're a teacher of the truth and the light. You have set your feet on a path of discovery right now. You are discovering how this works, where you are with it, what you're supposed to do with it, and where it will take you. I'm going to tell you, my dear, and I have a very strong feeling about this, that you have grown, energy-wise, as fast as anyone I have ever known. I don't know what you're doing, but whatever it is, you're surrendering to it. You're going to be stunned as to what happens for you."

I was taken aback, as I was just beginning to understand not only what a path was, but that I was on one.

He went on to say, "But somehow, you must have always known this. You must have known that you have a larger purpose."

Nodding in a cross between agreement and disbelief, I wanted to know everything right then.

Hans then softly asked, "What's the sadness, Alice?"

I answered haltingly, "I want to know what direction to go in. I'm stuck."

"No, you're not," he gently scolded. "You've just

started. They're giving you the tools. But, what do you want to do with the tools?"

"I want to be able to enjoy life," I responded. "Not just get up, go to work, and go home, just to do it all over again the next day."

That had been my dilemma for quite some time. I had become totally disenchanted and frustrated with the practice of law, the system, the clients, the process, the lies, the anger, just to name a few. There was too much negative energy surrounding me daily, and I had not yet learned how to protect myself.

In addition to not liking the work, my social life was at a dead end. I was not in a relationship, and I, of course, thought that would make my life perfect.

"And, what would give you that enjoyment?" Hans asked.

"I thought I was happy here, but I'm not. This is a stressful business. I'm also not happy in this city."

I figured that since I was with a genuine psychic, I may as well ask about my future. "What city would be a good area for me, where I could grow more and be happy?"

Hans answered me by passing on another message from my master guide, Ling. "Your friend says, 'Stay in this city a little while longer. Watch as we unfold your stuff. You won't stay here forever.'"

I didn't know it then, but it was very important for me to remain in Miami, so that the events, which would eventually lead to my meeting Dennis, could in fact unfold. There was still so much more for me to experience before I could be ready to love my twin soul unconditionally, and have him accept my love in return. First, I needed to learn how to love myself.

- *A Glimpse into the Future* -

I have come to learn that psychics see things that happen well into the future, and that time is a concept that is not often clearly defined because there is no delineation of time in the spiritual world. Time is past, present, and future, all happening at once. Time is merely an illusion, and psychics may see things as happening now that may not happen for several months or even years.

Hans then asked "Alice, when are you going to start a group?"

"A group of what?" I asked in a surprised voice, and we both shared a laugh.

"A metaphysical discovery and discussion group," he responded. "I want you to have six to ten people, no more, no less. Use a book that works for you as the focus for your group. You need to see how you are as the teacher and the clairvoyant. We will make the facilities here at MIEL available for you. What actually happens is that the group winds up conducting itself, but as you facilitate the group, you will hear things come out of you that you have no way of knowing. I think that the best way for you to get started is to see what a strong light you hold, and to witness what comes out of you as you facilitate these groups. You're a natural born leader. You're a natural born healer and clairvoyant. I want you to tape record the sessions for this reason. You might be very surprised at how you sound."

I was astounded by what he was telling me. How could I possibly lead a group when I was just learning these things myself?

Hans continued to describe what he saw ahead for me.

"Your job is to bring light into darkness. I have watched a transformation occur in you. You have already shifted out of the old and into the new. That's very unusual for someone in the early stages. That says that your soul has quite a large purpose and wants to get on with it in a hurry."

Hans then repeated, "You're a natural born leader. You'll be going on to do a lot of this work; a lot of motivational stuff; a lot of healing. You could make your living from this and do rather well."

As I write this, four years after that session, I am amazed at the clarity and accuracy of these early readings. I never would have dreamed then that I would have an on-going metaphysical anything. Yet, in late 1997, Dennis and I formed a metaphysical discovery and discussion group. We met weekly for a full year at Athene, a metaphysical center and bookstore in South Miami. Our purpose was to create a safe place for like-minded people to get together and freely share experiences and bare their souls. We had a wonderful class of 10 to 15 people who we trained and helped guide to be in touch with their own natural psychic abilities, such that each could easily become a group facilitator on his or her own. The scheduled time for the class was two hours, from 7–9 pm. However, we always stayed longer because no one ever wanted to finish. So, when the store manager needed to close and go home, the group would go a few doors away to the Chinese restaurant for a late dinner where we could continue our discussion. We had a terrific time and we all learned from each other. The friendship, eagerness, and loyalty of the group will always be remembered gratefully and forever in our hearts.

Chapter Eight

The Journey of My Soul

- The Relationships -

As for relationships, Hans touched on that in our second session. "'We understand your concerns, and your fears,'" my guide told him to tell me. "'Don't fret. You were not born into this life to be alone.'"

- Peter -

I asked Hans about my relationship with Peter, my second husband. As I asked, he wrote on the notepad he kept on his lap, "completed". This was true, because I had finally and at long last completed my ties to Peter.

It took a long time, but I have learned that in order to be ready to meet and recognize my twin soul, I needed to have total completion with past relationships. Of all my relationships, this had been the longest lasting, and the most difficult to sever.

We met in 1978. I was a legal secretary in a downtown two-attorney firm, and Peter had come into the office to get a divorce. It was perfect. I was able to learn first hand all about not only the man, but about his marriage and the reasons for the break-up. I knew that Peter was a good person, and the divorce was not due to any horrendous fault of his. We hit it off immediately, and ours was clearly a soul connection. Once Peter and I began our relationship about a month after meeting, his case became top priority, and, unfortunately for my boss, evolved into a non-billable file.

Peter was from Pula, Yugoslavia, and arrived in the United States only ten years before. He had his own successful business and was quite intelligent. He was also charming. I found his accent delightful and had no trouble communicating with him.

After two months of dating, he moved in with me on Thanksgiving Day, 1978. Justin was then 4 years old, and they got along beautifully. It was good for Justin to have a father figure since his own father was non-existent, and I thought it was perfect that we were a family unit. We lived together for two glorious years before getting married.

After his divorce, Peter's two children had moved with their mother to Texas. When she refused to allow phone contact or visitation, I encouraged Peter to petition for custody. The children were having problems with their mother, and I thought that Becky and Peter, Jr. would be a nice addition to our little family unit. I was wrong.

Becky and Peter, Jr. were 13 and 10 years old when they came to live with us. I recognized that our paths were destined to cross because of past life conflicts. My problem was that I did not know then how to work with the situation, so instead I fought it, which only added fuel to the fire.

When I first met Peter, he showed me school photos of his children. Just from those little square pictures, I felt an instant feeling of discomfort. I just didn't like them. As hard as I tried, it never got better. I was the original stepmother from hell, and I now accept full responsibility for allowing my marriage to be destroyed because of my own actions and feelings.

It took 13 more years, but I have made peace with both children, who are now adults. They understand, as do I, that we agreed to play out those roles in this lifetime. In order for me to be able to recognize and connect with my true twin soul, I had to experience and complete certain chapters in my life, no matter how troubled or chaotic.

Peter and I were married for only three years when we decided to amicably split. The marriage simply wasn't working out. It had become an issue of "my kid / your kids", and neither of us could see the other's view clearly. We still loved each other, but we couldn't live together as a family. Besides, I had already decided that I could not stick it out for five more years until his children were grown and out of the house. Patience was not my strong virtue then.

The year the marriage was ending, I had gone back to school to earn my college degree, and was already accepted into law school. I decided to give up a great lifestyle, which included a big house with a swimming pool and jacuzzi, no need to work, lots of travel and no money problems. These were all material things, which had suddenly become immaterial.

My sanity and my son's happiness were more important to me. What I had not yet realized is that it was my soul's chosen path that was creating all of these decisions and choices, and I was doing exactly what I was supposed to be doing. In essence, it was perfect.

The divorce was final in August of 1983. I began law school a week later, and didn't move out of the house until October of that year. We still shared the same bedroom and made love as we always had. We still went out with other couples. Nothing had changed except my last name, which had been shortened to "Best". In fact, my new name had been selected by the stooges at a "stooge lunch" honoring my decision to get divorced.

However, the problems with the children were also the same, and I finally moved out in October after a shouting match over some stupid thing I had said to his son. The night I left the house I was hysterical, and Sandra and Michael came to my rescue. They were there to help me get settled into the same townhouse Peter and I had first lived in during the early years of our relationship. The townhouse had been returned to me as part of our divorce settlement, so I felt like I was back at square one again.

It's funny what friends won't tell you until later, but both Sandra and Dee Dee later told me that they never thought Peter and I were meant for each other. They were wrong. Peter and I were absolutely perfect for each other. We had to have our life together exactly as it was. I had to know that feeling of ecstatic love and the destruction of it, or I would never have been able to know and love my twin soul without conditions or expectations. Even the negative experience of being a bad stepmother was essential to the development of my relationship with Dennis' children. We learn from experience, and I can finally say that I learned a lot from Peter and his children.

The story of my relationship with Peter doesn't end there. Our love for each other and our souls' ties were so strong that we continued a love affair for ten years after our divorce. I am not proud of this. It's just merely a statement of truth.

I cried the day he got married, only one year after our divorce. I cried when he told me his wife was pregnant. I cried when he told me she was pregnant the second time. His marriage has always appeared to be strained, however, he has two beautiful daughters. He loves them dearly, and in his own way, he loves his wife.

During those ten years, whenever I was involved in a relationship with another man, Peter and I never got together physically. While he wasn't happy about it, he respected the fact that I was with someone else. We also always kept our lines of communication open.

When I was not involved in a relationship, we were always there for each other. It kept me somewhat sane during the law school years and it was a perfect arrangement for me. I welcomed the comfort of being old friends and lovers without fear of commitments or responsibility. However, the pain was occasionally present, especially when he had to leave or the times when I was lonely and actually regretted our divorce.

The only people I ever confided in about my affair with Peter were Sandra, Michael, Dee Dee and Jerry. I tried to rationalize away the word "affair" by believing that since we had once been married to each other, and since I had no intention of breaking up his current marriage, it didn't matter.

I fondly recall the episode when Sandra called Peter at his home to let him know about my brain tumor. It was November of 1986, and I had been admitted to the hospital on an emergency basis and was being scheduled for surgery. Sandra and Michael had come to bring my personal things to me. It was late at night, and since Sandra knew Peter could not freely speak from his home with his wife present, she made the call short and one-sided. "Peter," she said primly and to the point, "this is Sandra. Alice is at South Miami Hospital. She has a brain tumor. she just wanted you to know. Good-bye." Peter was at my bedside the next morning at 6:30AM.

I never resented Peter's wife. She came into his life after we were divorced. She, however, never liked me. She even tore up old family photos that had me in them. Peter said it was because he still talked about me, and she believed that he never stopped loving me. I now know it was our souls' destiny, and she too, had chosen to be included in this journey.

It was late in 1993 that our physical encounters ended. It just happened. Peter and I had been lovers for 15 years; my longest relationship with anyone. But we had to play it out; to dance the dance; to create the scene that we had been destined to be in together.

My life was finally in the process of closing chapters, and Peter's chapter needed closure as well. It was as though we both knew I was preparing to meet someone new and very special. I could not be ready to have anyone in my life on an unconditional basis until I had complete and final closure with Peter. Even though he had been a main staple in my existence and he accepted the fact that whatever I was waiting for did not include him, he still continued to try. However, once Dennis came into my life, he never initiated another phone call. Somehow, he just knew this was "the one".

Peter and I continue to remain friends. I still call him every year on his birthday. Friends do things like that. I called him when my mother died in 1997. He loved her very much, and she had always blamed me for the failure of our marriage. I never argued with her about that. We will always love each other, but we never again need to be lovers. We played out that role to the fullest, and I thank him for the experience.

- Rob -

Peter was the first man I ever loved. Considering the fact that he was my second husband, that is a bizarre statement, but it's true.

My first marriage sort of just happened. I was twenty years old, and wanted to get out on my own. I became a mother just four months before my 25th birthday. In the early 70's, that's how we did it. You go to college; you meet a man, get married, and become a wife and mother. When I turned 25, I knew that I had made a mistake in getting married so young, and in not finishing college.

I believe that something magical happens at age 25. You awaken; you mature; you see that you have purpose and desires. While I will never regret that my son was born during that time period, I know that he was the sole purpose in my getting married to his father. I often tease him in new age jargon and ask, "I know why you chose me to be your mother, but why on earth did you choose Rob to be your father?"

Rob and I met in 1968 while I was a freshman at the University of Tennessee. We eloped in 1970, and lived in his hometown of Knoxville, Tennessee. We separated after six years, when Justin was only 18 months old. The divorce was final six months later, and Justin and I moved to Miami where I had grown up and where my entire family still lived.

The first seven years after the divorce were spent trying, unsuccessfully, to collect the small amount of child support I had been awarded. Rob was never an attentive father when we lived together, and he chose to totally ignore not only parental responsibilities, but also his financial obligations once we got divorced. I also resented his refusal to give Justin the Lionel model train sets that we had collected for years. The trains are quite valuable collector's items, and Rob had promised that they would be given to Justin, but he of course never kept his word. The trains played a role not only in our post-divorce litigation, but in my personal growth and closure process as well.

I was angry, but I never spoke ill of Rob to Justin. I decided success was the best revenge, and I went to law school in 1983, when Justin was almost 9 years old. That same year, I agreed that Rob could waive his parental rights. He hadn't seen Justin since his 3rd birthday, and Justin never really knew him anyway.

So, I was on my own. Sort of. Fortunately for me, I was blessed to have parents who were able and willing to assist me financially, and I am forever grateful and indebted to them for their generosity in putting me through law school.

The negative relationship with Rob was important to my personal and professional development. Because of my own life experiences, I was able to recognize and understand specific issues when they were presented to me in my divorce practice.

I had become the consummate client. I had two failed marriages, one bitter, and one friendly. I knew what it was like to not receive child support; and I knew what it was like to have a husband paying support to another. As a result of my first divorce, I knew firsthand what it was like to have had inadequate divorce counsel as well. I also knew, because of Peter and our respective children, what problems a blended family encounters. Because of that experience, I am able to realistically counsel clients who want custody changes or who are contemplating second marriages. I am, more often than not, quite candid and forceful with them when I ask them to be sure their love is strong enough to withstand the inevitable problems.

With the exception of domestic violence experience (thank goodness), I literally have sat in every chair, and I have participated in almost every aspect of divorce problems. Even when I served as a special master or mediator, I was able to see issues from the judge's perspective. While I did not realize it at the time each experience was happening, the Universe and my own soul were assisting me in my personal growth by preparing me for what was yet to come into my life.

I admire the young people today who take time to experience life and themselves before getting married. They have their own apartments or homes; they travel, work, and discover who they really are without the need for attachment to another. They live life. They create their own reality. When I was able to do just that for myself, I opened myself up to the Universe and its wondrous events began to flow my way.

- *Albuquerque, New Mexico* -

I was beginning to learn how to "go with the flow" and just let things happen. It was October 1994, and the Family Law section of the American Bar Association was having their fall meeting in Albuquerque, New Mexico. I decided to attend the meeting, and take additional days to tour the region, which made a nice vacation for Justin and myself. He took some time off from college to join me, which also gave him an opportunity to check out the college campuses in the area for a post-graduate program.

The annual Hot Air Balloon Fiesta was in Albuquerque, and it was the most extraordinary experience we'd ever had. With Justin's expertise in photography, and my point and shoot camera, we wound up with two volumes of spectacular pictures. The highlight was when we took a ride in a balloon the day before we left, and flew over the city. I hadn't taken a trip alone with Justin in many years and, now that he was becoming an adult this also gave us time to get to enjoy each other's company.

I had come to this meeting for the sole purpose of seeing New Mexico and getting more in touch with what I believed was my Native American ties from a past life. The fact that it was a business trip was a bonus. At that time, I was not dating anyone, and had not been involved in a relationship for many months. I knew absolutely no one in the family law section, but I knew that I would have no trouble meeting new people. What I didn't expect was that Justin would be a matchmaker of sorts.

Our first night in Albuquerque we decided to have an early dinner. It was early by New Mexico time, but late by our internal clocks that were still on Eastern Standard Time. It had been a long day of travel, and we chose to have a light meal at the restaurant in the hotel, and then go to sleep early. As we sat at the table deciding what to order, Justin noticed a man seated at a nearby table all alone.

He said, "I'm going to see if he's alone and ask him if he wants company."

"Don't you dare!" I laughingly replied. I laughed, but deep down I knew that Justin was up to something that he had to carry out.

With that, Justin got up and went to the man's table, which was on the next level below ours. It was situated so that I could see the table and place settings, but I could not see the man's face. What I did see was Justin sitting down at the same table, engaged in conversation with a total stranger.

Justin returned to our table about 10 minutes later, all smiles, and said, "He's a divorce lawyer from Texas, and he's all alone, too."

I was in shock that he had actually gone to speak with him, and still laughing, insisted that he tell me everything that was said.

He told me that when he approached the man's table, he said, "Are you here alone? Because I'm here with my mom, and she's alone, too."

"Omigod! You didn't! What'd he say?" I demanded, still laughing out loud.

He just laughed, and asked, "Does your mother know you're doing this?" Then he told me to sit down, and we just talked. I told him all about you."

That's my son... nothing scares him. Well, I always did encourage him to be outgoing and independent. We both inherited that gift from my father.

While eating our dinner, I looked up to see the man coming toward us. He was tall, lanky, good looking, and was wearing tight jeans and cowboy boots. Justin had done all right.

He introduced himself as Joe, and said that he was here for the Family Law section meeting, too. I apologized for Justin's escapade, and we shared a self-conscious laugh. We said we'd see each other around, and then he left as quickly as he arrived.

After dinner, Justin went to the room to unpack, and I went to find the registration and reception area for the section meeting which was scheduled for the next day. Of course, synchronicity being what it is, the first person I saw was Joe. We again shared a laugh and he asked me to join him for a glass of wine. We sat and chatted easily, as though we had been friends for a long time. He said he needed to go phone his son and I said that I needed to go to the room to unwind after such a long day of travel. He asked me to meet him later for a drink, and I said I would. However, when I got to the room, I realized how tired I was, so I telephoned him to explain and ask for a rain check.

At the seminar the next morning, Joe and I somehow connected up again. That was no small feat in a room of over 400 people. We sat together at all the sessions and shared all our breaks as though we had planned to be with one another. It just happened so naturally, and we were both delighted to have each other's company.

That first afternoon, I had planned to go to Santa Fe with Justin. Hans had told me about a bookstore in Santa Fe where he often did readings, and I had promised him that I would stop by to say hello to his friends who ran the store. Joe said he was going to Santa Fe, too, and asked if we wanted to join him. Justin had been away at college for two years, and I hadn't really spent much time with him, so this was to be our special day together. I told Joe that I had really wanted to spend some private time with Justin, and he understood. Also, I knew that we were going to the metaphysical bookstore, and I wasn't ready to hit Joe with all of that "aerie-fairy" stuff, as Hans jokingly called it. Joe appeared to be this straight conservative type from Texas, and I didn't really want to explain my spiritual beliefs to a complete stranger.

The Universe works in strange ways, and sometimes it takes a two-by-four and hits us across the head with it. The next day, while on a coffee break, Joe and I were sitting and chatting about our side trips to Santa Fe. He asked where I went, and I simply told him we had gone to a bookstore.

"Which one?"

"Oh, a metaphysical bookstore a friend wanted me to check out," I casually replied.

"I thought so. I just finished reading *The Celestine Prophecy*. I believe in that stuff, too."

With that, our conversations took off on a whole new perspective, and we were really able to communicate on a deeper level. I told him about the bookstore and the pendulums Justin and I had purchased for each other. I also told him about my involvement with MIEL, and how my life and my law practice had been changing lately.

I had just finished telling Joe about how Hans had brought me messages from Sherril during a recent reading. Within five minutes, a total stranger walked over wearing a nametag with the name "Sherril". I had never seen that spelling for anyone else before, and neither had this woman! She was from Indiana and was at the conference with her lawyer husband, Sam. I told her about my friend's name being spelled the same way, and that I had just been speaking about her.

Their first and middle names, "Sherril Ann", were identical and were spelled the same. To add to the magic of the moment, I told her that my friend Sherril's oldest son is named Sam. We kept the game going with more questions. The Indiana Sherril's maiden name was Katz. My friend Sherril's mother's maiden name was Kahn. At that, we stopped looking for comparisons.

I knew that this was a message from Sherril, letting me know that she was always with me. She was there showing me how synchronistic events happen and telling me that I should allow myself to be open to receive the many messages. The messages and signs are everywhere; we just need to listen and pay attention.

Joe and I hung out together the rest of the week, and Justin was delighted that he didn't have to stay with me the whole time, especially at the Balloon Fiesta where he was free to roam the many acres and take rolls of magnificent photos. It was also nice for me to have Joe's company during the meetings and special social events.

We continued our friendship by telephone for many months. We had kept our connection totally platonic, and it never progressed past that. We had actually planned for him to come to Miami to visit with me in February for my 45th birthday, however, literally at the last minute, he backed out. His excuse was lame, and I suspect it was just basic fear. Of course, that too, was perfect.

My first reaction was to call Michael, as he was my closest friend and confidante. Sobbing, I said, "Why does this always happen to me? Why can't I have a normal relationship?" He tried to console me by saying that it wasn't me, it was Joe, and I shouldn't be too concerned about it. Someone would come along soon. That was comforting, but what did Michael know? His own poor judgment and relationship track record since Sandra's death was becoming legendary within our circle of friends.

I celebrated that birthday by going to lunch with my office staff and a client who had become my friend. I received so many flowers that day from friends and clients, my home looked like a florist's warehouse. That night, I went to an automatic writing class at MIEL, and received a powerful message from Sandra. It turned out to be a wonderful birthday.

To this day, I have never quite understood why Joe and I were brought together, except to give each of us some friendship and comfort while we were each alone at a large conference.

And, once again, the message is clear that each relationship, no matter how brief, and even if platonic, brings us closer to meeting our twin soul. For that reason, I thank the Universe for the experience. I didn't know how many more test relationships were scheduled for my soul's journey, but I was getting rather anxious to meet this man Hans said was "on the way".

Chapter Nine

The Awakening Begins

- *The Third Reading* -

My spiritual growth process continued as I attended classes, seminars and weekend workshops at MIEL. My third reading with Hans was on October 24th, 1994. That was a remarkable day for me in many ways, and the beginning of an equally remarkable week. I knew that I was opening up and allowing myself to accept and acknowledge messages from multiple sources. The Universe was putting people in my path that not only needed my assistance, but also were to be in my life for some special reason, even though it might have seemed insignificant at the time.

I had just returned from my trip to Albuquerque and I excitedly told Hans about meeting Joe and about the synchronistic events that led to my meeting Sherril and Sam from Indiana. Hans told me in this reading that I had reached the next level in my spiritual growth.

He explained, "That's called evidence. They're giving something to you so that you can know they are around you to assist. You're going to begin to witness the power of your ability to heal. It's part of what your soul is here for. You provide an opportunity for healing. That's why they're saying, 'slow down'. I told you on the day that I met you that your soul has a destiny; it has something to do this lifetime. You shouldn't argue with that."

He continued with, "Having said that, I also want you to hear, that nowhere since I've known you these past three months have I seen that you came into this life to be alone.

But the person who comes to your wedding dressed in your clothes is a person that did not exist one year ago. You're not that child by any stretch of the imagination. You had to become that person."

He was almost lecturing now. "There is a saying, 'you have to get lost to be found.' You can't go from joy to joy; you have to go from despair to joy. As plants grow out of the darkness into the light, so do you. You have to grow that way. What I'm trying to get you to do is to honor what's already happened."

I sat there in awed silence as Hans told me that my life would certainly be changing. "Alice, you were meant to be in service. You have another destiny that can be a little more powerful than mine in many ways."

He had told me that during the first reading. However, he now stated what he meant in greater detail, "You have the power of the law combined with the power of the Spirit. I have the power of the Spirit, and the power of awareness. I know the laws of life. But you know the laws of the land."

I voiced my disbelief that I could have any such spiritual powers, and told him that lately I hadn't even been able to write in my journal.

"I feel that you've hit a plateau," he said. "When you hit that plateau, there's a little numbness that comes in, as if nothing's happening anymore. That's the exact time you know you've arrived. The Spirit must bring the faith back into it, and the only way to have the faith is to stop the momentum for a little bit. It's a true lesson in faith. Frustration, doubt, and all the old behavioral patterns will present themselves."

I felt then that rather than "arriving", I had hit a brick wall. Now, four years later, having studied the messages in

Conversations With God and other metaphysical books, and from the many workshops I attended these past years, I have come to believe and embrace the concept that there are only two emotions in the world: love and fear. Everything else is based on those two emotions. I jokingly refer to them as "subsidiary" emotions. I wanted to be in touch with Spirit so much, I was blocking my own emergence. I realize now that I was getting in my own way due to my own feelings of inadequacy stemming from fear.

Hans then elaborated even more. "But the difference is that I expect you to face them down. You no longer have to look at them in the old way because you have risen above those old patterns. Tell your guidance you want to be removed from your fears, and that you want to resume your journaling."

I said, "I am doing more writing now, and I know messages are being given to me. I just want more, and I want it now."

"You have merged with the energy as a type of quiet acceptance," Hans said. You're falling into your belief system. I want you to get a little more comfortable with your emotional energies," Hans said. "Your pendulum is also very important to you. That's one of the ways that Spirit is going to help you to receive. You're now in the space where the Spirit can use you. They're giving you the opportunity to understand that you can just speak things and they happen."

Aaron had taught me how to use a pendulum, simply by asking "yes" and "no" questions. With practice I became adept in the process, and soon I was teaching others to use pendulums to answer their pressing questions. The pendulum and automatic writing seemed to be my "tools" in enabling me to connect with my guides and spirit. When I focused my energy in the right directions, the plateau began to shift and my growth process was on the move again.

- *The Voice* -

Four days later, I was scheduled to meet with a potential new client. It was to be the first time I would hear a voice speak to me; a voice from somewhere other than my own thoughts.

The appointment was for a legal consultation with a woman named Carol who had been referred to me by an attorney who did not practice marital law. Carol told me that she had been married for 22 years, and her husband had just informed her he wanted a divorce. They had been college sweethearts, and she'd considered him to be her best friend. They had one son who was almost 18 and was graduating from high school.

After several years of deceit and denial, the husband finally had just admitted to her that he was having an affair with a female co-worker, and that the relationship was very serious. The woman in my office was obviously distraught. She quite simply could not cope with the situation that had just been thrown at her! She was experiencing the classic symptoms of divorce, all of which stem from the root emotion of fear: anger, guilt, anxiety, depression, and lack of self-worth, to name just a few.

During our initial conference, I kept hearing a persistent voice, which I knew was not my own thought. This voice quite distinctly said, "Ask her." It also refused to be ignored, and kept saying, "Ask her." That was the only message, but it was enough. Although I had never before heard this voice, I just knew what it was. Somehow, I also knew what it meant.

This was what I had been asking for; this was the voice of my guide gently giving me guidance.

I knew what to do, but I was just trying to avoid it. I was obviously concerned about the possible consequence, and was operating out of emotions based in fear. Here I was, an attorney sitting across from a potential client whom I had never met before. Though emotionally upset, she appeared to be quite prim and proper. I did not know her religious or spiritual beliefs, but during the initial interview process, she mentioned that her son attended Catholic school. Aware of what I was about to ask, I knew I would be taking a great risk professionally.

Nevertheless, I threw caution to the wind, and said, "Carol, I'm going to ask you a question that has nothing to do with legal advice, but I must ask how you feel about something." After a short pause, I then asked, "Do you believe in fate?"

"Well, sort of," she replied hesitantly.

Encouraged, I plunged ahead. "Are you familiar with metaphysics and new age books?"

"Not much," she said, "but I'm open to what they have to say."

I was surprised and pleased with her response, so I went further out on a limb. "Suppose I were to tell you that when you and your husband first met 27 years ago, this was already in the plan. This part of your life had been predestined, and no amount of crying, begging, or counseling would fix anything. Suppose for the moment that the sole purpose of the two of you meeting and getting married was to experience your lives together for all these years, and to have your son. Your son is now almost grown, and has turned out well. Now, it's time to move on to the next chapter of your lives, separately. If you believed that, would you feel better?"

To my even greater surprise, Carol nodded and said, "Yes, I think I would."

Once we had passed that hurdle, and the elements of anger and the need for revenge were out of the way, I was able to direct the discussion to legal matters of property distribution and support.

Within two hours, I'd been retained, and her husband even came to the office to pay the retainer fee for her.

That case settled after several months of negotiation, amicably and without any litigation. There were a few stumbling blocks, but with appropriate assistance, they were able to see past the initial guilt, anger, and pain. Carol was once again empowered and able to make her own choices. She and her husband were able to take control of their own lives, which enabled the attorneys to work together rather than against each other, to reach a fair and equitable divorce agreement.

What I said to my client that afternoon is what I have discovered I truly believe. If more people believed in fate, perhaps they'd accept uncomfortable situations without anger or remorse. They would be able to lead productive lives without worrying about results or what the other person is doing, thinking, or feeling.

The moral of that story is simply to listen to your inner voice. Pay attention to the signals and the signs that sometimes are subtle, and sometimes hit us between the eyes like sledgehammers. I listened and I allowed myself to act upon what I'd heard. That was a breakthrough for me, and I consider it a blessing that I not only heard it, but that I reacted accordingly. I have learned to be open to every message ever since, and am always thankful for the spiritual assistance.

- *Introduction to Metaphysics* -

A few days after having my first reading with Hans, I signed up to attend a class on tarot cards. When I arrived at MIEL that night, I was told that the class had been cancelled because there were not enough people registered. However, since there are no accidents, I met Lynn Schwartz, the head of the Angel volunteer" program at MIEL. Lynn and I hit it off immediately, and we sat for three hours and just talked. Somehow, with Lynn's influence and persistence, I found myself in a Tai Chi class that night and in an Angel training program the next day.

As an Angel volunteer, I became skilled in using the bookstore's cash register, which greatly amused those who knew me to be a successful lawyer. It was also no coincidence that my law office was located directly across the street from MIEL, and I was able to assist at a moment's notice if the need was there. It was fun giving of myself, and in the process I learned how to scan ISBN codes as well as incense, candles, and candy bars. I became a regular at MIEL and, at the founders' invitation, agreed to be on the Board of Directors.

One of the many benefits of being a volunteer was that I was able to attend all workshops and classes at a reduced rate. Therefore, I registered for every class and workshop that was offered. This enabled me to sample and experience the wide variety of topics and lecturers. I learned a lot, and was able to weed out which belief systems were not for me. I discovered an entire new vocabulary in the world of metaphysics. This included words such as guides, angels, Spirit, light workers, reiki and many others that I have yet to learn how to pronounce properly. Even the word "love" took on a whole new meaning when applied in the spiritual context. I attended meditation groups and learned not only that I have mind chatter, but that with practice, I can quiet it. However, I have still not taken a tarot card class.

- The First Workshop -

The first full weekend workshop I signed up for was to be facilitated by Alan Cohen. Alan was a personal friend of Aaron and Hans, and they both recommended his workshop to me. I had not yet read any of Alan's books, so I purchased his best selling book, *The Dragon Doesn't Live Here Anymore*. I began reading the book and loved it immediately. For some strange reason, I felt a close connection to the author, but I had not yet learned to recognize these signals. When I met Alan the first night of the workshop, we interacted as though old friends.

The workshop began on Friday night, and consisted of Alan's opening stories that are his trademark form of motivational speaking, combined with soul sharing exercises that allow people to open up and get to know each other. For the first time, I actually allowed myself to get into the moment and shared warmly with people I didn't know. It was the beginning of the tearing down of the wall I had carried around my entire life as my protection. That night, when Alan asked us to relate instances of how Spirit had helped us in our everyday lives, I shared the story about Carol and "the voice" with the group. It had just happened to me that afternoon, and was very fresh in my mind.

Next, we did a special exercise where we were told to choose a partner. Holly Schwartztol, one of the founders of MIEL, and I gravitated toward each other and made a connection that continues to this day. We both are very strong- willed professional women who don't usually allow others to see into our hearts and souls. Yet, the exercise we did opened us up and we each felt the immediate warmth and love for a kindred spirit.

What began on Friday as my awakening and acceptance of being open with strangers, continued in full force on Saturday. There were about 25 people in the Saturday workshop, which was facilitated totally by Alan. I had just begun my volunteer work at MIEL only weeks earlier, and didn't know most of the people there.

This was a new experience for me. I had never been one who could hug and share openly with strangers. I now know that my fear was that if people got through my wall, they might see the "real me." Until I knew who the real me was, how could I possibly let others in? Most importantly, until I liked and accepted the real me, how could anyone else?

Alan incorporates a lot of music and dancing into his experiential workshops and retreats. The type of dance he introduced us to was Sufi. By definition, Sufis are mystics on the path to their Beloved (God). Most Sufis are Muslims, followers of the religion of Islam. Some Sufis, primarily in the West, are involved with other religions, or follow no formal religion. They are essentially directed by the higher source of wisdom within the human heart.

One of the Sufi dances we learned consisted of two circles, one inside the other. Each circle contained the same number of people, with each person facing a starting partner in the other circle. The instructions were quite simple: each circle rotated to the left, which meant that a new partner was faced continually. As each partner was met, we were to honor him or her with special hand movements that would be mirrored by the partner. There was to be no physical touching and no speaking other than the words of the song. The souls were speaking through the eyes as they would meet each new person. The words of the song were to be repeated with each new partner..

"I am the light of the world; that is my only function. You are the light of the world; that is your only function. We are the light of the world; that is our only function. That is why we are here."

As the verses were completed with each new partner, we would honor the partner by bowing slightly and would then move on to the next person.

When we formed our two circles, one more person was needed for the outer circle. I was in the inner circle. Alan was the only person left, so he joined the outer circle and, as was perfect, chose the position across from me. The music began, and the two circles began their rotation.

As I faced each new partner, our eyes remained fixed while we sang the words and mirrored the hand movements of the other. I had never before felt so honest, open, and free with my soul and spirit as I did that day. The wall was definitely crumbling.

With each person, I felt more comfortable and enjoyed the moment. There was one man in the outer circle named Bob, who reminded me of Uncle Fester from "The Addams Family". But, he had the most incredibly piercing green eyes. Under normal conditions, Bob and I would not have connected as we did during this Sufi dance. For some strange reason, when we stared at each other's eyes during our partnering, I felt a warm and loving feeling emanating from him and, more to my surprise, from myself towards him. This was definitely a new experience for me; I don't believe I had ever felt such emotions toward someone in a totally platonic manner, without expectations. I was suddenly beginning to understand what this "new age touchy-feely" stuff was about.

Then, it happened a second time. When it came time for Alan to be opposite me, I immediately felt an incredible heat that generated from the field of energy between us. It was as though we were staring completely past each other's eyes and into our souls.

Later, we did another exercise where we were told to select three people from the group to give a message to. Four people came up to me with messages.

The first was Veronica, who was bubbly and came running up to me before anyone else could get my attention. She said, "I don't know why I have to meet you, but I've been drawn to you all day, and I feel that I just need to connect with you somehow. What do you do?"

"I'm a divorce lawyer," I replied.

She laughed and said, "That's it! I definitely need to talk to you!"

We hugged, and I gave her my business card and offered her a free consultation. Her guides were definitely with her, because I always charged my standard hourly rate for initial consultations.

The next person who came to me was someone I had been seeking out to give one of my messages. It was Bob. He told me I had incredible eyes and that he felt a strong energy from me when we were in the Sufi dance circles. I was amazed and told him that was exactly what I was coming to tell him! We gave each other a warm hug, and I knew at once that his eyes were truly the windows to his beautiful soul, in a less than perfect body and face. Sadly, Bob had an advanced case of cancer and died about five months later.

After exchanging messages and hugs with several other

people, I went to where Alan was sitting, quietly observing the interaction of the room. I told him about the tremendous energy and heat that I'd felt from him during the Sufi dance. I was quite surprised when he said he, too, had felt the energy field coming from me.

Weeks later, when I discussed the workshop with Hans, who had now become a personal friend, he said that Alan and I were no doubt experiencing a past-life memory that our souls had recognized. It wasn't until the next year when I re-read *The Celestine Prophecy* that I understood the concept of energy fields, and I was amazed that I had actually experienced such an event so early in my metaphysical training.

That Saturday night after the workshop, I wrote in my journal that my life was moving at an incredibly fast pace, and that it was wonderfully exciting. So much had changed since the days I felt that my life was mere existence without purpose. Had it really only been two months?

I called Hans and Aaron in North Carolina that same night and told them that I had decided to go to Alan Cohen's Mastery Training retreat. It was to be in Hawaii for one week in March, 1995. My 45th birthday was in February, and the trip would be my birthday present to myself. The only time I had been to Hawaii was with Rob in 1975, which had been toward the end of our marriage. After 20 years, I wanted to experience Hawaii again, this time with more positive emotions and memories. What I would discover was that my soul needed the experience even more than I could ever imagine.

- Meeting Nelly -

My client Carol and I had developed a close friendship, and she was also becoming very enlightened spiritually. In the early part of 1995, she called and in an excited voice told me she had just been to see a psychic.

She said, "You're not going to believe it, but your name came up in my reading!"

Carol began to describe the content of a private reading with a psychic named Nelly. A friend of hers had suggested that she go to see Nelly just for fun and to see if she could predict what would happen with her divorce situation.

She said that during the reading, Nelly asked, "Who's Alice?"

Carol told me that she was so in awe of what Nelly had been telling her that for a few moments she couldn't even remember who Alice was.

She could hardly contain her excitement when she repeated what Nelly had told her. She said that Nelly was quite specific and told her, "She's going to be very helpful. You are to listen to her."

Carol told me she almost fell off her chair when she realized that "Alice" was her divorce lawyer. She told Nelly that she completely understood the message.

Carol knew that I had been going to Hans for readings, and she said that I had to go see Nelly, if for no other reason, just out of curiosity to see what would come up in my own reading.

I was intrigued, so I called to make an appointment to see Nelly the next day. She did not know who had referred me to her, and it was never mentioned at that time.

When we met, our energies connected like old friends, and my reading was as spectacular as Carol had anticipated. Nelly went into a great amount of detail about what was happening in my life, and her accuracy was amazing.

She told me that she saw me going on a boat. "Do you like the water?" she asked.

I said that I did, but I didn't know anyone who had a boat that I would be going on. She kept insisting she saw me on the water, and when she finally used the word "ocean", I suddenly remembered that I was going on a weekend cruise with Carol in February the week before my birthday. It was going to be another birthday present to myself because I deserved it.

Nelly was quite serious when she told me to "expect a surprise" on the trip. She didn't know what the surprise would be, but it was going to be a gift from my guides.

During the reading, she suddenly asked, "Who's Carol?" I had to laugh, and I told Nelly who Carol was and that my name had come up during her reading, too.

That was the first of many readings I would have with Nelly over the next few years. The February cruise to the Bahamas was fantastic, and my guides came through with flying colors. My "gift" was wrapped in the uniform of the ship's chief engineer, a marvelous Norwegian who bore an uncanny resemblance to both Rob and Peter, my two ex-husbands.

I became an enthusiastic promoter for Nelly, and referred many people to her. Her method of channeling is completely different from Hans, however, her readings are every bit as powerful.

Chapter Ten

Alice's Onion Peeling

- *The Calm before the Storm* -

What I had planned as a combined vacation and spiritual retreat would become a major step in my growth process.

March, 1995 had finally arrived, and it was time to go to Hawaii for the Mastery training. I decided to fly out a few days early so that I could spend some time alone in Maui and also become used to the five-hour time difference. Alan had arranged for a small local hotel to offer accommodations at greatly reduced rates to his retreat participants. I made reservations to stay at The Mauian on Napali Bay for a few days before and after the retreat.

It was a perfect setting for being able to get away from the world and go within one's self. Each room faced the courtyard, which led directly to the beach. With the balcony doors open, the sound of the ocean waves flowed throughout the room, along with the salty, yet soft Pacific breezes. The rooms had no phones and no television; total solitude was the perfect prescription for me at that time. There was a guest book on the dresser that contained the signatures and hand-written comments from previous guests who had stayed in that particular room. It was so quaint, and I enjoyed reading what others before me had written. Of course, I joined the list and added my own reflections: *"First Day – First Impression: Delightful! After such a long trip, it's nice to know Paradise was and is the destination. This is far superior to any fancy, high-priced hotel chain. The warmth and friendliness of the place and people are*

evident, and I eagerly look forward to my stay here. Aloha!
Alice Best, Miami, Florida"

Those first few days were peaceful, and I enjoyed spending some quiet time to myself. This was a pleasant change and necessary relief from the daily stress I was used to in my law practice. The high point of the day was at dusk when the dolphins and whales would come close to the shore and put on a spectacular show for the tourists. It was so serene and wondrous that I knew I was in paradise. I felt a calmness about me that led me to believe I had lived here before. It was the same calmness I had felt 20 years earlier, but I didn't recognize it then. An old comfortable feeling came to me; a knowing that I had lived in Maui in a past lifetime.

The setting was so beautiful, that while I was there, a couple from California had their wedding ceremony on the beach, Hawaiian style. I was told that the couple had been repeat guests at The Mauian for twelve years, so this was the perfect location for their wedding. Their parents, children, and friends from California were all in attendance, each barefooted and adorned with traditional floral leis. The women wore flowing cotton sundresses, and had fresh island flowers in their hair. The men were decked out in Hawaiian tuxedoes, which consisted of black tie and tails with Bermuda shorts. The sunset was magnificent, and I was honored to have been included among the guests on the beach. I thought how wonderful it would be to have my own wedding in a setting such as that.

- *Synchronicity, Again Revealed* -

After three relaxing and wonderful days in Maui, it was time to fly to the Big Island to meet the people I would spend the next five days with. The retreat was being held in Kona on the island of Hawaii. It seemed that my life was being filled with synchronistic messages lately, and an interesting event happened on the way to Kona.

While waiting to board the small plane, which did not have assigned seating for such a short flight, I was concerned that there would be no space left for my carry-on luggage. I was one of the last people to board, and the plane was filling quickly. As I entered the plane, I was surprised to see that the very first seat in the front bulkhead row was empty. I asked the couple seated in the window and center seats if the aisle seat was available, and they said that it was. The man assisted me in putting my suitcase in the overhead compartment, and the three of us soon began chatting like old friends.

His name was David Moses, and he was a jewelry designer and manufacturer from northern California. His fiancée Debbie, who was sitting in the middle seat next to him, was strikingly beautiful and told me that she was an Apache Indian. I admired the necklace Debbie was wearing and she told me that it was a one-of-a-kind pendant that David had designed. As I looked at it closely, I saw the intricate detail and noticed that it was sterling silver and a signed piece with his signature "Moses".

Being a jeweler's daughter who loves unique pieces of jewelry, I asked to see more of his work. They showed me their catalog and promised to show me their samples when we landed. David explained to me that he had studied anatomy, so that when he designed his cuff bracelets he could be sure they would fit a woman's wrist comfortably.

Debbie offered to sell me the chain and pendant she was wearing. "I know the designer," she laughed, "and I can get another one." Without hesitation, I purchased both her necklace and a matching bracelet at an incredible discount.

They asked why I was so far from home, and I told them I was in Hawaii to attend a spiritual retreat. We spoke about destiny and agreed that the seat was obviously meant for me, which is why no one else seemed to see the empty seat when they entered the plane.

Debbie then told me that she had never worn that particular pendant and she really didn't know why she had it on that day.

With a knowing smile, I replied, "It's no coincidence that the seat was there for me so that I could meet both of you. For some reason, I am supposed to buy the necklace."

Synchronistic events such as this would continue to happen as I proceeded along my spiritual journey. I was opening up and allowing myself not only to see what was being offered, but also to accept the gifts as they were being presented to me, in any form. I believe that this was the Universe's way of letting me know and showing me that it recognized my existence and that I was indeed headed in the right direction.

- The Hawaii Retreat -

"This entire program is worth its weight in gold. This is a weeklong therapy session and we are each being healed as needed. Each time one person speaks, someone else is affected in some way."

I wrote those words in the small journal I kept with me for each part of the weeklong "Mastery Training", which was the theme of Alan Cohen's retreat.

There were 12 of us eager to bear our souls: 10 women and 2 men. The only staff members were Alan, his enthusiastic and fabulous assistant Samantha Freeman, and Carla, a medium who was there to give us channeled messages.

The retreat center was neither primitive nor rustic, as I had expected. Instead it was a modern building, large and roomy with high vaulted ceilings, and the meeting area had plush carpeting. We had professionally catered meals three times a day in the spacious combined kitchen and dining areas. The swimming pool and ample patio faced the ocean which allowed for a view that was magnificent all the time, but especially so at sunset.

The dormitory style bedrooms were quite comfortable for two people to share. There were no locks on the doors, but none were necessary. A nice thing about associating with truly spiritually minded people is that trust is always a given. We had been told that roommates would be pre-assigned by choice or by chance, and since I did not know anyone prior to my arrival, I let Spirit choose my roommate. As always, Spirit does everything for a reason and there are no "accidents". My roommate, Mary, was the perfect choice for what I needed to learn.

Mornings came early, and Samantha would stroll down the halls past the bedrooms to awaken us gently with her melodic singing. Amazingly, although there were only three bathrooms for fifteen people, I can't recall having any scheduling problems.

The first morning session was spent getting to know each other, and learning basic spiritual principles that we would use the remainder of the week and throughout our lives. My favorite sayings have become "your history is not your destiny" and "the Universe rearranges itself to create your own picture of reality". These simply mean that just because I've been accustomed to certain patterns during my life, I need not carry them with me forever. I am not "destined" to continue life as I've been used to; I have the power within me to change my own life and thus create my own destiny. Think you can or think you can't; either way, you'll be right. Whatever I can picture, I can create by merely sending that message out to the Universe.

It took some effort for me to believe and really know that I truly have that power, and as a result, I began to use those principles in my law practice. I am now able to assist clients in taking control of their own lives so that they can feel, believe in, and trust their own empowerment. However, I know that I wouldn't have been able to help others until I first learned how to love and empower myself.

The theme of our week in Kona was "self-worth". Most of us, including staff, were there to deal with self-worth issues. Another "new age" axiom is "The teacher teaches what he/she needs to learn." As it would turn out, Mary and Carla were there to be my teachers, and I theirs.

- In Your Face Productions -

We all learned from one another, and we only half-jokingly dubbed the week "In Your Face Productions". We each bring into our lives people, places or things to assist us in the demonstration of our own beliefs. Translated, that means that whatever I choose to believe at any given time, I will then manifest some person or thing to come into my life to demonstrate that same belief. Good, bad, or indifferent, the people, places, and events in my life are there at my request, and it is my choice to have them travel my path with me. The purpose is "to experience." When I remember that we are all spiritual beings having a human experience, then each experience is more easily accepted.

If it is my choice to have certain things, then it makes sense to believe that it can also be my choice to not have the same things appear in my life. What we learned to do in our mastery training was to upgrade our belief system; to shift the identity of "being" from victim to master. No one else has the power to make me a victim; only I have the power to create such a situation for myself. I am truly the "master of my own destiny" and therefore only I can choose to be the victim or the master.

The third axiom we learned was "My life is a reflection of what I believe I am worth." This is something I remembered hearing from my mother when I was a young child. She used to tell me, "If you don't like yourself, then no one else will." I had come to Hawaii to learn to like myself again. It was a tough struggle, and a real eye-opener. During the week, I was able to see myself as others saw me: sometimes I liked what I saw; sometimes I didn't. The healing through the onion peeling process was just beginning.

- The Peeling Process Begins -

With fifteen people continually interacting, the individual focus transferred from person to person as the need arose. My turn for healing came on Wednesday morning. It was during the "Tell me what's in your heart" exercise I had first experienced with Holly at the time of Alan's workshop in Miami. This was the exercise where each person is to bare the soul and tell the other what's in the heart. For some strange reason, it was during my partner's turn that I began getting emotional. My soul knew what was about to happen.

When it was my turn to answer, my own personal floodgates just opened and I couldn't stop crying; I couldn't even breathe.

Although there were seven couples performing this particular exercise, Alan observed what was happening with me and took control of the situation. As is customary in experiential exercises, the entire group comes together and focuses their attention on the one needing to process. They nurtured me and cradled me, which is an extraordinary emotional experience. The group formed a human cradle by standing across from each other in two lines, and joining their arms and hands to support a person's weight. I was then gently placed into their arms. While being cradled, I was sung to and showered with their genuine love and concern.

My emotions were so intense, I don't even remember what the specifics of that particular release were about. I do remember that it was powerful day, filled with emotional highs and lows.

After the morning session, I had a full body massage from one of the two massage therapists Alan had hired for the week. Part of the cost of the retreat entitled each of us to a full body massage and a private channeled reading with Carla.

The afternoon was scheduled for free time, and Samantha had a big surprise for us. She took us to the black sand beach, which turned out to be a nude beach. She forgot to tell us that on the way, and what an eye-opener we had when we arrived. There was no need for visualization that afternoon, and I was delighted that I had worn my contact lenses.

That night brought more fun and relaxation for the group. We learned how to belly dance, Hawaiian style. This was much more than just hula dancing, and I was glad that I brought my camcorder with me. The videotape is a hoot to watch!

After a very long and exhausting day, I just wanted to unwind quietly in my room, write of the day's events and record my thoughts in my journal. My roommate, however, wanted to chat, but she only wanted to chat about herself and her own feelings. At first, I put aside my journal and listened to her, but there didn't seem to be any end. I quickly realized that this wasn't a conversation, it was a monologue.

In retrospect, I should have given her the attention she needed and just listened, but it was frustrating to me at the time. Harsh words were said and I left the room. The day had begun emotionally, and ended the same way.

That set the tone for us for the remainder of the week, and it was uncomfortable. She thought I was self-centered and I, of course, thought the same of her. As I wrote about the episode in my journal, it became apparent to me that Mary was the "mirror" of my own flawed need to monopolize conversations.

The next day, during another experiential exercise, one of the women in the group faced each person and spoke to each one individually. When she faced me, she said she wanted to mirror my strength. Inwardly I had to laugh.

Because of my chosen career as a lawyer, I was aware that most people saw me as strong and confident, and even intimidating at times. I suppose the acting classes from my early childhood had finally paid off, since I was able to hide the self-worth issues I dealt with constantly.

The day was filled with experiential exercises, and during one of them, I wrote in my journal about my resentment toward Mary. Psychologist friends have told me that whenever you're sitting in a group, especially in a circle, the person you choose to sit across from is the one who will teach you the most. It was no surprise then that Mary and I were across the room from each other as our circle encompassed the room. At that time in my life, I had personal issues with some family members, and it seemed that Mary was the embodiment of them all rolled into one person.

Carla was speaking and said, "Everything that was ever done to you is a reflection of what you are." She suggested that we write a letter to ourselves as though it had been written from the other person who caused pain.

In "couples therapy", a similar method is used and is quite effective. A healing is often achieved by having one person read the letter aloud while the person who wrote it listens with eyes closed. The key, of course, is mutual and open communication.

During the exercise, we paired off and I was able to share my letter with Mary. I told her that she triggered negative emotions in me that I felt toward other people in my life. She responded by telling me that I had triggered in her the same feelings that she had toward her own mother. This was healing in action.

- Recognizing Sexuality -

The week would not have been complete had the topic of sexuality not been discussed. The following question was raised: "If, in using the two principles that 'life is a reflection of what you think you are worth' and 'the Universe rearranges itself to accommodate your own picture of reality', then how does sexuality fit into my life?"

After much discussion, I realized that I have always ended a relationship that was mediocre or less than "bells ringing, toes curling" status. I preferred to wait for what "felt right" rather than to just be with someone for the sake of having companionship. I wrote then in my journal, "I'm worth better and can be happier with someone who can meet me emotionally, physically, and intellectually, and be spiritually equal. It is better to be alone than to make do just because it's 'someone'."

It's okay to be alone, and there is a tremendous difference between being alone and being lonely. I also now know that you don't need to be "in love" in order to enjoy a relationship. Being "in love" is quite nice but it is not essential. Every relationship is important, in and of itself, by the very fact that each person brings you a gift. This gift may be good, bad, or even worse, but it is a gift of the experience just the same. When a relationship ends, it is never a "failure". Look at it as a completion, close the door tightly, and be open to moving forward. Each new experience and each completed relationship brings you just another step closer to meeting your twin soul.

- *The Next Layer* -

There was still another day to go, and it would be my most emotional yet. The deepest cleansing was about to hit me square between the eyes. Carla was my next mirror image and my greatest teacher of the week.

It was early evening and a period of free time, with people just milling around doing their own thing. I entered the main meeting room and saw Carla speaking with a gentleman who was visiting. I had not seen him before, and I noticed that he was smoking a cigarette. We were clearly in a no-smoking environment; the retreat center was immaculate. I was horrified that this intruder had the nerve to smoke inside, especially when there was no ashtray in sight. Without thinking (which was my first problem), I walked up to them and asked if he would please smoke outside. At least that's what I'd like to remember I said. I probably was much more blunt in my approach.

Carla's face registered horror and it was directed toward me. I was quickly told that the gentleman to whom she was speaking was the owner of the house and he could well do as he pleased. Even so, I still believe that he should not have been smoking in the retreat center where the air is kept pure and no one else was smoking. Besides, even if he was the owner, we had rented the property for the week, and our preferences should have been respected. But that's my personal view as a reformed smoker and a lawyer!

That one incident opened a Pandora's box. During the next gathering of the group, Carla openly told me what she thought of my rude conduct, and it went downhill from there.

Although displaying an outward appearance of being tough and confident, I have always been very sensitive and cried easily, especially in my earlier years. Everyone wants to be liked, and I am no different. I suppose that I often tried too hard, and so I may have appeared to be pushy and aggressive. I knew that I had a strong personality, but it pains me to think that I may have been perceived as being overbearing and unwelcome in the group.

The lesson I learned that day was a valuable one that will stay with me forever. Whenever I get too cocky or even think about interrupting someone else's conversation, I think twice. Only if the reason for the interruption can't wait, will I intrude. Even then, I attempt to do so apologetically and gently. The healing process is constant. Everyday brings a learning experience, just by living and by "being".

Carla never quite apologized for what I perceived to be her attack on me. Given her view of the situation, she believed she was absolutely correct. She did attempt to ease the sting of my pain by saying she had seen herself in me. I fully understood that concept, for I had seen myself in others the entire week. So here and now, I thank Carla for the gift she gave me that day in Hawaii. The gift of myself, of finally being able to see myself as others saw me. No better gift have I ever received, and I am grateful for the experience.

The notes in my journal from that day contain acronyms for ANGER and FEAR. I composed one for "ANGER": "all no good energy released". There are three for "FEAR": "face everything and resolve"; "fuck everything and run"; "false evidence appearing real". I think I made up the first two, the second of course being the antithesis of spirituality.

The last one is an established acronym in metaphysical jargon.

Whatever else can be said, no good comes from the emotions of "anger" and "fear". Negative emotions are a waste of energy. Once we recognize that concept, we can learn to deal with all emotions more realistically. We can then arrive at a better understanding of why others must create the experience for themselves. What I now understand is that no one else has the power to "make" me angry or afraid. In fact, no one has the power to make me "anything". Only I have the power to create such emotions or reality in myself. When I experience any emotion, whether viewed as positive or negative, I have created the experience out of my own reaction to a situation or to another person.

- Return to Maui -

The retreat had come to an end, and I was looking forward to returning to Maui to spend a few days by myself once again. I needed the time to reflect on the events of the week and to come to grips with the feelings I was experiencing.

I returned to The Mauian and spent much of the time on the beach, just being alone and enjoying the solitude. The dolphins and whales came by and put on their daily show as if to tell me everything would be all right.

I have come to learn a great deal about my own path, and the Mastery Training was an essential part of my growth. The issues I focused on then enabled me to move forward, especially as they dealt with self-worth. Many memories I took home with me were not pleasant, but I am now also able to recall the fun moments we shared. Time and new experiences have assisted the healing process. The layers of the onion were peeled off so that I could be prepared for the next chapters of my life.

- *Enjoying Life Again* -

The healing process that had begun in Hawaii was apparent when I returned home to Miami. I remember Lynn telling me one day at MIEL, "What happened to you? Where's the old Alice? You're so quiet!" It was quite noticeable and even I was aware that I was less boisterous than usual. I had come home from the retreat subdued and humbled. I realized that I also listened more to others around me.

The Universe was getting me ready for the next significant event that was to take place in my life. I was beginning to like my lifestyle and myself. I no longer resented going into work. Even Miami traffic became more tolerable. I was blessed with a good career, a good reputation, and a wonderful office staff. I was my own boss, and I had money in the bank. Overhead was high, but money came when needed. My demeanor in court became less aggressive, and judges and colleagues even noticed the difference. I was still a good lawyer, yet by choosing to tone down my personality, I was able to obtain quality results without unreasonable forcefulness. I remember a client saying to me, "You're so nice. Can you be a bitch?" I said that I could, but I chose not to if it wasn't necessary.

Suddenly my life revolved around home, the office and MIEL, all which were within a three-mile radius. My auto mileage was even low. Life was good and I was content. So, of course, I never suspected that my life was about to erupt and take off.

I had been back from Hawaii only two weeks when one night I watched a television show that I taped earlier in the day. There was a couple on who appeared to be quite mismatched. The woman was explaining that, in searching for her soul mate, she decided to write a letter to God, and ask Him to send the perfect man to her. On the show, she described how she wrote a very specific letter, citing each and every quality she was looking for in her perfect man. Within days of writing her letter, she met the man who was seated beside her. They were married and appeared very much in love and quite happy.

Up to that point, the relationships I'd selected left a lot to be desired. My philosophy has always been, "if you don't ask, you don't get. If you get 'no' for an answer, you're no worse off than if you hadn't asked." I figured that this method of asking for what you want couldn't hurt, so I, too, wrote a letter to God. I was very specific in my request, because I didn't want to leave any detail to chance.

A couple days after writing my prayer in my journal, I realized that I hadn't specified a date for this "perfect man" to arrive. So, in typical fashion of someone who grew up writing in a diary every night in junior high, I went back to the prayer I had written on March 31st and added these words on April 3rd, "Please, God, before the end of April, 1995."

- *Sam* -

My prayer was answered so fast, I didn't have time to even tell anyone about it. It happened exactly two days after I added the postscript to my prayer. I couldn't believe that what I had heard everyone at MIEL speak about was actually happening to me. The Universe had not only heard my request, but had answered it in record time! This was manifesting at its best.

I was speaking on the phone one afternoon with Dick, an attorney who had referred a case to me, and he was just touching base to see how it was going. It was getting late in the afternoon, and as we were ending the conversation, I casually asked, "By the way Dick, do you know anyone I could go out with? I'm not seeing anyone special and I'm ready."

He said, "Actually, I do. Someone just asked me the same thing a few weeks ago, and I didn't know anyone for him then. But, you're perfect for each other."

Dick told me his name and that he was also an attorney. I said that I knew the name, but that we did not know each other personally. He gave me the man's phone number, and said he would give him my number as well. Dick was such a romantic that he loved playing the role of matchmaker.

Minutes later, I called and asked to speak with Sam, the name I had written on the paper. He wasn't at his desk, but his secretary took the message. I told her why I was calling and that I'd be in the office a little while longer. I had plans to meet my client Carol and a friend of hers in Coconut Grove for "happy hour" after work, so I was just finishing up some work while waiting for the time to leave. Once again, synchronicity was knocking at my door, for I hadn't been to a happy hour in more than ten years! For the past eight months, my life had just been work, MIEL, and home.

My phone soon rang, and it was Sam calling me back. He had received enthusiastic phone calls from both Dick and his own secretary, and he was curious enough to call me.

I told Sam that I was meeting some people in Coconut Grove that night, and he said that was perfect since he lived in the Grove. He suggested that I meet him at his home, and we could go out to dinner. I decided that happy hour could wait another ten years. Carol understood perfectly and wished me luck.

This was clearly kismet, fate, basheirt, karma, destiny.

In any language, it was supposed to happen. I felt perfectly safe going to his house since he was an attorney with an excellent reputation in the legal community.

Dinner lasted four hours, and by the end of the evening, we knew something special was happening. Two months later, I moved into his house with my clothes and my dog. I would have made the move sooner if we had known that my dog, Whitney, and his cat, Spike, would get along as well as they did.

Sam matched almost every criterion I had written on my prayer list of desired qualities for my "perfect mate". He even played Scrabble. Looking back at my list, I realized that I had asked for my "soul mate". What I didn't know then was that I was searching for my "twin soul", who was still out there waiting for me to be totally ready.

The difference between a "twin soul" or "twin flame", and a "soul mate" is that everyone around you is a soul mate. Each person you come into contact with in this life is there because you agreed to come into life with them and have some sort of interaction. This interaction can be positive or negative. A twin soul, as defined by everything that I have ever learned, is "one soul that splits in two, creating two souls". One soul in two bodies; one taking the predominately feminine side, the other the more masculine, and both retaining a bit of the other for recognition purposes. Twin souls can also be the same sex, but the two will always come together in a "love" relationship, which need not be the case with soul mates.

If you are to find and recognize your twin soul, you must be at the point that you can love yourself. You must be able to look into a mirror and sincerely say, "I love you" to yourself and not fall down on the floor laughing or look away instantly in repulsion or disbelief. In other words, you must be able to look into the other's eyes and know you are looking at the other half of you. Again the old cliché comes to mind, "Before you can love another you must first love yourself."

The lesson I learned from Sam is that in order to truly know and understand what it is like to be loved, you must first know and experience what it is like to not be loved. True unconditional love is the aspiration, and to know and experience such love is wonderful beyond your wildest dreams. There must be no expectations and no preconceived notions; thus there can be no disappointments.

The problem came when I realized that I had fallen in love with Sam, and he couldn't voice the same feelings. He told his friends he was in love, but he couldn't tell me. His friends told me they had never seen Sam happier, and I was the first person he had lived with in five years. But he was deathly afraid of making a commitment, which clearly contradicted the fact that he had asked me to move in. He just couldn't say the three magic words.

We traveled many places together, and we got along great. We took a weeklong cruise and even in such close quarters, we had no problems. I met his entire family and cadre of friends in Chicago and in Detroit. We had mutual friends in the legal field, and everyone thought we were perfect for each other. However we did more with his family and friends than with mine, which should have been a clue to me.

Our kids were all in college, and none lived at home. I kept my house intact, and only cancelled the newspaper. We moved my pots and pans to his house because he liked mine better, but he was not ready for me to move my personal bric-a-brac. Then someone asked me if I wanted to rent out my vacant house to some "snowbirds" for the winter months.

When I discussed it with Sam, he practically hyperventilated. That should have been a clear message, but I couldn't see beyond my own hopes and dreams.

Sam and I were definitely soul mates, but we were not twin souls. We were each destined to meet and be with the other in order for each of us to be prepared to meet and recognize our own twin soul. Sam had to let me be free so that I could meet Dennis, but I had to be hurt, completely devastated, and deeply pained before I could understand the concept.

I had moved into Sam's house in June of 1995. The month before, I had purchased a copy of *Conversations With God, Book 1*, by Neale Donald Walsch. I began reading it, but I obviously was not ready to receive the information because it became a bedside book for many months. You know, one of those books you buy, start and never finish. It just sits on the night table and after a while, you don't even realize it's there. I wasn't supposed to have the book's message yet, because I would have realized then that this relationship was not going to work out. This was something I needed to discover on my own, by experiencing the emotions I was about to encounter.

By late September, Sam fully realized that he was being suffocated by the feelings I had. Even though I had never yet told him I loved him, it was all over my face, and in my actions.

That particular weekend, I attended an intensive experiential workshop at MIEL and had my own revelation during one of the exercises. We were in a guided meditation, and one of the instructions was to think of what made us truly happy. I couldn't think of a thing that could make me smile; I could only cry.

It was at that moment that I realized that I had never

told Sam I loved him because I was waiting for him to tell me first. I discussed my concerns with a married couple who was at the workshop. They shared their own similar experience with me from early in their relationship, and they both encouraged me to go home and confront Sam with my feelings. Whatever happened, it was important for me to communicate and express myself completely.

When I went home on Saturday night, I told Sam about my experience in the meditation and we discussed our own situation. He had already made up his mind, and was now letting me in on the decision. Our live-in arrangement was not working out, and we agreed that I would move back to my own home. However, we agreed that we would still continue to see each other, to see where our relationship would go.

In fact, that next weekend, we took a trip together to Gainesville, Florida, to visit his two children at the University of Florida, and attended a football game with them. We had a wonderful weekend. Nothing had changed except my address and phone number.

On November 19, 1995, Sam accompanied me to the wedding of my dear friends, Tom Chasteen and Dale Edelman. I was performing the marriage ceremony, and Justin had come home from college to attend the wedding. As a notary public in Florida, I am authorized to officiate and legalize marriages.

I first met Tom when he came to me five years earlier as a divorce client. We later became friends, and when I met Dale, we hit it off immediately. Dale filled the void in my life that had been present since Sandra died, and we are still close friends. From the onset, Tom and Dale's families welcomed both Justin and me into their family circles. To this day, we are still included in their birthday and holiday celebrations. I have photo albums filled with wonderful memories of the Chasteen parties. Tom's dad, Eldon, loved to tease me about who my date would be for the next dinner party.

The wedding was at Cheeca Lodge in the Upper Keys, and the outside setting was beautiful, as was the day. The Atlantic Ocean was behind us, and the morning sun was quite cooperative and splendid. This was not the first marriage ceremony I had performed, but it was the first time I was doing it in front of such a large crowd.

The ceremony was lovely. Dale is Jewish and she and her family have always celebrated the traditional Jewish holidays as I have. Tom is not Jewish; however, he and his family have always respected Dale's faith and honored both the Jewish and non-Jewish holidays. The comic relief came when Tom was ready to break the glass as part of the Jewish tradition, and I had forgotten to bring the glass to the podium. I simply took my plastic water cup, emptied it onto the beach, and handed the empty cup to Tom, who obediently smashed it with his foot.

After the traditional and lavish wedding reception, we went back to Tom and Dale's home in Key Largo, and enjoyed some less hectic time with a smaller group of family and friends. Justin had come in his own car so that he wasn't tied to our schedule and so that he could drive back to Orlando that day since he was still in college.

Late in the afternoon, Sam and I decided to leave. The hour-long drive home was quiet, but I thought it was because we were both tired. Sam had spent the night before at my house so that we could get up early to be in the Keys for the morning wedding. We hadn't been in my house for more than ten minutes, when Sam abruptly informed me that this simply wasn't working, and that we shouldn't pretend it was going to get better. This had obviously been on his mind for quite some time, and he was determined to do it quickly. He was breaking off our relationship, totally. This hit me from left field, and I was in shock. He was out the door before I could even catch my breath.

Once I realized what had just happened, I broke down and cried like I had never cried over any man before. In retrospect, I knew that this had happened to me because I had never before experienced such hurt and pain. This was actually the first time any man had ended a relationship with me without the feeling being mutual.

When I read *Conversations With God*, I discovered that this was the only way that I would learn how to recognize true unconditional love when it came to me. The pain was so strong that I couldn't eat for weeks. In the past, I would have binged on junk food. That in itself was a new experience, and my weight loss actually was a bonus benefit! I learned for the first time what it meant to eat to live, because I literally had to remind myself to eat during the day, as I had difficulty getting through the day's altogether.

Friends tried to get me to go out just to keep me company, but I refused to be social. I couldn't trust myself to not cry. I cried at stoplights; I cried whenever I had a moment alone to think. This was such a new and difficult experience for me that I guess I just had to experience it and live through it. At the time, I just didn't understand why it was so important for me to be in that moment. As I later studied and opened up to the messages in *Conversations With God*, I understood that everything was exactly perfect as it happened. I even came to understand that this was my own personal choice, and Sam had nothing to do with my pain. This was a more difficult concept to grasp, but nevertheless, I know it to be true.

During my period of mourning the breakup with Sam, I still clung to some hope that we would get back together. I knew he was seeing someone new, but his friends told me that even they thought he was crazy because I had been the best thing that ever happened to him. I thought so, too.

His birthday was coming up right after Thanksgiving, and I sent him a birthday card. Nothing mushy, just a nice card. Of course, he called to thank me and of course, there was a method to my madness. He did not have plans for his birthday, and asked if I would like to have dinner with him. Would I? My spirits were lifted. Why wasn't he taking out the new woman he was dating? In reality, I had no great expectations. I knew that Sam was very stubborn. He simply wasn't in love with me, and once he made up his mind, that was all there was to it.

We made plans to go to dinner for his birthday and then to see the Miami Panthers play hockey at the Miami Arena. We were just like old friends going out together. Nothing special, and no concerns about how the evening was going to end. I surprised myself at how well I handled the situation. I suppose I actually thought that if I played it cool, he might realize what a mistake he had made. But fate had other plans for me.

Chapter Eleven

Moving Toward Love

- Healing on the Rebound -

Justin and I spent Christmas Day with Tom and Dale and their extended and expanding family in Key Largo. We drove down in two cars, and on the way, I stopped at the outlet mall and got side tracked in a shoe store. Shoes have always been my source of solace; some people buy hats, I buy shoes. Quite frankly, it's because shoes are the one item of clothing that won't change sizes on me! Anyway, as I was at the counter paying for my purchase of six pairs of shoes, my cell phone rang. It was Justin, complaining that everyone was waiting for me to arrive at Tom and Dale's. The Christmas presents were in my car, and they were waiting to open them! I had totally lost track of the time, and said I'd leave right away. My shoes became the joke of the day, and the story still remains fodder for laughter when relationships are mentioned. I had given Dale a "Cathy" Christmas card that was a classic. The gist of the card was that the purchase of shoes was a substitute for sex, and I joked that since I wasn't having sex, I was making up for it by buying shoes...six pairs at that!

I had presents for everyone. For some unexplained reason, I had even wrapped a gift for Bill, a friend of Tom's who was visiting from Chicago. We were introduced on the day of the wedding, and he had also been at Tom's for Thanksgiving dinner. Bill was an avid fisherman who loved the Keys, and he spent his entire vacation time in Florida. I didn't really speak with him on Thanksgiving Day, since I was wallowing in self-pity at that time.

On Christmas Day, I was in slightly better spirits, but there were so many people around, we never had time to talk to each other. The gift I gave him was a signed poster of the "Conch Republic". The artist, J. Brian King, was a former client of mine, and it was a perfect gift for anyone in love with the Florida Keys. Fate was obviously guiding my decisions since my own mind was mush.

The next week was going to be tough, as I had no plans for New Year's Eve, a holiday for lovers. Justin had returned to college, and Tom and Dale insisted that I come down to spend the weekend with them so that I would not be alone.

As fate would have it, Bill and his 10-year old daughter were also spending the weekend at Tom and Dale's house. They were using the downstairs room, and I was content to sleep on the sofa bed upstairs in the living room. I had spent many nights at the Chasteen home over the years, and I was completely comfortable being with these wonderful friends. I had watched their children grow and mature, and I loved them all.

Tom is quite the joker and fancies himself to be a matchmaker. It was December 30th, and Tom suggested that Bill and I go out and enjoy an evening at the club featuring "Big Dick and the Extenders". Yes, that's really the name of the band, and they get rather raunchy in their lyrics. It was, of course, a perfect suggestion! We went out as friends, and had a wonderful time. We danced, and something magical happened. I began to loosen up, and forgot to feel sorry for myself for being without Sam. When we got back to the house around 1 o'clock in the morning, we weren't tired and we had not yet talked ourselves out. We were discovering that we really liked being together and we didn't want the night to end. So, we found ourselves in the hammock downstairs on the back porch overlooking the beach, and we talked until the sun came up. We were clearly smitten with each other, and enjoyed the excitement of a possible romance.

The next day, we sent the kids to a movie, and we took separate naps. That night was New Year's Eve, and we made plans to have dinner out together. The New Year's celebration was terrific, and we watched fireworks at the local Marriott, and had a few fireworks of our own. Tom was quite pleased with himself and teased us endlessly. Bill was seven years younger, and this was the first time I had ever been involved with a younger man. A true boy-toy. I felt wicked and wonderful.

Bill and I began a long-distance relationship that lasted through March. He came to Miami several times, and I visited with him in Chicago in February. I chose the coldest week of the winter, but I finally got to wear a winter coat I had purchased three years before and had never worn.

It soon became apparent that the relationship was not going to work for several reasons, including geographic incompatibility. We mutually agreed to end the relationship, knowing that we would eventually meet again at future parties at Tom's house. We knew that when we'd see each other again, we'd probably be with other people, and that would be okay. We were friendly enough that there would never be any jealousy or awkwardness in being introduced to new significant others.

Our short-lived relationship had been absolutely perfect for me. It gave me confidence in myself again, and allowed me to totally close the door to Sam. I knew that someone special was out there for me, as Hans had told me in my first reading. I was still getting ready. But, I was also getting impatient.

It is imperative that all doors to past relationships be completely closed before a new door can be opened. There is a great deal of truth to the saying, "When one door closes, another door opens." Yet, the feelings have to be completely healed before a new relationship can be cultivated and developed. I discovered that with Peter, and again with Sam. The pain has to be completely healed in order to move on.

This is a concept that I try to instill in my clients and at mediations with couples who cannot comprehend how they can ever get to this phase. The love and fond memories can remain, provided the yearning and hope for reconciliation are gone. Sometimes there just needs to be closure. Sometimes the love was never strong enough to last so it is not required for complete closure. The trick is to get past the anger and negative emotions.

I will always love Peter and Sam for the journeys we shared together, however, I knew that my doors had finally closed. Having experienced this genuine healing and complete closure, I feel very fortunate that I am able to maintain a friendship with both of these men I had once been deeply in love with. To this day I treasure those friendships and my memories. And I thank each of them for the gift of allowing me to move toward my final relationship with my twin soul.

- *Opening the Door* -

Now that I was living alone again and was not involved in any relationship, I was able to stay at home and read the books that had formed a stack on my night table. My stack of books was typical of a novice student of metaphysics. Books are purchased with every intent to read through to the end; however, then a new book is recommended and purchased, a few chapters are read, and it too soon finds its way to the stack.

The time had at last come for me to finish reading the book that lay unread on the night table when I lived with

Sam. It had been exactly one year since I dealt with the self-worth issues at the retreat in Hawaii, and I knew that I was finally ready to move on with my life. The Universe knew, too. When a book suddenly calls you to read it, you know it is time to learn the message within. *Conversations With God, Book 1* was such a book for me.

Of course, the timing was perfect. The author, Neale Donald Walsch, was scheduled to be in Miami in April of 1996, and an entire weekend at MIEL had been set aside for his workshop. My friend, Ron, another lawyer and regular at MIEL, invited me to be a part of a small group of patrons who were sponsoring the author's workshop. "Sponsoring" meant paying extra money above the registration fee for the purpose of assisting with expenses and providing scholarships for some people to attend who could not afford the cost. Money was a little tight for me when Ron first asked, but when he called the second time to remind me, I was in a better financial position to say yes, and I did.

We had many organizational meetings at Ron's house to plan the event, which was billed as "The Awakening". Neale and his wife, Nancy, were to be guests at Ron's home for the weekend, along with Will and Rose, members of Neale's staff. The weekend workshop was to consist of a lecture on Friday night, an all-day experiential workshop on Saturday, and another workshop on Sunday afternoon. Neale had also graciously agreed to be the guest speaker at the Sunday morning spiritual church service at MIEL, which enabled people to hear him speak at no cost to them.

I had been reading the book, and its content and the messages astounded me. From some spot deep within me, I had a strange feeling that I already knew everything the book was telling me. But I don't believe that I fully comprehended the divine messages until I attended the first Friday night session.

That Friday was April 12th, 1996. I had been preparing all week for a very intense divorce trial. I represented the husband, and his wife had already moved out of Florida with their two young children. We were thoroughly prepared, and I felt confident that the facts and the law were on our side. However, in any litigation, nothing is certain and I never give guarantees. The trial lasted all afternoon, and was going well, but it was getting late as I presented my closing argument. The judge had not yet made his ruling, and looking at the clock, I knew that the evening session at MIEL would be starting within an hour. Finally, he ruled completely in my client's favor. It was a total victory, and my client was delighted. But I had little time to rejoice as we hurried to leave the courthouse and downtown Miami. My client had left his car at my office, and I needed to take him there to pick it up. He still laughs and calls me "Mario Andretti" when he remembers that 15-mile ride.

I was glad that MIEL was across the street from my office, and I rushed into the building like a maniac. I didn't want to miss a single word from this man whose book had specific messages just for me. The room was filled to capacity, but fortunately, since I was a patron, a seat was reserved for me up front.

Neale Donald Walsch had just been introduced, and he had taken his place at the front of the room. My seat was on the left, and as I entered through the side door, I almost knocked over a stand holding fresh flowers. Naturally, while trying to avoid attention, all eyes were on me as I heard Neale say to the group, "Ah, here comes my next wife." The crowd laughed and I was to learn later that Neale's prior history of failed marriages could have made my career quite prosperous with just him as a client!

The evening was a huge success as Neale was a dynamic speaker. The messages he gave us were thought provoking and powerful. At the end of the evening when he told a parable about "the little soul and the sun", I was visibly moved. The parable was in Book 1, but when he told the story and acted it out, it all fell into place for me. I at last understood what the message of the book was all about. I now understood that my life's purpose was to just "be"; to simply experience life in all its splendor, savoring each and every moment to it's fullest.

This was just the beginning of Neale's speaking engagements on the road, and this weekend was the first workshop he'd ever taken out of his home state of Oregon. I was eager to begin the next day, which would be an intensive workshop.

Neale's staff members had brought brochures promoting the upcoming 5-day retreat that Neale would be facilitating at a monastery in Baltimore two months later. The retreat was scheduled to begin on Monday, June 10th and end at noon on Friday, June 14th. This was no coincidence; this was clearly fate in my face. I was going to be in Washington, D.C. beginning that same Friday for the weekend bar mitzvah celebration of Sherril's son, Sammy. I'd already made the hotel reservations, but I had not yet made flight arrangements.

I took home the brochure about the retreat and said I would think about giving my deposit the next day after the workshop. I was concerned about my financial condition, because lately, my business income was just enough to pay for overhead at the office and my necessary living expenses. There was very little left over for me. But, hadn't I just learned that the Universe provides for us at the perfect time? Where was my faith? What about the "coincidence" of the dates? Wasn't that a clear message to me? Seeing the synchronistic force in this, I knew that Sherril and destiny had intended for me to be at both the retreat and the bar mitzvah. I decided to take the entire week off from the office and made plans to fly to Washington on Monday, June 10th and return to Miami on Sunday, June 17th. I knew that I was supposed to be at the retreat in Baltimore that week. I just didn't know why.

I stopped by my office early Saturday morning and took a check with me to give a deposit to Will. The decision had been made, and the gears were in movement. The Universe had some major work to do in the next two months to improve my financial situation.

So it was no surprise that the issues I dealt with at Saturday's workshop involved relationship and finances. I finally was at a point where I liked myself, and I did not need to focus on any self-worth issues. Through Neale's method of processing, I learned that every part of my being must be ready to manifest my own thoughts so that each thought could and would become a reality. This was further confirmation of the principles I learned in Hawaii.

The important lesson for me was to not be attached to a result and to have no expectations. I needed to just believe. This is not an easy task, but it is essential to spiritual growth and development.

What I discovered about my relationship with Sam was that there never was any "relationship". The notes from my journal that day in the workshop are quite revealing. I wrote, "Sam could not relate to me because he didn't love me as I loved him. Therefore, there was no relationship, so what is gone? Nothing. Nothing is lost. Move on and let go."

"The expectation of return from the other is disappointing," my notes continued as though the message was being channeled. "Life is not about what I'm going to get from the other, but what I can <u>give</u> to the other."

I had finally gotten it! Suddenly I understood that I didn't lose anything because I never had it in the first place. I was healing and ready to move on. However, I recognized that we did have a relationship; it just wasn't a love relationship. The door was really closed this time and I was able to look forward again. I also stopped "wanting" a relationship to be a part of my life. It was no longer essential to my existence; I was no longer obsessed with the idea that a man in my life would make me complete. Once I stopped "wanting" and "needing", the Universe made preparations for the delivery of what I no longer felt was lacking.

The workshop ended on Saturday night at 11:00 PM, but the night was not yet over. During a break earlier in the evening when Neale signed my book, we had a chance to speak privately. He told me that his non-profit organization, ReCreation, was considering expanding by developing an intentional community in Colorado. He asked me if I would be interested in becoming a part of the community by serving as staff counsel. I was honored and flabbergasted at the same time. On my desk at the office was an application to the Colorado Bar. I had requested the application two years earlier, yet I had just never gotten around to sending it in, partly because there had never been a reason to do so. Here was this synchronistic energy again, tugging at me to wake up and pay attention to the signs. We agreed to meet at Ron's house later that night to discuss his proposal in further detail.

When I arrived at Ron's about 11:30 PM, Ron, Neale, and Will were already relaxing in the hot tub. I politely declined the invitation to join them, and spoke with Neale from my chair outside the tub area. He described his vision about the intentional community and after further discussion, we agreed that since I would be at the retreat in Baltimore, we'd wait and see if this would be the path I'd follow.

- *Miami to Baltimore* -

It was June 10th, 1996. I didn't know it then, but my life was about to change. I was going to the retreat in Baltimore. Other than Neale, Nancy, Will, and Rose, who I had met in April and who were all part of the ReCreation staff, I didn't know any other people who would be attending the retreat. Traveling and attending retreats on my own had never bothered me, so it was with great excitement and anticipation that I packed my bags for the five days I was to spend listening to this gifted author of *Conversations With God*. I had no idea what to expect, but I know I was fully prepared to accept whatever happened. I was about to discover that I was not prepared at all.

My flight was scheduled to leave at 7:00 AM. Who else did I know that could take me to the airport at that early hour but Peter? I had asked Peter if he would drive me to the airport, and he gladly accepted. In fact, he somewhat jokingly asked if he could come over to my house earlier and help me get dressed. Of course, as our physical relationship had been over for quite some time, I declined his offer and asked if he would please just pick me up in time to get me to the airport. He gladly did so and I was on my way. Neither of us knew then that what was about to occur in my life would forever dowse his hope of any possible further relationship between the two of us. I suppose it was apropos, if not an omen, that the first man I had ever truly loved would be taking me to the flight that would eventually take me to meet the next and last man I would ever love.

When I arrived at National Airport in Washington D.C., my first order of business was to take a taxi to the ANA

Hotel where I would be spending the following weekend for Sammy's bar mitzvah. The bar mitzvah was to be a bittersweet weekend in that the entire Siegel and Starr families would be celebrating with Sammy, while at the same time mourning the absence of his mother Sherril, and feeling our great loss of her.

I checked in with the hotel concierge and arranged to store my extra suitcases there during the week while I was in Baltimore. I had systematically packed so that all of my dressy clothes that I would need for the bar mitzvah festivities would remain in the suitcases at the hotel. The suitcase with the jeans, T-shirts, and sneakers would go with me to Baltimore. The hotel was large and beautiful and was in stark contrast to what I would soon have as my living quarters for the next five days.

There was no pre-arranged transportation to the Baltimore retreat location for those of us who were coming in from other cities. So I fumbled my way with the mass transit system available in the D.C. area, and finally managed to figure out where my destination would be, and how long it would take to arrive. First I took a taxi to the location where I was to pick up the bus that would take me to the retreat area in Baltimore. Being geographically challenged as I am, upon arrival in the general vicinity of the monastery in Baltimore, I took another taxi directly to the retreat location.

When I finally arrived at the monastery at about 1:00 PM, I immediately noticed this would be a self-help, "schlep your own bags to your room" facility. I entered through the back door and was dragging my bags up the two flights when I saw a familiar face. There was Will to greet me and give me a warm welcome hug. It was wonderful to see him, and I knew then that my week had just begun.

The first order of business was to choose a room, and as one of the early arrivals, I had my choice of single rooms from which to select. Since there are no accidents, Room #216 was available and it was the perfect choice. My birth date is 2-16, and has always been a favorite number of mine. The Universe was sending me a not so subtle message that this was to be another day of birth for me and in fact it was to be my rebirthing. I naturally chose that room and settled in.

As I walked toward the dining room to have lunch, I met two of the people also attending the retreat. Pat and her friend, Trouda had just arrived from West Virginia, and had chosen rooms across the hall from mine. Pat's husband was dropping off the ladies for their week of "whatever silly things they were up to". Pat was delightfully fresh and outspoken, and she contributed a great deal of humor as well as insight to the week. She was just the first of several people that I would recognize as having been a part of some other life I may have known in the past. The connection was strong and immediate, which is common when old souls reconnect.

After lunch we all kind of lazed around and relaxed, unpacked, and got used to our sparse living quarters. There were no phones, no TV's, no luxuries of any sort; simply a bed, a sink, a mirror, a desk and a simple closet containing a few wire hangers. There was also no air conditioning. Coming from Miami and being used to central air-conditioned housing, this was a real surprise, and I was not looking forward to the hot summer days and nights. As it turned out, the heat presented no problem and I enjoyed every minute of my stay.

When it was time to assemble in the large meeting room for the beginning of the first session, I saw a woman walking down the hall who was also alone. I approached her in utter amazement, as she looked totally familiar to me. When I stopped her and said, "You look so familiar," we played "where do I know you from?" for a while and discovered we had never been in the same place and that we had never met before that day. Obviously, this was another remembrance of a past life connection.

The woman was Margaret, a psychologist from Vermont. We quickly became friends and hung out together the entire week. After a couple of days the realization hit me that Margaret, at the time of the retreat, looked almost exactly like Sherril looked when we were teenagers. They had the same slender body shape, and had the same mannerisms. They also had a general sense of slight self-consciousness about them. They both, of course, were nothing of the sort, as both Sherril and Margaret were quite educated and very accomplished professionals. I know that Margaret was there to connect with me and be my friend, as this was to be a very important week for me. Sherril, from the other side, was instrumental in tying the whole thing together and she was loving every minute of it.

It was around 3:00 or 3:30 PM on Monday when we assembled in the large meeting room. I selected a large Naugahyde chair next to where Margaret was seated. We settled in for what was to be the first of many long and comfortable sessions (and some not so comfortable) throughout the next five days. That first meeting was just a quick get-acquainted and briefing session about what to expect for the remainder of the week.

- *The Retreat Begins-*

It was 6:00 PM and we had reconvened in the large meeting room after dinner in the communal dining hall. Dinner was simple, but tasty and better than we had expected to be served in a monastery. At least it wasn't all vegetarian.

The Brothers, dressed in their robes, were quite cordial, but kept to themselves during mealtime.

This time, for the evening session, I had chosen to sit on the floor and used the large square sofa cushions to prop myself up against the coffee table. I sat next to CarolAnne who had just joined Neale's staff as his personal massage therapist. She was from North Carolina and displayed an outward softness, yet at the same time, she possessed powerful spiritual strength. Her strength became evident later on in the week when she helped me in processing through some emotions I was dealing with.

Neale had begun the evening session, and was seated at the front of the room. We were getting ready to go through the exercise of memorizing and recalling everyone's first name. We had done this at "The Awakening" workshop in Miami in April, so I was familiar with this exercise and the reasons chosen for this game to be played within this type of group. It's an excellent tool for not only learning first names, but for breaking the ice in a group full of strangers.

Just as we were about to begin the "name game", the door in the back of the room opened, and Neale said, "Ah, we have a late arrival."

The Love

Chapter Twelve

The Baltimore Retreat

Dennis' words are in regular font - *Alice's words are in Italic Bold.*

- *Late Arrival* -

I arrived at the monastery at about 5:50 in the evening, so I felt good about being there early. I walked into the dining area and looked for someone familiar. There were a few people there, but it appeared that everyone was leaving. It also appeared that the buffet containers of food were being taken away and I was famished. Then I saw Will and Rose.

They both came over to give me a hug and Will asked, "Why are you so late, did your plane get delayed?"

"Late?" I exclaimed. "I thought I was 10 minutes early!"

"No, everyone was supposed to be checked in by 3:00 this afternoon," Will stated. "So you are almost three hours late," he added chuckling.

"Well, I'm really hungry and being diabetic, I have to eat something. I'm also very hot and sweaty and I need to clean up."

"Oh, no problem, let's get you something to eat, get you a room, and then join the group. The session's starting in 20 minutes or so."

When we got upstairs, Will said, "You can have any room here on the 3rd floor."

I chose a room, put my stuff in it, took a quick shower and changed my clothes. Then I went downstairs to where the group was meeting.

As I quietly opened the door and entered, I felt like Dorothy when her house landed in Oz, full of anticipation of what lay on the other side. The large room was filled with big Naugahyde covered couches and chairs. They were the kind that make you sweat when it is hot and it was a very hot, humid day in Baltimore. Fortuately, the in-the-window air conditioner was blowing cold air like a refreshing chilly north wind.

I quickly scanned the room to see how many people were there and if I recognized anyone. I saw Neale and Nancy in the front of the room. Rose and Will were off to my right sitting on a couch near the back of the room. That's when I realized I hadn't entered as quietly as I had hoped. There were at least a dozen pairs of eyes looking at me as I rushed to sit down.

A woman on the left side of the room blurted out laughingly, "Oh my God, look at his shirt, look at his shirt. I love it!" The shirt that I had put on was a special T-shirt that I had gotten at the previous retreat. I wore it in honor of "The Awakening" that I was going through. I felt that it was appropriate for the way I was feeling, especially after the way this day had gone. It had a line drawing of a man with a beard on it. Under the drawing it had the words, "God In Training" emblazoned in gold. Everyone turned to see, but I had already sat down.

So the woman, who I came to know as Marie and a wonderfully playful being, said, "Stand up, show them your shirt."

At that same moment, Neale said, "Ah, we have a late arrival. Let me introduce Dennis Jackson from Seattle, Washington. He and his lovely wife, Jackie, have started a support organization called 'Friends òf Recreation'. It was set up to help support the efforts of Recreation, our CWG foundation."

That is what happened at the beginning of this retreat, at least for everyone else. For me it was a little different.

Well, it was a little different for me, too.

Just as Neale said, "Ah, we have a late arrival", someone seated on the side of the room was laughing out loud and shouting to this new person to show off his shirt. At that moment, I turned my head around and saw a very tall and husky looking man standing there in a purplish colored T-shirt with a caricature line drawing on it. I couldn't tell what the drawing was, but I really didn't care about the shirt at that particular moment in time. Who was that man? And why was I suddenly drawn to him?

Then, Neale began introducing him to the group. All I heard him say was, "Dennis and his lovely wife, Jackie..." Oh, great. He was married. Oh, well. I turned back to where I was sitting and faced the front of the room to listen to what else Neale was saying.

- Instant Recognition -

This is the part of the story where my life does a 180° turnaround. As I entered the meeting room I was floating. With the events of the day very much in my mind, I scanned the whole room. In the front I saw two people seated on the floor. They were sitting on and leaning back against cushions that had been removed from the sofa and placed against a coffee table. From their positioning, all I could see of the two people seated there were the backs of their heads.

The person with dark hair, I didn't even notice, but the person with the red hair affected me in a way that I will never forget. I didn't even know if these people were male or female.

As I looked at the back of the red-haired person's head, a strange, yet comfortable feeling came over me. It was a feeling of recognition, of knowing, of having found something that I had been searching for all of my life. It was as if someone had hit me in the face with a sledgehammer filled with molten love. Soft and flowing, encircling my soul and me like a million tiny butterflies fluttering their wings and giving me tingles that went from the top of my head to the tips of my toes. I know now as I write this story, that it was what can only be described as "love at first sight". Literally, it was like falling into a big billowy cloud made of cotton or soft feathers. A wonderful feeling of having just had an experience that could never be equaled. It's what I have come to call a peak experience.

As Neale was introducing me to the group, the two people in front turned around and I then saw that they were both women. I recognized the woman with dark hair as CarolAnne, Neale's personal masseuse whom I had met in Oregon, but I didn't know the red-haired woman at all. There was something here and I instantly felt that this woman was having the same feelings as I, that we were connected and our souls had recognized each other. A bond had been remembered.

I was buried in these feelings; kind of hearing what Neale was saying and kind of off lost in the clouds. Just as Neale said the words, "Dennis and his lovely wife, Jackie..." the connection was torn away and, as I was to later discover, a wall built by this red-haired woman that blocked the bonding process. It was as though someone had come up between us and cut the connection with a sharp knife, severing the link. I wasn't able to understand the reason that this happened until later.

All I had was this incredible need to know who she was and what this feeling was all about, and I was determined to do just that during this week.

Unfortunately, I also had a whole mess of issues that I had to work on concerning myself, my relationship with my wife and my marriage that had to come first. So I decided at that moment, that my focus had to be those issues. After all, I had come here to try and come to a decision about what to do. I owed that much to myself and to Jackie.

- *The Name Game* -

I had moved over to a chair that was next to the air conditioner to keep cool, and still have a full view of the room. I wanted to be able to see everyone in the room, and I knew Neale was going to start the introduction game. That is when everyone gets to know everyone else. Neale and Nancy had done this at previous retreats, with Nancy usually going first, like this; "Hi, I'm Nancy". Then Neale would say, "Hi, that is Nancy and I am Neale." The next person would say, "That's Nancy, that's Neale, and I am John," or whatever their name was. It would proceed around the room in that fashion until the last person is naming off all 27 people in the room and then his or her own name. It was always a blast, because everyone was doing it with each person as they went around the room. The last person always had it the toughest. The funny thing is I had been wondering what this mystery woman's name was and as it turned out, she was the last person to do the name game.

Then she stood up and said laughingly, kind of half joking, half serious, "Ok Neale, you want me to do it backwards?"

Everybody laughed, especially when Neale said, "Sure, go ahead," and he began to laugh too.

Amazingly, she did exactly that and didn't make one mistake. She got a rousing round of applause. Her name was Alice.

Everyone was eager to join in to learn the names of the people we would be living with all week. I was the last to participate, and when it came time for me to recite all the names, I jokingly asked Neale if he wanted me to do it in reverse. Well, he challenged me, and I did it! My name was also the last name anyone heard, and for some reason, I wanted the new man in the back to know who I was.

- What is Love? -

Love, what is it really? For me it was a feeling of connection. A feeling that I am connected to the one who is so special to me, to the one with whom I had chosen to spend my life. That connection to my wife had become very strained and the feeling was quickly disappearing.

I had come a long way in the feeling of love. I now have come to understand that the most important love that one can have is the love for one's own soul. The "self" we all hear about. Loving one's self is the most important aspect of life. The old adage, "You can't love anyone unconditionally if you don't first love yourself" holds such truth for me now.

I had awakened at the first retreat, and had worked through anger and hurt at the second. Now was the time to get in touch with the real me and to learn how to love *me*. That is what my crystal was saying. "U LUV U." It was written right there in plain black and light. This time, at this retreat, I needed to focus on myself and "who I really am". I knew then that my life was in an incredible changing phase.

At this time my plans were to become even more involved with Neale and work as part of his staff, but I had much processing to do. I had to decide if I was going to do this as part of a married couple or as a single man.

- Processing Begins -

As the first evening progressed, I watched the woman named Alice from across the room. I was taken with the fact that she looked so familiar. Now her face seemed even more familiar than earlier in the evening because, after coming back from a break, she was wearing a pair of greenish-blue framed glasses.The glasses, for some reason, sparked a recognition in me that I still have not, to this day, figured out. I know it has to do with one of our past lives together, and we are exploring those as we write this book. The glasses were in sharp contrast but complimentary to her short red hair. I was hoping to talk to her after the meeting broke up for the evening, but the opportunity didn't come that first night.

The next morning I awakened to the sounds of people talking in the hall. I got up, showered, and then went downstairs to breakfast. As I walked into the dining room I scanned the room to see if Alice was anywhere to be found. I spotted her sitting at a table with three or four other people. I saw also Neale, Nancy and Will at another table and decided to go and sit with them.

In previous events that I had attended, I was always drawn to sit with anyone with whom I connected. I had immediately felt the connection with Alice but I needed to focus on my marital issues. I knew that if I sat next to her during the workshop I would not be able to do that. So when we gathered in the large meeting room, I chose a seat alone.

During the morning session I had a chance to relate the

story about my crystal to the rest of the group. I was actually able to demonstrate how the light refracted through the crystal to make the letters of light, U LUV U. It was just as awesome for me then as it had been the day before. I felt like a kid again, trying to get the new girl's attention. I didn't know why I wanted her attention; I just did. I was happy that Alice was among the group of people who came to the window to see the crystal's letters and I knew that Spirit was moving us ever closer. Spirit was in this process every step of the way, from the first moment we had seen each other.

Dennis told a fascinating story about a crystal he had just purchased the day before. I actually saw the reflection of the letters he'd described. But, what affected me most was this big man's sensitivity. He appeared to be so gentle and loving, such a rare quality in men these days. I was intrigued, but cautious.

- Quiet Time -

The monastery where we were staying was a very peaceful place with large green lawn areas and lots of trees surrounding the buildings. It was a park-like setting without all the people, so it was easy to get away from the group for some quiet time. I did this often to contemplate what had gone on during the previous session and to center myself to be ready for the next round of emotion grabbing interaction. I also used the time to try and figure out what the connection with Alice was all about. I remember thinking that maybe Alice would come out for a walk and we could "happen" to bump into each other, thereby giving us a chance to be alone together.

So, that's where you disappeared to so often. I often looked around to see where Dennis had gone, but I never even thought to walk around the grounds. I wish now that I had taken the time to enjoy the surroundings more, but I've never been the out-doorsy type. So I just stayed inside and socialized with the others.

As I contemplated all of the processing that I had done up to that point, I was really moving toward a feeling of letting go. I had been through so much, that I just needed to stop trying to force my marriage back together. I think that was the moment I made the decision to allow Jackie to be free. At the same time I was freeing myself. I don't remember verbally or even mentally saying that then, but I had this feeling that I couldn't fix it anymore. I couldn't keep the marriage together no matter how hard I tried. There had been too much water under the bridge; too many problems, and too much pain and damage.

- First Contact -

When I later walked into the lunchroom in anticipation of what was to be served, I was hoping that it was not a vegetarian menu as it had been at the two previous retreats I'd attended. Much to my surprise I saw hamburger patties in a pan. What a feeling of relief that was. I would be able to eat regular food here. As I walked up to the line, I saw Alice standing across from me on the opposite side of the buffet table.

I remember that when we both reached for the hamburgers from opposite sides of the buffet table, we looked at each other and laughed. It was comforting to know that we could eat meat without feeling guilty. I couldn't understand why I cared what Dennis was eating; I just recall that it made an impact on me.

A few minutes later I got up to get some iced tea and Alice came up at the same time. The pitcher was empty so we had to get someone to fill it. While waiting, we stood there and made small talk about the retreat and how it was going for each of us. I think we even chatted about the brand of tea and about how good it was. Nothing major, but I still felt that connection and still couldn't figure it out. "I know you," I thought. "But from where?" Must be a past life thing, I rationalized, not knowing how right I was.

The iced tea took longer to arrive than we expected, and we stood at the back table nervously talking with each other. It had been quite some time since I'd been nervous while speaking to anyone, so why was this happening to me? It was as though we didn't really want the tea, but it was an excuse for us to talk and begin interacting with each other.

As the processing within the group sessions continued, so did the processing in my head. I was going through an incredible battle that no one in the room could see, but I felt that probably everyone else was doing the same thing. That's the way it is at these retreats. There's always someone processing orally while the rest of the group is processing internally at the same time. The benefit of workshops such as this is the incredible healing effect on everyone involved.

I was in turmoil over the events that had transpired between my wife and myself during the last six to eight weeks. Yet, even during this personal processing I would look across the room and see Alice sitting there. I felt even more of a recognition when she would wear her glasses instead of her contact lenses. She looked so familiar that each time I would think, "Now where do I know you from?" Then I would go through a thought process about how to get to talk to her on a personal basis.

At one point I recalled how my friend Lori had blown an energy ball at me. I remembered how it had hit me right in the chest and radiated out to all my extremities, so I did that to Alice. I worked up this energy ball and softly blew it at her. Nothing, just nothing, no reaction, nothing. "Oh well," I thought, "maybe I am imagining this connection."

Nothing? Let me tell you it wasn't "nothing" at all. Every now and then I would look across the room at Dennis and he would be looking at me. Sometimes it unnerved me, but sometimes I thought, "This is cool. What's happening here?" I couldn't fault him for looking at me when that's exactly what I was doing to him. I couldn't understand the feelings, and I had a strange sensation that we were being drawn to each other. But why?

Once, when I looked up, I saw him holding his hands slightly cupped near his face. Then he blew a puff of air toward me, as though blowing a kiss in my direction. It hit me right in the center of my chest and I literally couldn't catch my breath. No reaction? I had stopped breathing!

For the rest of the retreat I would look over at Alice and it seemed as though every time I would look at her, she was looking at me. I knew there was something here; I just needed to talk to her to figure it out. I needed to make that connection and I only had two and a half more days to do it.

Sometime during the next break, Margaret, a woman I had met at a previous retreat, asked me if I would do a reading for her. She had discovered on the last day of the previous retreat that I was a psychic/medium.

I said, "Yes, I'd be happy to give you a reading," and we agreed on a time.

Then she asked if I had done very much medium work and I said, "Yes, why?"

"Well," she replied, "I would like to contact my dad, if possible, and talk to him."

"Sure, we can do that after the evening session is over, but I'm leading a meditation first and you're welcome to join us."

"Perfect, right after a great meditation!"

I had told Alice earlier in the day that I really needed to talk to her and we agreed to meet during one of the breaks. It didn't work out that day, but I was hoping that maybe the next day we could talk. I was still going through this recognition thing. I would not be satisfied until I figured out why I felt I knew her.

Dennis had asked me to meet him outside during a break because he wanted to talk with me. My first reaction was ok, but then some inner feeling came over me, and I just couldn't be alone with him. I think I wanted to, but for some reason, my soul was not quite ready for me to meet him eye to eye. I did look for him later that day, and found him downstairs in the small room that housed the only phone in the building. We all took turns making long-distance phone calls. When I saw Dennis on the phone he appeared to be very engrossed in his conversation, so I just waved and went back upstairs.

- Sherril Shows Up -

That night after the meditation, Margaret and I had been discussing the session we were going to have later and Alice said that she was also interested. She asked if she could stay and watch.

I said, "It's ok with me if it's ok with Margaret."

Without hesitation, Margaret said, "Sure, it's fine with me."

We chatted while we waited for the rest of the people to leave the large room so we could have our private session.

While we were speaking, it came out that Alice, during the first part of her career as a lawyer, worked for Janet Reno as an assistant prosecuting attorney in Miami. I remembered that Lori had said she worked at the Justice Department and that she now worked for Janet Reno in Washington, D.C. My immediate thought was, "I can use this to get Alice alone, if I can arrange for her to meet with Lori." I knew Spirit was working its magic for us.

By the time we started with Margaret's reading, it was getting really late. This was a very personal session that involved Margaret's father and grandmother and turned out to be a successful healing for her.

It was such a good session that Alice asked me to see if I could connect with her grandfather or anyone that she had known. As soon as she asked the question, a vision of a woman, similar in build to Margaret, came to me. She was dancing around, smiling and just having a great time. I saw her wearing a black and white dress.

I told Alice all of this and she immediately recognized the woman as her friend, Sherril. Alice explained that the dress was the one that Sherril had worn to Justin's bar mitzvah, two months prior to being diagnosed with cancer. She died one year later. It was very moving for Alice, and I felt as though I had gotten a little closer to her because of her friend.

I couldn't believe that Sherril had come through Dennis, but I was delighted. Margaret's session was amazing to watch, and I just sat by quietly while Dennis recreated an entire scene for Margaret. Her father and grandmother had come through, and Margaret confirmed everything Dennis had told her. So, when he told me he saw a woman with thin arms and legs, laughing and dancing in a black and white dress, I immediately saw

Sherril in the zebra patterned dress she wore to Justin's bar mitzvah. Now I knew that Sherril was instrumental in getting me to Baltimore. What else was she up to?

After Sherril came through, and Alice confirmed the information to be accurate, I felt more connected to the spirit world. So, when she asked me if I would do a regression on her, I agreed to try.

For two years I had been going to people who attempted to regress me to a past life, and I was never able to experience anything. I recall a specific time lying on a regression therapist's couch for two hours and seeing just blackness. Nothing came through and I was totally disappointed. I paid for the time I had taken, and never went back. I was exasperated at not being able to be regressed. Why could others see things so clearly, even down to the specific clothing worn, and I saw nothing? Hans and I once discussed this, and we both felt that I was probably trying too hard. I wanted it so badly, that I was blocking my own energy channels.

Dennis told us about his experiences from his own regressions, and I was fascinated. He told us about seeing himself in vivid detail when he was Joshua Abram, a printer from St. Louis, and then as Reginald May, a pilot during WWII. I wanted to have experiences like that, and I asked him if he could do a short regression on me then.

He said he would try, and I just felt it was safe to allow him to do this. Yet I was still cautious about opening my soul to this man, so I asked Margaret to stay with me. She sat close by and observed the whole thing.

Dennis' method of regressing people is quite safe and simple; there is no deep hypnosis involved. We sat in chairs facing each other, and as I sank back in the large comfy chair, I closed my eyes. He began by guiding me in a meditation and I was totally relaxed. His voice was so soothing. Then, he simply asked me what I was seeing, if anything. As the visions appeared, I was surprised that I actually was seeing clear pictures for the first time. I slowly described out loud what was coming to me.

I immediately saw a blonde woman at an outdoor café seated across from a man at a small table for two. The era appeared to be around the 19th century. She was wearing a blue dress, and her hair was in a bouffant style, not smooth. I then saw glimpses of a jewelry store and clearly saw large display cases with jewelry in them.

Dennis asked me if I knew what their names were. He had already instructed me to always go with my first thought and to not try to edit any information that would come through.

I said, "Joan; Joan and Fred Taylor." The spelling could also be Tailor; I wasn't sure.

"Where are you now?" Dennis asked me softly.

"Frankfurt," I replied. I didn't know whether that meant Frankfurt, Germany or Frankfurt, Kentucky.

"I see cobblestone streets," I continued.

"How many children do you have?" Dennis wanted me to try to get a full picture of this woman's life.

"Three children," I quickly said. "Two are boys."

The pictures began to fade and I came out of the meditation and back into the room. It had been an incredible experience, and I was so thankful that I had finally been able to get a glimpse of something! The pictures of the scene were vivid, but I told Dennis that I had not been able to see either person's face. I only saw the back of her head and felt the energy of the man.

"That woman sitting there was you," he told me with the authority and confidence of a psychic who had just observed the scene as clearly as I had.

It had been a powerful evening and I felt even closer to Alice by having been able to glimpse one of her past lives with her. When telling Alice that she was the woman, I left out the fact that the man with her was me. I knew that telling her this would have to wait because she was definitely not ready for that just yet. By the time we were done it was 3:00 AM and we were all very tired. Seven o'clock would come early.

- *Window to the Soul* -

The next morning, as I came into the dining room for breakfast, I saw Alice and Margaret sitting together at a table. They motioned for me to join them and I did. From that moment on and for the rest of the retreat, I would always sit with Alice at mealtime. Either she would save a seat for me or I would save a seat for her, but we never sat together during the sessions. I still felt that if we sat together, it would somehow take away from the total effect of the processing that we each needed to do separately.

When I sat down, both Alice and Margaret thanked me for the previous night. I told them it was my pleasure and a feeling of warmth came over me. Again there was that slight feeling of movement closer to something of which I was not really sure.

I had mentioned to Alice the day before that I would like to talk to her privately. So, when we took the first break in the day's sessions, I asked her if she would like to join me at one of the picnic tables. They were placed along the large grassy area across the street from the back entrance to the monastery.

"Sure, why not." she said, and agreed to meet there in a little while after taking a bathroom break.

I went out to the picnic table and sat waiting for this woman that I didn't really know and had no idea what I was going to say or do when she arrived. Nervously, I waited. I had no idea why I was so nervous, but I was.

When she got there we again made some small talk about the retreat and how interesting it was.

She asked me about the psychic stuff and then I said to her, "You know, the eyes have a way of being a window into one's soul. I'd love to look into your eyes and see what I could see. At the same time you could look into mine and see what you could see. Interested?" I asked.

"Ok," she nervously said, "I guess so."

I detected her nervousness and when she took off her sunglasses, I still felt her wall and I couldn't really see or feel much, but I did get a glimmer of something. I am very honest when doing such a spiritual act so I related what I saw and felt.

"You know, we were lovers in a past life!" I just blurted it out.

As soon as I had said that, I realized how it sounded. It was like a pickup line from a cheap "B" movie.

She said, "Yeah, right" and started to laugh and put her sunglasses back on. That's when I started to feel kind of weird. I was being who I really am and relaying exactly what I had seen and felt. I suppose at that time it was not something she could accept. We talked a little more until the break was over, then went back inside for the rest of the morning session.

"Yeah, right," I told him. What I was thinking was, "You're full of it. I bet you tell that to all the girls!" There was no way I was going to let him look into my eyes, and just who did he think he was? I actually did take off my sunglasses and we tried to look into each other's eyes for a brief moment, but I immediately put them back on. It's difficult to describe the feelings I was having. Again, my soul was in charge of dealing with the issues, and had not yet let me or my mind in on the game plan. My mind wanted to know who and what this man was about; my soul was saying, "Not yet." My years of metaphysical training had taught me to listen to the inner voice, and I did.

As the day's events progressed, I was able to see another side of Dennis. He truly was a sensitive being; not the typical man on the make. His sincerity and sensitivity came through in everything he did and said, and more and more I found myself watching him from across the room.

- Sad News -

That Wednesday was a day I will never forget. At about 11:00 AM we were in a particularly emotional session when someone came into the room and got Nancy to take a phone call. She left and when she came back in, I could tell something was wrong. She was visibly upset and as she whispered something to Neale, the color drained out of his face. I knew something heavy had just happened.

Neale very calmly looked out to the group and said, "Heartlight has just burned down!"

Heartlight was not only their retreat facility in Oregon,

it was their home. I felt very close to Neale and Nancy, and my heart was breaking for them and for Heartlight. I had attended two retreats there and had a sense of attachment to it.

At that time in 1996, Neale's third book in the *CWG* series was still unfinished. One of the concerns among the participants at the retreat was whether the manuscript was ok. It was.

I had never been to Heartlight, but we all felt the pain Neale, Nancy, and the others were going through. When Neale and his staff members left the room, the rest of us got into our own discussion about what we had just been told. When we learned that their dog, Lady, and the manuscript were unharmed and safe, we were able to carry on. After all, the other material things could be restored or replaced.

It was during the afternoon session that I received a phone message from my office that Tom's father had passed away. Eldon had been diagnosed with cancer in January, and we knew the end was close. I last saw him in the hospital the day before I left for Baltimore.

I called and spoke with Tom, Dale, and Tom's mother, Louise. They told me that Eldon had the most beautiful day right before he made his transition. He was at home and had been able to have all his family surrounding him to say their good-byes.

After making the phone call, I went back into the meeting room and told the group about my friend's father. The strange thing about this entire process was that just that morning I had presented my own issue to the group and they assisted me in processing through my fears and pain. My personal difficulty had been focused on dealing with deaths of my close friends. My two closest friends of

*my life had died within a three-year period, and I was
afraid to get close to anyone, for fear they would die and
I'd be alone again. It was an emotional processing, and
I remember that Neale played a special song for me, "The
Gift You Are" sung by John Denver. That was when
CarolAnne came over to me to help me feel complete in
my processing. She stayed in the room with me, long after
the rest of the group left to go to lunch. This was
appropriate assistance. That's what I needed and did not
receive in Hawaii. My processing was complete, and I
was ready to move on.*

The rest of that day was very intense for me. I was
thinking about Heartlight and how nothing is set in stone
and feeling like my life absolutely had to change. While
processing very intense things about my marriage, I reflected
back on my life as a husband and father. I was feeling very
successful as a father, but not so much as a husband. I had
been involved with other women during my marriage and
wasn't feeling too good about that. I also realized that
nothing happens without a reason, and that everything during
the last six-month period had been leading up to this moment.
The moment I finally said to myself, "It's over", was very
freeing.

Even though I knew it was over at that moment, I still
could not take responsibility for ending it. I contemplated
calling Jackie that night but I decided to wait until the end
of the retreat. I would call her in a few days while I was
staying with Lori and Greg for the weekend.

- Grandest Version of the Greatest Vision -

During the afternoon session, we wrote down our five
"grandest versions of the greatest vision" we'd ever had for
ourselves. I started writing them down and reading them
back to myself. That's when I realized that everything that

I had written down had to do with leaving my marriage and moving on with my life. The one major item was "to let my wife go". So when Neale asked if anyone wanted to share what they had written, I volunteered.

I said, "My grandest version of the greatest vision of myself is to be completely giving and to allow my wife to move on in her life, which in turn, will allow me to move on in mine. I'm going to ask for a divorce when I get home."

I had said this in front of the room for me as my personal declaration, but I also wanted to make sure that Alice knew that I was now "free and unencumbered". I didn't really know that then, but in retrospect, that is why I announced it the way I did.

I listened to what Dennis was saying and my eyes never left his face. If what he had just said were true, then he wasn't as "married" as I thought he was. I allowed myself to open up more to see what, if anything, would develop from the friendship we were establishing. Something was happening inside of me; the feelings I had were stronger than I wanted to deal with at that time. I reminded myself that I was there for a specific purpose: the retreat.

One of the benefits of attending a retreat such as this is that when we listen to and observe others doing and sharing their individual processing, it's for all of us. "Jointly and severally", to quote legal terminology and give it new meaning. Each person benefits from the experience. Just as our group in Hawaii was dealing with "self-worth" issues, our group in Baltimore was together for a purpose. My soul knew precisely what it was; it just wasn't ready to let me in on it.

We were then asked to describe the "most outrageous adventure" we'd ever had. I'd done many outrageous things over the years, but what was I willing to tell 27 other people? The first thought that popped into my head was what I decided to go with. I shared a story about my trip to Club Med in Cancun, Mexico. It's a story I'll never forget because it was so outrageous and out of character for me.

It was September, 1978. I decided to go to Club Med with Ginger, an old friend from high school that had just gotten divorced. We had reconnected our old friendship at our 10-year high school reunion the month before. Our sons were the same age, and we decided we both needed a vacation and time away from work and single parent responsibilities. I left for Cancun the day after my first date with Peter, and in fact, Peter drove us both to the airport.

When we arrived at Club Med, the rooms weren't quite ready, so we hung out for a little while at the pool and bar area. Within moments of our arrival, a man came up to me who looked as though he could be Peter's twin. He even had an accent; it was Israeli, but it was still an accent. Well, we connected...all week long. It truly was an adventure for me. The outrageous part was that we made love on the moonlit beach that first night and had no concerns that anyone was around us.

As I told the story to the group in Baltimore, I knew exactly why I wanted to tell the story out loud. It was my way of sending a clear message to Dennis that I was free and uninhibited.

The story that Alice told the group did not come across as pointed in my direction. In fact, up until that afternoon, Alice had sat on the opposite side of the room. During this session, she chose to sit on the same side as me. I was still in my usual spot near the air conditioner and was seated slightly to the left and behind Alice, such that her back was toward me. My attention at that time was focused on my processing. When she told her story, I thought "What a free spirit! I hope that I can get to that point after my divorce." To be able to open up and be ok with myself would be a tremendous accomplishment. I also began to look at Alice from a different perspective. There really was a sensitive, sensuous being behind that wall; a being that I needed to get to know. I just didn't know how, yet.

Later we all got together and decided to do a group meditation before we broke for the night. Margaret and Alice had asked me to do another session with them so we all stuck around afterward. I was especially looking forward to working with Alice again; I just didn't know why.

- A Visit from Charlie -

During the session with Margaret, I was able to bring her brother through, which helped her to move closer toward resolving some of her issues. I knew she had more work to do and I expected that she would be able to do that the next day with Neale.

After Margaret's session with Dennis, I took her aside and asked her to please stay in the room with me. I told her that I had asked Dennis if he could bring someone through for me, and I didn't want to be alone with him. I finally trusted him; I guess I just didn't trust myself.

The high point of that night was when Alice asked me if I thought I could bring her grandfather through for her. I told her I was willing to try. We were sitting in two chairs, one facing the other and I started going into the meditative state that overcomes me when I do this type of reading. I was going very deep and beginning to feel the presence of a male entity.

I described the vision I was having. "The man that I am seeing is an older man. He is wearing glasses and a white shirt and tie."

"Ok, so far so good," Alice said with a slight bit of skepticism in her voice.

"He has stains on his tie and thick glasses that are very dirty. This guy is kind of a slob." I was giving her a detailed description of the person in my vision.

Surprised she said, "That's not my grandfather; he was impeccable. It actually sounds like my ex-father-in-law, Charlie."

She then added with a laugh in her voice, "I'm glad I'm not paying you. I didn't enjoy talking to him when he was alive and I certainly don't want to talk to him now."

It was at this point that the spirit started sending messages that were very strange. I felt slightly embarrassed to be bringing him through, but I continued. I had made an agreement with my guides and God to not edit anything that was to come through. As I was getting ready to tell Alice the next message, I moved my chair back, slightly away from her because I didn't know how she would accept the message she was about to hear. I didn't think she would slap me or anything, but you never know how someone will react in this situation.

A lump was growing in my throat as I started thinking about what I was about to pass on to Alice. Here I was, finally in a position to get to know this person better, and I was about to insult her.

I nervously said, "Yes, this feels like your former father-in-law. Before I pass on what he is saying, I have to ask you a question."

"Go ahead."

I cautiously asked, "Did he ever call you 'Fat-Ass'?"

"Not to my face," she laughingly but hesitantly said. "Why?"

"Because he is saying 'Tell Fat-Ass hello for me'."

"That's definitely my former father-in-law you've brought through, she groaned. "But now I have a question for you."

"Ok."

"If he is so enlightened that he even made it to the other side, which amazes me, how could he say that to me?"

"Well, if he would have sent through, 'tell Alice hi', it would not have been as obvious it was him. Therefore, for you to *know* that it was Charlie, he had to be true to the personality that he had while living, and he had to insult you. Is there any doubt that it was he who came through?"

"None whatsoever."

That's Charlie. Ever the obnoxious personality. I used to tell him that he'd outlive me just for spite. Fortunately, I got out of my marriage to Rob and felt as though I'd divorced his parents as well. As an only child, Rob had always been close with his parents, but more often than not, their constant presence in our lives was smothering and destructive to our marriage. This message from Charlie, coming through Dennis, shocked me. Not so much as what he said, but that he was there at all. I had many friends and all of my grandparents who had passed to the other side, any one of whom I would have preferred a visit from. Of all those people, why was it only Charlie who came through that night? What was the purpose of his being there?

At that time, I needed to know that Dennis was truly in touch. A nice gentle hello from friends or my grandfather wouldn't have made the impact Charlie's insult did. Clearly, Dennis was not just telling me what he thought I wanted to hear. I began to look at Dennis in a new light, and recognized that he truly had a gift to share. The real purpose of Charlie's visit would come to me months later.

The three of us stayed up again until about 3:00 AM, just chatting and talking about many spiritual things. I finally got too tired and excused myself. After doing a couple hours of readings I was very tired, but at the same time I was feeling wonderful and even more connected to Alice.

- Closer Yet -

The next morning started off great. Although I was really tired from staying up so late, I was feeling especially good about the sessions the night before. I was on kind of a high when I went down to breakfast. I sat with Alice and Margaret and we had a great time talking about what we did the night before.

Alice was wearing a T-shirt with two jumping dolphins on the front. I immediately received a vision of the two of us being in Atlantis together.

"That's where we were," I blurted out.

A name suddenly came to me, which I felt was Alice's in that life. It was 'Shanta Blue' and I told her. She chuckled and jokingly made some off-handed remark about it. But that was the first point that I really knew I had to talk to her, one on one, and without the wall. I didn't have any idea why or for what reason, but I knew that it would happen at the perfect time and place. After breakfast we all went in to begin the morning session. There was much processing going on during this, the last full day of the retreat.

Dennis' comment to me about my dolphin T-shirt was perfect. I had purposely chosen to wear a shirt from Hawaii, because of my own special feelings and beliefs that I had a past life there. I was fully aware that I wore it hoping that it would spark some recognition in Dennis, and it did. Even his remark about Atlantis didn't shock me. While I had not been successful in my own regressions, I had been told several times that I played an important role during the time of Atlantis. It did not surprise me to know that Dennis had been there, too. We had now begun our path of remembering, and our own re-membering and re-connecting of our souls.

- The Reprimand -

Later on in the morning there was a long break just before lunch. I was sitting in the large meeting room talking to a couple of the people when Will came in and told me that there was going to be a meeting upstairs on the third floor. He said that Neale wanted to talk to all of the staff.

"Ok," I said, "how long do I have before he wants to meet?"

"He is up there right now in room 301. Just go on up."

As I went up the stairs my thoughts were wandering and I wondered what the meeting was all about. Little did I know, but I was the only one to be 'invited' to this meeting with Neale.

"I guess I am the first one here, eh?" I jokingly asked Neale when I entered the room.

It was then painfully obvious I was going to be the only one there besides him. He was sitting in a chair with a very serious look on his face. I felt the heaviness in the air and instantly knew what he was going to say next.

"You are the only one here for this meeting," he quietly stated.

He then continued, "Dennis, I have to tell you I am not very happy about what I have heard today. I understand you were working with Margaret last night, that you did a reading for her and were processing with her about some issues surrounding her father."

His voice was strained but low and quiet like only Neale can be. It was kind of fatherly like, but with an edge. I knew he was very upset about what I had done.

He continued with, "I have to explain that what I am upset about is that you didn't come to me with this information. I am the facilitator at this retreat and you, as part of the staff, should have come to me. I must have control during these retreats or we would have everyone doing this work. Being one of my staff I feel like you have not held up your part of the bargain." He went on to say that from then on I was to come to him with anyone who came to me needing to process."

"Ok, will do," I said as I sat there stunned and suddenly at a complete loss for words. I felt that I had done nothing wrong, yet I could say nothing.

He went on to tell me that it was not a personal thing, but it had to do with the insurance. He was the facilitator and if anything was to go wrong, he could be liable. He also wanted me to know that I was not fully trained and he felt I wasn't ready to do the facilitating yet. He basically was being very nice about it, but stern at the same time.

I explained to him that I had done a channeled reading for Margaret and that I thought that what I was doing was not in the scope of facilitating. I understood that his perception was that I had stepped out beyond the boundaries, but that I felt I had not. I then told him how sorry I was and I went on to say that this would not happen again.

We parted and I went downstairs, dealing with a new set of feelings that I was unsure of. The episode was quite reminiscent of the reprimand from Sylvia, and if I had been able to read that sign, it was saying, "Go your own way. You will not be working with this man until you reach an equal level in the human world." Maybe someday Neale and I will work together, but right then I knew that I could never work **for** him. I loved him dearly, and I continue to regard him with the utmost respect to this day.

Even though I heard this message loud and clear, I continued to try to keep the connection open through the "Friends of Re-Creation" network that we were trying to establish.

That afternoon Neale had the opportunity to work with Margaret on her issues and I feel as though it all worked out for the best.

I believe that even the reprimand was for a worthy purpose. Had Dennis not worked with Margaret the night before, and had Neale not been made aware of it, perhaps Margaret would not have brought her issues to light. Ultimately, Neale had to be the one to assist Margaret in the processing of her emotions, and Dennis may have just been the catalyst. As for myself, I needed to observe the process in order to allow Dennis to do the reading for me. It was all perfect and each person's role served a purpose.

Earlier that morning Marie had approached me and asked if Dennis would do a reading for her. I thought it was interesting that she was coming to me to act as the communicator to Dennis. Were we being perceived by the others as a "couple"? Anyway, I told Dennis that Marie had asked for some time with him, and he told me that he could not do any more private sessions with anyone. He explained what Neale had told him, and I told Marie to speak with Dennis directly. Although she was disappointed to not have her chance at a reading, she understood the reasoning.

I was touched that Dennis had confided in me as he did. It seemed to bring us a little closer, as I felt his pain. Again, each step of our path was being artfully choreographed.

- The Graduation -

I had spoken on the phone with Lori during the day and told her about Alice and the fact that she used to work for Janet Reno. I said, "You guys should meet and have a chance to talk. I think you would hit it off really well."

She replied with a knowing smile in her voice, "Well Dennis, if you like her, she has to be great, so bring her over if she doesn't have to leave right away. I would love to meet her."

That was the first time that I felt that my path was going to be shifting. I suddenly realized that the retreat was almost over; there was only half a day left. I was beginning to feel these feelings that I didn't recognize. I knew my marriage was over and I knew that I was about to embark on my next adventure.

I had to get Alice alone and talk to her to find out what this was all about. I don't know what I expected to be revealed, I just knew that I had to be alone with her and become truly transparent.

I needed to get a message to Alice. I had to let her know

that there was something else going on here. I didn't know how I would do that, but I should have known that it was already taken care of by the Universe.

It is customary for Neale to close his retreats with a parting ceremony, a type of graduation for our week's achievements. Before the parting ceremony, everyone is asked to bring a gift to put on the table in the center of the room. Everyone is also asked to write on one piece of paper what it is he or she is leaving behind or sending away. On another piece of paper they are to write what they are taking with them, or what they gained from this retreat. Each person is given the opportunity to read their notes out loud to the group.

We took a break just before the ceremony and everyone went to get his or her gift for the table. I really didn't have anything, so I went to my room and got a piece of paper and a pen. I wrote a poem to Alice on the paper and hooked the pen to it. It read as follows:

This pen is for your thoughts,

Write them with great care,

Love everyone you meet,

And let them know you are there.

"SEIZE THE MOMENT"

On the outside I had written "WITH LOVE FOR YOU" and had underlined it twice. If someone else happened to get it, then it would mean "Universal Love", but somehow I knew Alice would get it. It was either my psychic ability, my guides or just my soul remembering what was going to happen.

When I got back to the meeting room, I went straight to the table and laid the poem and the pen down. There were a few gifts already there, and I saw a dolphin T-shirt and instantly a mental image of Alice placing it on the table came to me. I really wanted the T-shirt, because I knew that Alice had put it there, and I knew that if it were still there when I went up, then I would take it.

On the table with the gifts, there was a large porcelain dish with a candle burning in the middle of it. Each person was to take the paper on which they wrote what it was they were leaving, light it on fire and leave it burning in the dish. It is symbolic for getting rid of an emotion or weight that is holding you down. After burning the paper, each person is asked to select a gift to take away from the table

Alice was the first one to get up and tell everyone what she was taking and leaving. When she was done she reached down and picked up the pen and poem. She looked at me and smiled. I felt a warmth come over me and realized right then that something special had happened between us. The rest of the people went up one by one, each person declaring what he or she was taking away from the retreat and what they were setting free. Patty from Dallas got the T-shirt before I was able to get it, so I knew that it was meant for her.

Ok, I admit it. I was sitting in my Naugahyde chair when I saw Dennis come into the room holding a small yellow piece of paper with a pen clipped to it. I tried to be nonchalant and not look at him as he approached the table. I felt strange because I thought that I had cheated. For some reason, then unknown to me, I needed to retrieve Dennis' gift. The only way I could be certain that I would get the paper and pen was to be the first to announce my declarations to the group. In reality, I didn't cheat at all, everything was perfect. I was supposed to get the pen and paper because Dennis had written it just for me.

We had learned from Neale and from studying the message in <u>Conversations With God</u>, that we should walk into a room with the intention of showing up that way. Well, I walked up to the table and boldly announced, "That which I choose to bring home with me is all the love, wisdom, clarity, honesty, awareness, responsibility and tolerance that I now recognize I have always had. These are my own truths. I also take with me all the wonderful memories of this outrageous experience of all the souls who have reconnected this week."

I sat down and waited for the rest of the group to make their statements and to remove a gift from the table. I kept wanting Dennis to get up so that he could take my T-shirt. However, it was absolutely perfect when Patty, who had been sitting next to me and with whom I'd had a special connection during the week, lifted the gray shirt from the table and hugged it to her chest.

Dennis waited until the very end and finally got up to make his proclamation. When I heard him declare that he had made the decision to allow his wife to have the freedom she desired, I felt my wall begin to slowly crumble around me.

After the ceremony concluded, we all hugged and stayed around to socialize and take pictures. I was having some problems with my camera, and while I was perfectly capable of fixing it myself, I asked Dennis if he would take a look at it for me. He did, and it gave us some time to sit and talk alone. I can't believe I pulled such a "helpless female" trick like that.

Our conversation wasn't earth shattering, but it was revealing. Something was said about birthdays, and Dennis and I discovered that we both had birthdays in February. Mine is February 16th; his is the 19th. We were born the exact same year. Up to that point, I thought he was younger because he looked much younger to me. Actually, I was right; he is exactly three days younger! He loves that, and calls himself my "boy toy" for three days every year.

After the ceremony was over a group of us were sitting around chatting and I asked Margaret for a ride to the Baltimore airport the next day.

Then I turned to Alice and said, "Lori invited you to come with me to visit her tomorrow afternoon since you don't have to be in D.C. until the evening. We're done here by noon and I'm picking up a rental car at the Baltimore airport. I'll gladly give you a ride to D.C. in time for your dinner, and I'd love to have a chance to talk to you some more. I think you and Lori would hit it off really well because you both worked for Janet Reno." I waited nervously for the negative answer that I hoped that I wouldn't hear.

"Ok," she said quickly, "that sounds like fun. I would love to meet her after hearing all your stories about her energy work."

"Great," was all I could say, but inside I was shouting "YES!!!" I would finally get a chance to talk to her alone.

I was delighted that Dennis had found a way for us to extend our time together. Without hesitation, I accepted his invitation and looked forward to getting to know him a little bit better.

- The Last Day -

After plenty of hugs with everyone and some tearful good-byes, Margaret, Alice and I were on our way to the airport. We laughed and chatted and joked all the way to the airport. We talked about how CWG had changed our lives and was still changing our lives.

It was very busy at the airport so Margaret just dropped us off in the front and we worked our way to the car rental booths. While I rented a car, Alice took the time to try and turn in her shuttle ticket she had for her trip to National Airport in D.C. She had an interesting story to tell when she came back about her being an angel to someone. It seems that she was going to ask for a refund but she suddenly decided not to.

When I had first arrived in Washington on Monday, I purchased a round-trip shuttle ticket from National Airport in D.C. to BWI Airport in Baltimore. Then, from BWI, I took a bus to the general vicinity of the monastery, and then a taxi directly to the door. So, I still had the other half of my shuttle ticket to National Airport, and now, I didn't need it. I had already given the other half of my round-trip bus ticket to Gloria, one of the women from the retreat who needed an earlier ride to BWI.

When I entered the airport in Baltimore, I went to the shuttle counter, and asked if it were possible to obtain a refund for an unused ticket. I was told that it was possible, and that the counter to get the refund was on the other side of the airport.

"How much would the refund be for half of a round-trip ticket?" I asked.

"About $10," the man behind the counter told me.

"Oh. Just give it to the next person that comes up to buy a ticket to Washington," I said. "Tell them it's from an angel."

Then I went off smiling to find Dennis.

After we got in the car we had great fun trying to figure out what the big box-like gadget on the passenger's side was. After a little investigation, we discovered it was a satellite tracking system called "Never Lost". It was a computer mapping system and you could input an address and it would give specific directions on how to get to your destination. It was awesome to use. Alice was like a kid with a new toy. She had a great time getting to Lori and Greg's. It wasn't perfect, however, because we still had to call them and get detailed directions.

By the time we finally got to their house, we were getting much more comfortable with each other. It felt as though we were going to see old friends. It was weird, but I felt like Alice and I had known each other forever. It was such a comfortable feeling that I forgot that we had only met four days before for the very first time. We arrived at Lori and Greg's safely and had a nice visit for about two hours.

Lori had just gone through surgery and couldn't climb the stairs to go up to her bedroom. Because of that, she had set up a sofa bed in her living room. At one point, Alice was reclining on the sofa bed chatting with Lori, who was also there resting. I was seated on a chair next to the bed. Alice was sitting in such a way that her leg was stretched out and I noticed that she wore an ankle bracelet. I reached down and touched it and commented on how beautiful it was. The electricity that passed between us was so intense that it gave me a jolt. That was a changing point in the relationship between us. It went to the next level and we never looked back.

What Dennis didn't know was that my wall had completely shattered the moment he touched my ankle at Lori's house. It was as though our souls had finally connected and were allowing our minds to recognize the incredible energy passing between us at that moment. I was so comfortable with him that I felt as if I'd been with him all my life.

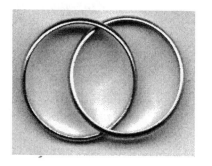

The Naked Place

The "Naked Place" the computer map read
The words were crystal clear.
I saw them and smiled.
Then, I looked again.
The words were just not there.

My surprise was shown and I looked at your face.
You smiled and said, "You saw 'Naked Place'".
You said you'd seen it, too.
The "Naked Place" we saw on the screen
was there only for me and for you.

So what next to do but to follow our souls.
The message was clear; it spoke true.
Go to the "Naked Place"
and get to know each other
Heart, soul, and mind; body too.

This much we discovered and more
Our love was at last found again
in the "Naked Place for me and for you.

Chapter Thirteen

The Naked Place

- *Souls Touch* -

When we left Lori's house, the air around us had a thickness you could cut with a knife. The emotions that were overcoming me were intense. Up until that point, other than the trip over, we had been surrounded by other people and that took away from our energy flow. However, when we got back in the car that all changed. We were finally alone, with no one to interrupt the moment for at least an hour on the trip to D.C.

It was like being a teenager again, like the first time I had ever been with a girl on a date. The feeling of slowly putting my arm around her shoulders, making sure never to touch her, until my hand was all the way around on the other side. The tension you feel. The incredible overwhelming excitement of not knowing whether she wants your arm there or not, but at the same time "knowing" deep inside that this is right. That was the feeling of that moment.

As we drove away I said, "Alice, I'm having these feelings I MUST talk about. Could you drop that wall you've had up all week?"

She looked at me and softly said, "It's been gone since your hand touched my leg!"

That is when it escalated to a fever pitch. I reached out and touched her hand and my pulse raced. My heart was in my throat, my palms started sweating and I knew this was something very special.

Holding onto her hand, I said, "This connection is so incredibly strong, and the feelings I'm having are so intense, I don't quite know what to do about them!" But I really did.

I began looking for a place to pull off. I couldn't drive another foot. I had to stop, get off the road. I HAD TO KISS HER! I was being driven to touch my lips to hers.

As we approached the onramp to the freeway, there was an open area alongside the road. I pulled off. Pulse racing, palms sweating, heart pounding in my throat, totally excited, I turned to her.

As my gaze met her beautiful blue eyes she said, "You read my mind!"

I couldn't believe that Dennis had pulled the car over. Just moments before, while driving through the residential area, I was thinking, "I wonder if there's a place where we can pull over so he can kiss me."

This is what the culmination of the search came to. When we kissed it was the single most powerful moment in my life. The world didn't exist! There was no freeway, no onramp, no city, no cars, no world. There was nothing but the sound of our breath, the feel of our lips together and our arms around each other, the aroma of her and the sweet taste of our love intermingling. I was knocked off my feet! I was, in an instant, totally and unequivocally in love with this woman I had practically just met. I knew that she was "the one".

It was while in that moment that a vision also came to me. I was seeing in my third eye pictures and flashes of faces that she had been in some far off past lives. I was recognizing her and not really realizing what all this meant. I was so blown away by the sheer energy that was taking over my soul and my body that the magnitude of this reconnection wouldn't register until much later. I had just kissed my "Twin Soul", and the pictures were of her when we were together in many, many past lives. These past lives would reveal themselves to us slowly as we traveled together again through the next few years.

After we kissed a few more times, and caught our breath, we drove on toward Washington D.C. This would turn out to be one of the most significant rides in our lives.

The kiss was the single most incredible kiss and electrical moment I'd ever experienced. The feelings were coming from a depth I'd never known. I knew this was special, and that Dennis and I had just embarked on the most joyous and spiritual moment of our lives. We had re-discovered our souls' desire.

As we proceeded on into the next part of our journey, a very familiar feeling was coming over me again. A feeling of knowing that "who I really am" was coming to the surface. For some reason I was feeling like I had just found a lost part of me. A final piece to the puzzle that had been eluding me. At the same time my mind was awash with question upon question. "Who is this woman? Why has she come into my life at this time and why do I feel this way." Then I would look over at Alice and just gaze in awe. I couldn't believe how overcome I was. I would look into her eyes and these wondrous feelings of love would permeate my whole being. How could I love someone so much in such a short amount of time? These questions would be answered in the months to come, but for now I was lost in a sea of emotion.

We found ourselves doing things that couples do only after they have been together for a long time.

At one point, I heard Dennis say, "That feels great. Thank you."

I realized that my left hand was no longer in my lap, but was gently rubbing his neck while he was driving. It had been a totally unconscious reflex and felt very natural and comfortable. I also remember calling him "honey" during one point of the trip.

"Did I just call you honey?" I laughingly asked, without any embarrassment whatsoever.

Everything was moving so fast, we felt as though we'd known each other forever. The comfort level was such that it was as if we were just picking up from a past life, re-connecting, and moving forward now that we were together again.

- Never Lost -

As I mentioned previously, in the car that I had rented was a system called "Never Lost". It was a satellite tracking system to help guide you to your chosen destination. Alice was busy toying with the system, scrolling down the list of items.

There were destinations that we could pick, or we could insert our choice of an address for it to guide us to. It had maps, and after a location was inserted and it had determined the best route, it checked up on us. When we would go off course it would announce in a computer-like voice, "You have left the chosen route, please come back on course or choose another route." It really was very adept at not letting us get lost.

As Alice was scrolling down the alphabetized list of places like "The Capitol," "Jefferson Memorial," and "Lincoln Memorial," she came to a listing that caught our attention. At almost the same instant, we looked at the screen and then we looked at each other.

With a surprised look toward me, Alice asked, "Did you see that?"

I immediately responded, "You saw "Naked Place", didn't you?"

"You saw it too?"

As we both looked back at the screen, we saw the words, "Named Place".

Well, we knew that this was some kind of sign. We were either supposed to go someplace and get naked, or it was pertaining to the fact that we had just gone through a week in a retreat that was emphasizing "transparency". It was about allowing the true self to come to the surface. It also inspired the poem at the beginning of this chapter.

It then came to us that we were supposed to "get naked" in a metaphoric sense and find out who each of us was. It was then that the walls really came down and we started communicating more deeply, and for the next two days we discovered who we were in relation to each other and to ourselves.

I really did see the words "Naked Place" on the screen, and I was astounded when Dennis told me that he saw the same words. If anyone else had ever said they saw at the same time what I'd seen, I'd say, "Yeah, sure."

But, I hadn't told him what I saw. I only said, "Did you see that?" He was the one who said, "You saw 'Naked Place', didn't you?"

To this day, whenever Dennis and I have a conflict, or if I ever have the slightest doubt about who and what we are, I think back to that day and those simple words on the screen. It's the same experience Kevin Costner and James Earl Jones had in "Field of Dreams". The words on the billboard were meant just for their eyes to see and for them to understand.

The signs and messages are everywhere if you just take the time to look and then appreciate their meaning. Some messages are subtle and may be passed off as "mere coincidence", such as Dennis and I being the only two people from the retreat who were staying in the Baltimore/ D.C. area. Other signs will hit you right between the eyes, such as "Naked Place" and others that keep happening to us all the time.

You can't ignore these messages, because if you do, you may be missing the opportunity of a lifetime. The Universe will keep trying with new signs and messages, but why wait? Be impulsive; be impetuous; live life to the fullest NOW while you can appreciate all it has to offer. Every cliché fits here... "don't put off until tomorrow..."; "life is short, enjoy it while you can"; "live, love, laugh"; "time waits for no one". Sandra's favorite saying was, "Life is uncertain, eat dessert first." Go for it, and you'll not only find your twin soul, you'll recognize your special love the exact moment it happens, and will be ready to grab hold with all your strength and all your heart and soul.

- The Hotel -

When we reached the D.C. city limits I knew that I would be seeing this city a lot in the next couple of days. It was about 6:00 PM when we finally got to the hotel where Alice was staying, and she was supposed to be at a cocktail party at 7:00 PM. She didn't make it.

As we pulled up I looked at her and said, "Shall I drop you off, or do you want me to come up?"

She replied coyly, "Just valet the car!" and then she smiled a knowing smile.

When we got to her room, it seemed like the bellman would never leave. He took his time about bringing in her bags and then went through the room checking everything. In my mind I was thinking, "Will you just get on with it and get out of here so I can take this woman in my arms and hold her, squeeze her, kiss her and press my body into hers?" He finally left and I did just that, and so did she.

We were finally alone and in a hotel room. We could do anything that we chose to do, including getting naked and merging our physical bodies together. We chose to get partially naked and just touch our bodies together, to press our heart centers together and "feel" the energy that was pulsing between us. There would be more time later for the merging of our physical bodies.

We were discovering, through our talking and touching, who we really were in relation to each other. That was the first time we felt that there was something more than just a physical attraction. This was something that was bigger than either one of us could envision.

We spent the next hour just lying on the bed talking and feeling the energy that was flowing between us. Alice was supposed to have been at a cocktail party at 7:00 PM but chose to miss that to spend a little more time with me. Finally she had to get dressed for the evening festivities that were to begin at 8:00 PM. We continued our conversation while she was dressing. It was during this conversation that the thought came into my mind, "What happens now?" So I asked.

"Where do we go from here? I don't want this to end."

"Neither do I, but I have to be here for the party tonight and the bar mitzvah reception tomorrow night."

"What about during the day? Do you have anything

planned? I would love to see the sights of Washington with you." And without even thinking or skipping a beat I continued, "Would you like for me to come back tonight?"

Without batting an eyelash Alice responded, "Absolutely," and then we sealed it with another deep soul reaching kiss.

"See you tonight," I said, "but it might be very late. Lori and Greg have invited some people that we met online to have dinner together tonight."

Smiling, she replied, "That's ok, I'll be up and waiting."

It was time for me to get ready for Sammy's bar mitzvah dinner. After all, that's why I was in Washington. I hadn't even seen or spoken with any of Sherril's family members yet, and I was very much looking forward to seeing them all again.

I asked Dennis if he would wait for me while I showered and dressed for dinner. He said he would, and I couldn't believe how comfortable I felt about changing while he was in the room. Something strange was certainly happening between us, and I wasn't going to try to fight it or even analyze it then.

I think my real reason for wanting Dennis to stay was that I wanted him to see me all dressed up. All week long, he had only seen me in jeans, T-shirts, and sneakers. When I was finally ready to go, I must say that I looked great! My weight was down to a decent size, and my hair and make-up were perfect. I was wearing a new outfit that even surprised me to see how I looked. From the expression on Dennis' face, I think he was quite pleased.

Yes, I was.

By the time we left the room, the cocktail party crowd

was leaving the atrium where the party was held, and they were moving into the large dining room for the dinner. Dennis and I kissed good-bye, and he said he'd come back later that night. I told him that the dinner party would be over by midnight or so.

It was wonderful seeing everyone, and I was told by some of the others that I hadn't actually missed anything by not attending the cocktail gathering. It was held in the hotel's outdoor atrium, and there was no air-conditioning. By arriving just in time for the 8PM dinner, everything worked out perfectly.

- Back To Baltimore -

As I drove back to Baltimore for the party with the people I had met online, I was deep in thought about what would happen next. Where do I go from here?

When I arrived at Lori's house, Annie, from New York, had already arrived. We greeted each other with hugs and smiles. She was a nice looking young woman, about 20, with long brown hair and a great smile. She had a warmth about her that one could feel from across the room. I had met her online about six months earlier and had chatted many times, so we were somewhat familiar with each other even though we had never met.

About fifteen minutes after I got to Lori's, Laurie from York, Pennsylvania, and her husband Skip arrived. Laurie and I had also established a friendship online and over the phone.

I had recommended to her that she read the book *Conversations With God, Book 1*, and she had. After reading it we had many conversations over the phone and online concerning the book's message and her personal feelings. She was having trouble letting go of all the old "stuff" to become who she really was. This was an opportunity to meet in person and actually be able to work through some of it. I was looking forward to conversing with her in person, and passing on the messages that I was psychically getting for her.

- The Phone Call -

About 10:30 PM or so I felt I should call Jackie and talk to her about what I had decided during the retreat. I wanted to ask her how she felt about the marriage and if she wanted it to continue or get a divorce. It seemed that simple. I went downstairs while everyone was still talking and made my phone call. When Jackie answered the phone, I said "hello" and talked a little about what was going on with the people from online.

After about four or five minutes of talking she said, "I thought you were not going to call."

"Well, I have to ask you a question."

"What's that?"

"I just want to know if you want to continue on with this marriage or do you want to get a divorce?" I blurted it out.

"Why don't you just come home and we can talk about it?"

"No, I think I want to know now," I stated flatly.

She said, "Well if you want an answer right now the answer is no, I don't want to continue. I want to get a divorce!"

I was somewhat surprised at the answer even though I knew what it would be. I felt the same way. I didn't want it to go on, but for some reason, I couldn't say it first. I guess at that time I needed for her to say she wanted out. It is very hard for me to admit this, but I just felt like I couldn't be the one. I sat and contemplated what was ahead for me. I had no idea how this was all going to turn out, but I wasn't worried. I really can't say that I was upset; I was just stunned.

I went upstairs and everyone noticed a difference in me. I didn't think I was acting any differently, but they all seemed to notice. Lori was the first one to say something.

"What's wrong, Dennis? You look upset."

"Really?" I quipped. "Does it show that much?"

"Yes it does," Lori answered. "What happened?"

"Jackie said she doesn't want to continue the marriage," I said, adding "but that's alright, neither do I. I'm just stunned that it is real."

They were all really nice and very supportive about my situation. We chatted for another hour or so, and then I said, "I'm going back to Washington D.C. tonight to see Alice, so I'll bid you all goodnight. I need to find out what this is all about. I'll let you all know later what is going on."

I told Lori and Greg that I would be back the next day and hoped that we could do some sightseeing during the day, and then I left.

- Moving On -

Driving back to D.C. was a little different this time. I had a reaction that I didn't expect. I broke down in tears and cried my eyes out. It was as if I had to cleanse this part of myself before moving forward with Alice.

I had all kinds of feelings about what was going on

with me. I felt one life ending and almost instantaneously another one beginning. It felt so right, but at the same moment, so strange. I know some people might call this a rebound, but it just didn't feel that way.

At the time I asked for guidance from my guides and felt a "go forward, don't stop" feeling come over me. In fact, I went through so much internal dialogue in the thirty-five mile ride to D.C. that I felt as if I had just gone through two years of counseling. After all the processing was done I knew that it was perfect, and I was ready to move on with my life.

The party was wonderful, and I was able to spend time with Sherril's mother, brother, and sister. I was seated at a table with Sherril's cousins that I had also known since my childhood.

We talked about the week I had just spent in Baltimore, and the conversation quickly turned to metaphysics and spiritual beliefs. Sherril's cousin, Cathy, had died five years before Sherril, and her sisters have always kept her memory alive.

At the end of the evening, I told Sherril's cousin, Denise, about Dennis, and that he was coming back to the hotel later that night. Since my hands were full with my purse and my camera, she helped me carry two glasses of champagne to the room. We thought that would be a nice romantic touch when Dennis arrived.

When I got back to my room, I changed into my long nightgown. I don't even know why I'd packed it, because I knew I'd be alone the whole trip. My usual bedtime attire was a nightshirt, one-size-fits-all. At that moment, I was glad to have the sexy gown, and admired my image in the mirror. I freshened my make-up and perfume and waited for Dennis to arrive.

I decided that I just had to talk to someone about what had happened that day. Who else to call but Margaret? When she'd dropped us off at the airport, she'd handed me a book and told me I had to read it. She had already inscribed it to me. The book was The Eagle and the Rose, by Rosemary Altea.

Margaret and I had really become friendly during the retreat, and I felt the closest with her. Now I wanted to share my feelings, and besides, who better? She was a psychologist! By now she would have arrived safely at her home in Vermont, and I dialed her home number.

Although the hour was late, she was happy to hear from me, and was flabbergasted when I told her about Dennis and me. She said that when she left us at the airport that afternoon, it didn't even appear as though we liked each other. Oh well. So much for a therapist's insight.

Margaret and I spoke for more than an hour, and I was still on the phone with her when I heard a knock at the door. We quickly said good-bye and I raced to the door, with my heart pounding.

- Back to Love -

As I walked up to the door of Alice's hotel room, I started feeling butterflies of anticipation in my stomach. It was like a first date all over again, but I knew that when I stepped over the threshold of that room my life would never be the same again. I was now truly starting the next chapter of my life and there would be no going back. I raised my hand to knock on the door and stopped, but only for an instant because I knew that this was right. This was perfect. This was someone who was connected to me in ways that I was just beginning to realize. I had a long way to go to understand it, but I just knew that it was supposed to be this way.

I knocked and almost instantly from inside the room I heard Alice's voice asking, "Dennis, is that you?"

"Yes it is," I replied.

The door slowly opened, but just enough for me to slip through. Alice smiled at me from behind the door as I walked into the room. As she closed the door I was gifted with the vision of the most beautiful woman I have ever seen, wearing a very alluring burgundy colored, lace fringed, nightgown. I took a quick gulp of air as my heart went up to my throat and my palms began to sweat in anticipation of holding this woman close to me again. She came into my arms with her face lifted, her moist lips slightly open and her beautiful blue eyes sparkling and filled with the look of love. I slowly bent down and pressed my open lips to hers. Our tongues played like two slippery snakes whose only intent was to intertwine in a thousand ways. As I pulled her closer, I could feel the line of her body under the nightgown and I knew that I was now moving on with my life.

When I opened the door, we fell into each other's arms and time stopped again. We never even got to the champagne.

- Changes Happen -

When I awoke the next morning, I was sort of disoriented. It took me a couple of minutes to get my bearings. When I did, I felt totally comfortable being there. I didn't feel out of place or have even the slightest bit of remorse. I knew it was supposed to happen this way.

When I opened my eyes, I was lying on my left side. What I saw in front of me was the vision of a beautiful woman lying on her right side. Our eyes were locked instantly in an embrace many thousands of years old. The warmth and love that I felt coming from those beautiful blue eyes looking back at me was overwhelming. I felt so comfortable and had such an intense feeling of love toward the woman lying next to me that I didn't care if I ever got out of bed.

Unfortunately, we had to leave our nest because Alice had to go to temple for the morning bar mitzvah service.

I went back to Baltimore to hang out with everyone at Lori and Greg's. I was supposed to go back to D. C. and meet Alice when she was done. I had my phone on and was expecting her call about noon. I began to worry a little until she finally called around 2:00 PM. She explained that she had been trying to call since just before noon, but couldn't get a connection with her cell phone. I bid my farewells to all and headed for D.C.

Morning arrived sooner than we wanted, but we still took time to drink in the experience of lying comfortably in each other's arms. We had spent a great deal of time the night before really talking and getting to know each other again. At that point, we just knew that we were picking up from a previous lifetime together.

We agreed that I would call Dennis around noon, as he said he wanted to come back into the city to see me before the evening party I was to attend. I thought that would be a lot of driving for him, but he said he didn't mind at all. We just wanted to spend as much time together as we could.

The Saturday morning bar mitzvah service was beautiful, and we were all so very proud of Sammy, who had performed magnificently. He was 13 years old, and had grown up to be a tall and quite handsome young man. He looked so much like Sherril, and had her slender build. He most certainly had her smile, and I was thrilled to be a part of the celebration. One of my fears had been that Sherril's family would shut me out after she died. Her mother, Connee, was always like a second mother to me, and she made sure that I remained a part of the family.

Sammy had finished the traditional bar mitzvah boy's speech, and I just sat and observed him. He nervously sat on the pulpit's bench and waited for the rabbi to conclude the Saturday morning Sabbath service. Next to him on the bench were the books and kiddush cup (an Israeli wine cup) that had been gifted to him during the service by the temple sisterhood. The kiddush cup, which was not in a box, was standing upright next to Sammy. Suddenly, a thought came to me, and I knew that Sherril was up on the pulpit with her son.

"Ok, Sherril," I thought to myself, "show me you're here with us. If you're up there with Sammy, knock over the kiddush cup."

I briefly looked away, and when I looked back at Sammy, the cup was lying on its side, still on the bench.

I was surprised, but not totally blown away. I knew this was Sherril, but would anyone else believe it?

Denise and her mother were sitting next to me. Denise's mother and Sherril's father were sister and brother, and the two families were extremely close. I had always envied their closeness. It is often said in metaphysical circles that people will choose to leave the earthly world on a special date or anniversary that has meaning for a close family member. Sherril's father, Joe, had died on Father's Day in 1984; Sherril died on the exact same date in 1989.

When I saw the kiddush cup on its side, I leaned over to Denise and said, "If I tell you something, will you promise to not think I'm crazy?" Denise, who is a psychologist, promised me she'd listen to what I had to say. Besides, she'd known me most of her life, and we both knew I could tell her anything without fear of judgment.

I told Denise what I'd said to Sherril and what happened next with the kiddush cup.

She squeezed my hand and said softly, "I know that Sherril's here, and I feel her presence, also. Cathy is here, too."

There was a buffet lunch after the service, and we were all ready to leave the temple by 12:30 PM. I had tried to call Dennis, but I couldn't get service on my cell phone. I even tried using a calling card several times to reach his cell phone, which was a Seattle phone number, but I never got through to him. I was frustrated that I couldn't get in contact with him as we had planned because I so wanted to spend more time with him. I decided to go back to the hotel and wait for his call. He finally called me as he was driving into D.C., and I changed into something more comfortable.

The closer I got to D.C., the more I felt the reconnection with Alice. We were talking constantly on the phone as I was driving back. When I arrived, Alice was waiting for me with a nice warm soul-connecting kiss. We were communicating on so many levels at one time it was hard to keep up with all the feelings that were washing over me.

We were lying on the bed just talking and kissing and holding each other close, while exploring our lives. There was so much to talk about and so much to find out about each other. We were remembering who we were.

What I mean is that we were having metaphysical experiences that gave us insights into our past lives. At one point we made such a strong connection it startled both of us.

We were lying face to face on the bed with our chests pressed together and our arms encircling each other. There was a burst of energy from both of us toward the other and our energy co-mingled. It was so strong it felt almost like an orgasm. That was the first of many times that our souls would connect on a much higher level than I had ever experienced before.

This was truly an incredible experience that reminded me of the scene in the movie "Cocoon" where the alien's entire soul enters her lover's body as pure energy and light. I can only describe it as a "spiritual orgasm", and highly recommend it!

At some point during the afternoon, I realized that my time with Alice was going to be very short because I was scheduled to catch a plane the next day at 7:00 AM. It was then that I decided that I had to stay longer. I discussed it with Alice and we both agreed to change our flight times. I changed mine to 7:00 PM Sunday evening and Alice changed hers from 3:00 PM to 5:00 PM Sunday. It was such an incredible feeling that she changed her time, because she could only add on two hours to her time with me, but it cost her $50.00.

I called the airlines to see if I could change my flight to coincide with Dennis' new departure time. I spent about 30 minutes on the phone with a really helpful woman who searched the system to accommodate my request. When the only time she could come up with was only an extension of two hours, I said I'd take it.

"Perfect," I told her, "book it."

She was shocked and asked, "You want to pay $50 to change a flight for only two hours?"

Looking over toward Dennis, I grinned and was laughing when I responded, "Trust me, he's worth it!"

That evening Alice had to attend a party with all of Sherril's family. She had asked me to go with her but I hadn't brought anything dressier than jeans, so I had to decline. I was also to get together with my friends from online to have some of the famous "Baltimore Blue Crabs".

- Dinner with Friends -

When I arrived back at Lori's, everyone was there and looking forward to dinner. After greetings, hugs and general chatting like old friends, we all went to a restaurant just down the street from Lori's house to finally have the famous "Blue Crabs" that Greg had been raving about. I have to say that they were well worth the wait. They were excellent, but I had trouble with the very spicy exterior. It was very salty but had a wonderful flavor.

When we arrived at the restaurant, Laurie (from York) sat across from me and it gave me the opportunity to dive into a psychic reading for her. With the help of my guides, I gave her some things to think about that were important for her to know. These readings with Laurie would continue online for the next two years with some interesting results. The nice thing about the people in this little group is that we were all very spiritual and were quite comfortable with the psychic world.

We all had some laughs, great food and some stimulating conversation, and then we went back to Lori's house for some coffee and more conversation. I stayed very late before leaving for D.C. to be with Alice. When I left, I said goodbye to Laurie and Skip because they were leaving to go back home to York, PA. I said goodbye to Lori, Greg and Annie, because at that point I knew that I was leaving for Seattle at 7:00 PM the next day and I wouldn't be seeing them again.

When I got to the hotel around 1:00 AM, Alice was already sleeping. She had given me a key to her room before I left because I knew that I would be late and she would be very tired. When I came in, I entered quietly and woke her with a tender kiss, but when she awoke she wasn't quite coherent or responsive. It was very strange trying to talk to her and explain to her what was happening.

It was the strangest sensation and quite difficult to describe. It was as though my body was in the room, but my soul had left temporarily. I'd never experienced any out-of-body travel before, but that's the closest explanation I can come up with for the feelings I had that night.

Dennis had come into the room, and from somewhere far off in the distance, I heard a door open and felt a presence of someone entering the room. When I tried to sit up and focus, I couldn't. There was no feeling; no thought process; just nothingness. I remember opening my eyes and not knowing where I was or even who I was. It was eerie, and a feeling that I've not experienced since.

My personal belief is that this was my soul traveling for the purpose of getting in touch with my higher self. It was a period of growth and expansion of my soul's being. Having reconnected with Dennis' soul, I was now getting prepared for my own spiritual growth process.

The next morning was Sunday and we rose bright and shining. It was a new day and one that Alice and I wanted to fill with wonderful memories to look back on. We did not know if we would ever see each other again. What we did know was that we wanted to spend the whole day together and do some sightseeing. Alice was scheduled to check out of her hotel that day so we packed up everything, paid the bill and checked out.

When we left, we decided that since Alice was leaving on her plane at 5:00 PM, we should store her bags at the airport in a locker until time for her flight. The plan was that I would take her back to Washington National by 4:00 PM, then I would drive to BWI in Baltimore to return the rental car and catch my 7:00 PM flight back to Seattle.

That was our plan. But, as the saying goes, "Life is what happens while you're busy making other plans."

An odd thing happened while I was attempting to store my suitcases at the airport. Dennis waited for me in the car while I went into the airport alone. I had never before used storage lockers at an airport, and I wasn't familiar with the system that I encountered. I located the locker area fairly quickly, but I discovered that the system required pre-payment in order to activate the locking device.

With all my luggage, I needed two lockers and several dollars worth of quarters. When I checked my wallet, I didn't have enough coins, so I looked around for a change machine. I needed only two more quarters to complete the process, and I really was in a hurry to get back to the car and Dennis.

At that moment a porter came up to me and asked if I needed assistance. I said that I did, and I asked him where I could get some change. He pointed me in the direction of a corridor that would have taken me far from the lockers and my luggage, but I didn't want to leave the luggage unattended. The porter told me that he was not permitted to stay with unattended luggage, and I would have to take it with me.

A thought suddenly came into my head that told me to check my wallet again. I did, and I couldn't believe what I saw. In the coin pocket were two quarters that weren't there the last time I'd looked, only moments before.

"Now, where did these come from?" I asked. "They weren't here a minute ago."

The porter looked at me, shook his head and chuckled, and walked away, muttering, "Women!"

I pulled out the two quarters, put them in the slot of the second locker, and walked out of the airport laughing silently to myself. Nothing surprised me anymore, and it was certainly nice to know that my guides and guardian angels were with me even for mundane things such as airport lockers.

- More Openings -

After leaving the airport we decided to drive around and see the sights. We drove by the White House, the Washington Monument, the Capitol building and the Lincoln Memorial.

We left the car parked at one point and walked to the Vietnam Veterans Memorial to view the names of the people killed during the war. I found a childhood friend's name listed there. It was a very emotional time for me because I could feel each and every person on that wall. I saw souls walking around with each of the visitors, and I felt that they were the people whose names were on the wall, greeting and accompanying their families and guiding them to the correct section. I couldn't stay long; it was just too intense for my soul.

We went from there to the Lincoln Memorial and the reflecting pool. It was all an awesome sight and very moving to see so much history in one place.

I could feel my soul recognizing each of these places. It was as if I had been here before, in another life, and I have no doubt that I was. As I would visit each place, I would see scenes in my head of things that had happened at that spot. I could feel the emotions of everyone around me. The whole day was very intense, what with my feelings for Alice and all the other feelings combined.

It was about 3:00 PM and we hadn't eaten lunch yet, so we went to a local hamburger place before I took Alice to the airport for her 5:00 PM flight back to Miami. While we were eating, I started to feel sadness overcoming me because I didn't want this day to ever end. I was getting to know this person whom I felt I had known forever. I was having experiences that I wanted to share with only her. I was truly falling in love with Alice as I had done many times before in past lives. The only option that I could see was to extend my time with her in D.C. for as long as I could.

As we were leaving the restaurant, Alice excused herself to visit the ladies' room. I took this as an opportunity to call the airlines to see if I could extend my stay until the next day. I was hoping to get it done before she was out of the restroom and surprise her. I had no idea what would happen, but I felt that she wanted to extend our time together also. It worked perfectly and Alice came back just as I finished my phone call.

When we got back in the car I said, "Alice, I don't want to leave today. Can you stay until tomorrow?"

She smiled at me and said, "I was thinking the same thing. Yes, I can stay until tomorrow, but I must leave then.

I have to go to Eldon's funeral Monday night so I have to be back."

"Ok," I said, "I've already made arrangements to catch my plane at 11:00 AM. Why don't you see what you can do."

I no more than got the words out of my mouth, before she was on her phone calling. She was able to get a flight at 1:00 PM on Monday, so she would go to BWI with me and catch a shuttle back to Washington National after I checked in for my flight. I also called Lori and set it up for us to spend the night at her house because Alice had checked out of her hotel and we didn't have any place to stay.

The rest of the afternoon was also wonderful. We continued to sightsee with stops at the Washington Monument and The White House.

The time we spent together that day was perfect. We were reconnecting our souls, and behaving as though we'd been together as a couple forever. There was none of the awkwardness that people have when they first begin dating. In fact, we marvel at the fact that we've never had a date. We just picked up where a past lifetime left off, and the momentum never stopped.

We took lots of pictures and completely played the tourist bit. The nation's Capital is a great place to visit, especially when funds are limited. I wanted to capture these moments, and I shot six rolls of film just that day alone. When Dennis said he couldn't have any photos of me on his camera, reality struck us as we realized that he was still married and would be going home to his wife and children.

It was at that moment we began seriously discussing, "Where do we go from here?"

- *Reconnecting with Lori and Greg* -

We left Washington D.C. behind and headed toward Baltimore and Lori's house. As usual, Lori was a wonderful host. She is such an incredible person, I know we have been here together before as brother and sister or something close like that. She welcomed us into her home with open arms and gave us a place to stay for the night. She was very supportive and helpful to me at that time of my life.

It was nice coming to back to Lori's house with Dennis again. When I'd first met Lori and Greg on Friday, only two days earlier, I was there as Dennis' friend from the retreat. Now, we were there as a couple in love, and the energy was completely different.

Lori started walking around her living room until she came to an item she'd been searching for. She picked something up and came over to me with it.

"Here," she said as she placed the object in my hand. "This belongs to you."

I looked at the object and saw that she'd given me a quartz crystal. I could feel the energy emanating from it, and was surprised at what she'd just done.

"What do you mean?" I asked her.

She replied humbly, "I feel that you used to own this crystal, and you've now come back to retrieve it. It's yours and I want you to have it again."

I was so touched by her generosity, and I have treasured that moment and the crystal ever since. When I returned to Miami, I had it set as a pendant in sterling silver and I wear it as a source of energy and protection.

Alice and I went out that night to have a quiet evening

and a nice steak dinner. Lori suggested a restaurant across the street behind her house. I don't remember the name of it but I will never forget the place. It was a steakhouse and karaoke bar combined. Needless to say, it wasn't quiet.

At least it wasn't quiet as far as anyone else was concerned. I was so intensely connected to Alice, enjoying our conversation, that I really didn't hear anyone else or realize that it was a karaoke bar until we were ready to leave. Then we realized at the end of dinner, while having coffee just how awful the woman that was singing sounded. Then we started laughing and also realized it was so loud that we couldn't hear ourselves laughing. It truly was a very funny moment and it was very revealing as to how we were beginning to feel about each other. The world around us had become non-existent.

We went back to Lori's and sat around talking to Lori and Greg for a while until they got tired and discreetly went next door to Greg's house to sleep. They let us stay at Lori's alone and gave us privacy.

I asked Lori if I could use her computer to check my e-mail. When I got online, I could see from my "buddy list" that Jackie and Jeff were both online. For some reason, I couldn't handle seeing them together in a private chat room, and I reacted in a very negative manner.

Alice had been watching what was going on and suddenly left the room. She went upstairs to go to bed, and in the state of mind I was in, I didn't understand why she left without saying anything to me.

I went upstairs to ask her why she'd left, and she said, "I don't understand why you have the need to deal with them now, and I don't enjoy seeing you get upset."

In retrospect, being diabetic, I realized that it was my

elevated blood sugar level that had played havoc with my emotions. It is important for me to pay close attention to what I eat to keep my blood sugar level under control. Alice was not used to that.

Even though she had just seen a very negative side of me, we worked through it and got to another place. We got to a place of total connection and love for each other. This was a sign of things to come, how we would process through issues and get to a very spiritual place.

We were beginning to realize that we had a connection that was going to show us new methods; new ways of processing to overcome disagreements. We fell asleep in each other's arms.

- A Difficult Time -

The next morning was very difficult emotionally. We were going to the airport and there would be no more flight changes. Alice was leaving for Miami and I was leaving for Seattle. We had slept late and had to quickly take showers and get ready for our respective flights.

At the airport I turned in my car, and Alice walked with me to check in for my flight. Luckily she had not gotten her luggage out of the locker at Washington National, so she only had her carry-on bag with her. Alice was getting nervous about missing her plane, so as soon as I was checked in she left to catch the shuttle to Washington National.

Now that our flight plans had changed yet another time, I needed to take the shuttle back to the airport in Washington. We'd spent the night in Baltimore, and now Dennis' plane was scheduled to leave before mine. I needed to purchase a shuttle ticket from BWI to National, so I went to the public transportation counter while Dennis was checking in for his flight. The same man was there, the one I'd given my ticket to on Friday.

I said, "Hi. Remember me?"

He smiled broadly and replied, "Why yes, I do. You're the angel lady."

We laughed and I asked, "Did you give the ticket away?"

"Oh yes. The very next person who came up got it."

"Well, I need to buy a one-way ticket now, please."

With my ticket in hand, I went to where Dennis was standing in line with his suitcases. Our eyes met and we couldn't believe that the time had finally come for us to be apart.

To this day and forever, I will never forget that moment. We gave each other a deep heart to heart hug and soul-reaching kiss and then she turned to walk away. I think it was at that moment that I realized this was not going to end here at this airport. I knew that we would be seeing each other again, but it was very painful watching her leave. When she finally disappeared down the hall, I turned, wiped the tears from my eyes and headed into the waiting area to board the plane for my flight back to Seattle and the changing of my life.

Chapter Fourteen

Decision Making Time

- Detaching -

The plane ride home was uneventful, except for the fact that I was missing this wonderful woman who had just entered my life. I was feeling a bit apprehensive during takeoff, because the engine on my side sounded weird. I asked my guides if I was going to die now that I had finally met the other half of me and I was given a resounding "No!" I thanked them, but the engine still sounded strange. After about ten minutes the noise smoothed out and I became a lot calmer.

When I landed in Seattle, I realized that all I had been thinking about during the entire flight was Alice. I had been remembering the whole weekend, every moment with her. I realized on the flight home that either I would be moving to Miami, or Alice would be moving to Seattle, and soon.

I was now faced with a more pressing task, getting home to the kids and facing Jackie.

I caught a shuttle from SeaTac airport, and as I got closer to home I started to feel uneasy. I had some tough stuff ahead of me and I wasn't looking forward to it. We had talked over the phone about divorce, but now it was in my face.

When I arrived home, my kids came running out to meet me, their faces beaming with big smiles. I was really happy to see them too.

However, there was a lot of what I now know to be

negative energy coming from Jackie. I wasn't sure why or what it was all about, but it confirmed my feelings about this marriage being over. Here I was, back in the feeling of not being able to be who I really am. God, I hated that feeling. It took me back to the feelings that I had during my onion peeling and I really was not ready for that. The difference now was that I was the one pulling away and moving toward a new love.

Over the next two weeks Jackie and I started talking about what we were going to do next. I told Jackie that I had met a woman in Baltimore and that I had very strong feelings for her, but I never told her that I loved Alice. I remembered how I had felt when she let me know that she loved Jeff and I didn't feel like doing that to her right then. I did tell Jackie that I was entertaining the idea of moving to Florida to be with Alice.

We talked about how we were going to divide up the assets, whatever there was. We also agreed that she would keep all of the items she had inherited and I would keep the things that I used, i.e. my music equipment, stereo, tools and hunting gear. She would keep the camping equipment to use with the kids. It was very, very strange to be talking about our lives in this manner. Dividing up almost 23 years of marriage is not easy any way you look at it, but we did the best we could and both of us seemed to be ok with it.

We sold the boat and the motorhome tow car through "want ads". We then had a big blowout garage sale and sold everything we could sell. Anything that didn't sell and neither of us wanted was donated to charity. We tried to sell the motorhome, but it didn't sell while I was in Seattle. It finally sold months later after the divorce was final and the money was used to pay off debts.

I must say this was one of the most amicable divorces

that I have ever seen or heard about. It was actually pretty laid back and I think that most of it was due to the fact that Jackie was, at that time, emotionally involved with Jeff and I was moving toward Alice.

Jackie was having thoughts about moving to be with Jeff, but as long as she was married, that wouldn't be possible. He wouldn't allow that to happen. Jackie told me many times that all he had to do was ask and she would be on the next plane to Utah.

I also knew that I was going to be moving to Miami and I really didn't know what I would need to take with me. I didn't want to take anything that would deprive my children of things they enjoyed or what they had become used to having.

Jackie and I got into many discussions and a few arguments over the next two or three weeks. Sometimes about something that one or the other of us was doing, sometimes about nothing. She would probably have a much different view of this, but that is understandable. We had many moments that were poignant; times when we would put aside all the "stuff" we had been through and see each other like we were many years before. Then reality would come slamming down on us and "POOF" back to the real world we would come sliding.

- The Decision -

One night Alice and I were talking on the phone, as we did everyday, four or five times each day. We had talked in great detail about one or the other of us moving. We had pretty much agreed that since she had an established law practice, it would be better if I moved to Miami. I could set up my computer repair/consulting business anywhere.

I remember the first time I brought up moving to Miami,

I said, "Why don't I just move to Miami?"

Alice replied without any hesitation, "Sure, that sounds great to me. Are you sure you want to move here?"

To which I replied, also without any hesitation, "Absolutely!"

During this particular conversation we were also discussing getting together for the Fourth of July weekend. Up to that point, Alice was going to come to Washington to see if what we felt was still there, but then she said, "Why don't you just come to Miami and see if you like it here? That way if we still feel the same way, you'll know if you really want to move down here."

"But I can't afford a ticket to Miami," I told her.

She quickly responded with, "Not a problem, we can just use the money I was going to spend for a ticket to Seattle. You can pay me back some other time."

"All right, if you're sure you want to do that."

She coyly replied, "Consider it done and pack your bags!"

Alice and I discussed it further and we agreed that I would spend the Fourth of July enjoying fireworks with the kids, then fly to Miami on the fifth.

When I announced that I was going to go to Miami to see Alice and find out if what I had felt in Baltimore was real, Jackie sternly said, "Before you go to Miami, we are going to file for divorce."

"Of course," I replied sarcastically, "I wouldn't think of doing it any other way."

I really don't know what was going on with her then, but I felt like she was not sure of what she wanted. In her own way, she was giving me the responsibility of the divorce. It was as though it was my fault, but I know there was no one person at fault. We were both just moving off in different directions and were trying to figure it all out as we went.

On July 2nd, 1998, we filed for divorce in Snohomish County. In the state of Washington, a divorce has a 90-day waiting period until it is finalized. That date would be Oct. 2nd, 1998. There was no fighting, no lawyers and very little anger, at least on my part. We simply agreed to part and did what we thought was best for our children.

Dennis and I had been speaking on the phone at least four or five times every day since we'd left Baltimore. Our love for each other was growing stronger, and we knew that we'd be together eventually. We just didn't know when it would happen.

We began writing poetry and would read the poems to each other on the phone. Then, I'd enclose a copy in the greeting cards I was sending to him everyday. He'd fax his poetry to me straight from his computer to my fax machine. I wasn't Internet savvy at the time, and I had to rely on the regular mail system.

The odd thing about the poetry is that I'd never before written anything that wasn't sing-song iambic pentameter. But the words that flowed from my pen were actually beautiful, and I was amazed at what was coming through. I knew that this was a part of my automatic writing, and once again, my soul was sending messages loud and clear.

Dennis' poetry was so beautiful, it was startling. I'd never before known a man who could be so strong and yet so sensitive at the same time. We cried when we read our poems out loud to each other, and we knew we were moving closer to spending our lives together.

So, when Dennis asked me what I'd think if he moved to Miami to live with me, I didn't hesitate for a moment. I told him that it would be wonderful, and we began discussing the logistics of how and when we could work this out.

I spent the Fourth of July at my parents' condo for the bar-b-q their building had every year. My parents had become actively involved in their condo association, and they enjoyed showing off their children to all the others. My sister and brother-in-law, Norma and Howie, went with me. I knew that I was going to tell my parents that Dennis was coming to visit, and I wanted to have some moral support. Even though I was 46 years old at the time, I still wanted their approval. My track record for relationships was not great, and it was important to me that they liked Dennis.

As luck would have it, or in this case, I knew that my guardian angels were still hard at work, my parents took my announcement with surprising calm and acceptance. My mother's two closest friends were also there and wanted to hear the story about how Dennis and I met. We all soon got into a very enjoyable discussion about psychics and synchronistic events. The day went better than I'd expected, and my parents were looking forward to meeting Dennis.

- Miami Bound -

As the plane was descending into Miami International Airport, I was starting to become apprehensive. I didn't know what to expect. My soul was saying, "Don't worry, this is perfect," but my human side was asking, "What if she decided that she didn't want me?" I know I was just buying into the fear of the unknown, and I wasn't paying any attention to my psychic ability. Of course I knew she still felt the same, but I still had this fearful vision of getting off the plane and Alice not being there.

Well lo' and behold, I got off the plane and she wasn't there! I was very surprised, but I figured that she was either late or waiting at the baggage area. I found out later that at MIA, because of security reasons, they do not allow people to come to the gate area to meet passengers.

While walking up the hallway toward the baggage area, all sorts of thoughts were flying through my head, but as I rounded a corner, I heard this very familiar and distinctive laugh and knew that Alice was here to meet me. I couldn't see her because there was a group of people coming toward me, blocking my view.

As they passed, we saw each other, and I could hear her laughingly say to the person she was walking with, "There he is, thanks for your help and good luck finding your wife."

"Hi," I said, "you look incredible!"

"So do you."

With that we embraced. My heart was in my throat, pounding at a thousand beats a second, my palms were sweating and excitement filled my soul. It was that familiar feeling of connecting with myself, my other half. My arms encircled her and the closer we embraced, the stronger the feeling became. Our lips slowly moved, as if in slow motion toward each other, my head started spinning, and I was totally aware of every nerve ending in my body. When our lips touched it was like the completion of an electrical circuit, the final connection of the soul.

Then the energy started to flow between us. Our knees buckled and we had to lean against the wall. I immediately knew that 'it' was still there in full force. There was only one other question to be answered, and that was, when do I move here? That question would be answered during this weekend.

I arrived at the airport with what I thought was plenty of time to meet Dennis as he came off the plane. I knew that I couldn't go to the gate because of tight security, but I'd be there when he came through the doors into the main terminal. Well, the plane arrived a few minutes early, and with the weekend holiday traffic, parking was at a premium. When I finally got inside the building, I was rushing to find the gate number and then the concourse. There was a man standing next to me who was also checking the monitor to see about the flight arrivals. Again, no surprise to me, he was meeting the same flight! We both raced to the gate and when I saw Dennis coming toward me, I said, "There he is."

Dennis and I looked at each other and I knew we were both concerned if "it" would still be there. It most certainly was, and still is. His kisses still go to the depths of my soul and take my breath away.

- *The Weekend Begins* -

After getting my luggage we left the airport and drove to Alice's house. The rest of the evening was spent getting reacquainted in the most intimate way that two people completely and wholeheartedly in love can do. We joined our souls and our bodies that night numerous times and, if it is possible, grew in love all over again.

The next morning was Saturday and here I was in a strange place and I was about to be exposed to lots of new people. Alice had planned to take me to her friends' house in Key Largo for the Independence Day extravaganza they put on every year. I was feeling a bit apprehensive about the whole thing but I knew that I would be just fine because

I was with a woman who was becoming my complete focus.

Before leaving, we needed to prepare some deviled eggs to bring to the gathering. We had a great time making them and discovered that we loved to work together in the kitchen. I enjoy cooking and although Alice doesn't like to cook, she doesn't mind cleaning up because she enjoys being with me in the kitchen. The deviled eggs were a hit and everyone made fun of Alice because they were surprised that she brought something homemade. They accused me of making them and giving Alice the credit. The standing joke is that Alice believes that "cook" is a four-letter-word.

And it is! So is "oven".

When we finished making the eggs, we packed up our swimsuits and cooler and headed toward Key Largo. But first we had to make a couple stops on the way.

The first stop was at Alice's sister's store. There I met Norma and Howie, Alice's sister and brother-in-law. They owned a gift and jewelry store near Alice's home. They were both really nice and seemed to welcome me with open arms.

From there we went to the local store for some sodapop, chips and film. As we left the parking lot, I called Jackie from my cell phone and told her that I made the final decision to move to Miami. She was a bit shocked to say the least, but at the same time she was very accepting. We chatted for a few minutes, she asking if I was sure and me assuring her that I had truly decided to move to Florida.

- *The Everglades and The Connection* -

We were driving along toward Key Largo and because I had never been there, Alice drove so that I could watch and enjoy the passing scenery. There were all kinds of things to see. When we drove through the edge of Everglades

National Park, I was in awe. There were exotic birds, trees with moss hanging off of them, and many more things that I had never seen, having grown up in Eastern Washington State. It was so cool to see all this and I let Alice know how I felt.

She said with joking arrogance, "So what, what's so exciting about the Everglades? I see it all the time! There's just a lot of grass and mosquitoes."

I said also in a joking way, "And I suppose you don't go crazy when you see pine trees?"

"I don't know, I've never seen pine trees."

"Well, there goes that argument!" I said and we both laughed out loud.

About that time I was getting really thirsty and I thought to myself, "A diet coke would really taste great right about now."

As if the Universe wanted to give us more proof of our incredible connection, Alice said, while pointing at a cup in the cup holder, "There is diet coke in that cup. I put it in there with ice when we left."

You could have pushed me over with a feather I was so blown away at the statement that she had just said. I slowly asked, "Did you read my mind or something?"

"Why? What do you mean?"

"I was just thinking that a diet coke would really taste great right now, and you answered me almost immediately."

"Wow, I knew we were connected, but isn't that cool to know we are so in tune?"

I simply replied, "Very."

Then in a loving tone I added, "And by the way, I love you."

"And I love you, honey," I softly replied as I squeezed his hand tightly.

- Tom and Dale -

We arrived in Key Largo at Tom and Dale Chasteen's home for their Independence Day celebration. Alice had been Tom's lawyer during his divorce and had performed his marriage to Dale five years later. She had become very good friends with both of them and had been accepted as a part of their extended family. Therefore, because I was with Alice, I was also accepted and made to feel completely welcome.

When I met Tom he was in front of the bar-b-q cooking hamburgers, hotdogs and ears of corn. We spent the day with them eating and just generally having a great time. I played horseshoes, a game that I had not played in years, and had a great time.

Alice and I went out in a paddleboat onto the small man-made lake in back of their house. We were sitting in the middle of the lake hugging, kissing and generally enjoying each other's company. We suddenly realized the mosquitoes were thick and had decided to have us as a feast of their own. Until that moment we had planned to stay out and enjoy the fireworks, but after getting bit a few times we madly paddled back to shore while laughing and swatting them.

"Welcome to South Florida," Alice quipped.

After watching the fireworks from the safety of a screened porch, we headed back toward Miami and Alice's house. On the way, Alice mentioned that we were going to go over to her parents' home the next morning for brunch.

She was excited to have me meet them, but also a little nervous.

I told her, "All mothers love me", and it was true. Her parents and I got along very well.

- *Marcia and Dave* -

Sunday morning we went to brunch with Alice's mom, Marcia and her dad, Dave. The first thing that struck me about Marcia, is the elegance with which she presented herself. It was very easy to see where Alice got her sense of dress and makeup. Neither a hair out of place nor a lipstick smudge in sight; she was impeccably dressed and coiffed at all times.

Marcia was a very short woman and I do mean short. If she were 5' tall I would be very surprised. Her stature as a person belied her physical size. She was very traditional in her ways as a Jewish mother and at the same time, very open to learning new things. She asked me many questions about the psychic world as I got to know her.

When I first met Dave, I was completely comfortable. I felt accepted by them and I also felt a feeling of thankfulness from both Marcia and Dave that I was with Alice. It was a connection that had to have been set up before we got here because they instantly accepted and welcomed me into their lives.

Dave is much different than Marcia about the psychic world. I think he just tolerates our after-life beliefs. I think he would like to believe, but his upbringing won't allow it. I also think he would be more accepting with some sort of physical proof.

It was very interesting meeting her parents. They were the classic example of a happily married couple. It was obvious that they were totally connected and very much in love even after 60 years of marriage.

Their life personified what I would call the all-American story of success in the United States. They both came from rather poor families, born to parents who emigrated from Russia. Dave's parents escaped during the Russian Revolution with four small children under the age of nine. Marcia's left long before the war started, but still felt the repercussions.

Marcia and Dave grew up in the Philadelphia area and met when they were 16 and 19. They got married about three years later and then moved to the Miami area after WWII. They established a very successful jewelry business and had four beautiful daughters, Diane, Norma, Linda, and my twin soul, Alice.

After I moved here and got to know them better, Marcia asked me if I would give her a reading.

I immediately replied, "Absolutely, I would love to. We don't have time right now, but the next time we are here I'll do it. Is that ok with you?"

"Sure," she replied. "I can wait."

I felt that she really did want a reading because of the sincerity in her voice, so I planned on it. The next time we were over, she asked again.

I said, "Do you want to do it right now?"

"Yes, if that is alright with you."

Norma and Howie were over at the same time. We had all eaten dinner together in the restaurant downstairs, and were now at Marcia and Dave's for coffee.

We went over to the dining table and Marcia asked me

what she should do. I explained that she didn't have to do anything but listen. I started into the reading telling her about many different things.

Norma, Howie, Alice, and Dave had all quietly left the room to give us privacy, when suddenly there was the spirit of a woman in the room with us.

The spirit started explaining that she was Marcia's aunt. She told me that she knew that she was Marcia's favorite aunt and that she was always around Marcia. I described her aunt for her, and she rushed to bring in some old pictures. We had pictures and all sorts of things on the table.

Well, Marcia was ecstatic with this news. She told me that nobody knew about the relationship that she had with this aunt; that she'd died a very long time ago. This was proof enough for her.

That is when Marcia said to me, "I have enough proof that you are what you say you are, so I have one more question."

"Ok," I said, "What is the question?"

"When am I going to die?" she blurted out and then continued, "Am I going to live a long time or go real soon?"

I saw the number 96 flash in front of me and without batting an eye, I told her exactly what spirit gave me, "Oh no, you are not going to die until you're 96." She was 80 at the time.

She then said laughing, "Oh good, I just wanted to know whether or not I should give my jewelry away."

She was not in any way worried about, or scared of dying. She was ready; she just wanted to make sure her jewelry was distributed fairly. What a lady.

She died approximately 96 days later in October, 1997, suddenly with no warning or prolonged illness.

The information that came through was perfect for her at that time. If the information that had come through had been translated to be 96 days, Marcia would have lived her life much differently and a healing amongst her daughters would not have taken place. The number 96 was really very significant because Marcia's mother had lived to the age of 96.

My mother died as she had lived...always a gracious and elegant lady. She always said she would never become a burden to her children, and she never wanted to be in a nursing home. She played cards on a Tuesday, and died from a stroke the next day. The sadness is we never said goodbye.

It was important for me to have Dennis like my parents, and for them to accept Dennis as a part of my life. As it turned out, I worried needlessly, and my parents came through with flying colors.

They were gracious and welcomed Dennis into their home. They seemed to be genuinely fascinated by our "story" of how we'd met, and Mother wanted to know more about Dennis' psychic abilities. I believe she knew on a spiritual level, that Dennis would be her connection to us after her transition. We are fortunate that she comes through often.

The story that kept my mother captivated, was the one about Jackie and Jeff. She was always asking if Jackie had met Jeff yet, and how that was going. Stories about Internet relationships were all over the news and she just couldn't quite understand or relate to this on-line energy stuff.

- *The Computer Connection* -

The rest of Sunday was spent helping Alice buy a computer for her home so she could become Internet savvy and we could chat online after I returned to Seattle. We still wanted to talk everyday, but we didn't want to continue paying large phone bills. What we didn't expect was that this would put us in contact with who we really are, twin souls.

Alice had arranged for us to have dinner on Sunday night with her friend and fellow stooge, Dee Dee, and her husband Jerry. We met at their favorite Thai restaurant and had a wonderful dinner. I had never had Thai food so this was another first for me. Alice was purposely having me meet all of her closest friends so that I'd feel comfortable in my decision to move to Miami. Dee Dee is very spiritual and knowledgeable about the metaphysical new age world. I knew that we would get along really well.

Monday we spent most of day finishing setting up the computer and getting Alice online so our communication would be easier when I was in Seattle.

- *Nelly* -

That day we also went to see a local psychic that Alice had come to know. Alice thought she was good and told me she felt she was being guided to take me to see her. She said that her name was Nelly and that she spoke Spanish, but that she did speak some English.

The instant we met there was a connection that was rekindled. I remember walking into her home and feeling very comfortable. It felt as if I were walking into an energy that I had known before.

Nelly said she felt the same connection, and as she went

into her reading, she described scenes from a village in South America where she felt I was her brother. At the same time I was feeling like she was my mother in yet another life.

But in the life Nelly was describing, I was a traveling minstrel and her brother. When I arrived in town all the people in the village rushed toward me. I was given a hero's welcome and showered with love and praise. I was carrying a guitar and I would sing beautiful love songs to all the villagers.

Suddenly I was overcome with the vision of a man standing beside Nelly. He had white hair, a white beard and was wearing a white suit. He was standing next to a white fence of some sort. As I described him to Nelly, she went into another room and came back with a book. It had a picture of a man with white hair and a white beard. It was the man I was seeing at that moment. He was telling me that he was her personal guide.

She told us a story about him. Through his many books, he was her spiritual teacher. He had passed on to the other side several years before and was now around her. She was so happy that I had seen him and confirmed he was indeed her guide.

We were both so emotionally overcome by all this that we were in tears. Then she got up and walked to her kitchen. She came back with a bottle of brandy.

Nelly said, "The guides say we drink a toast! We are back together again."

"No, I'm sorry, I don't drink," I declined politely.

She then insisted that we drink this toast and I felt that I would be insulting her if I didn't partake of the toast and I couldn't do that. She also said, "The guides say it will be ok, it is just a ceremony."

I was feeling the same feelings of love and connection with this lady that she was feeling with me. I felt like I had found my mother, my sister and a soul connection all rolled into one. It was very strange for me to feel these feelings. So when she poured the brandy into small shot glasses, we all clinked and drank the toast to our reunion.

I was pleased that Nelly and Dennis hit it off as well as they did. When I had my first reading with Nelly, we literally felt a tremendous flow of electricity pass through us when we touched hands. Haydee, my law associate, was in the room with us when it happened, and it actually frightened her.

So, when Nelly and Dennis made their connection that day and were both able to recall their past lives together, I knew that Nelly had been brought into my life for this purpose. When we entered her home, it was for the sole reason to have them meet briefly: one psychic to another. I never imagined the memories it would trigger, but nothing surprised me anymore. I have learned to go with the flow and accept whatever the Universe places in my path. I'd come a long way since my first workshop at MIEL.

The four days I spent in Miami made everything more real for me. I knew then that I wanted to spend the rest of my life with Alice and I felt the same feelings from her.

Alice took me to the airport on Tuesday, July 9th. As my plane left, I knew that I would be back very soon. We had discussed it over and over and had come to the conclusion that we needed to be together as soon as possible. We set up a tentative date of August 1st. I went back to Seattle with that date in mind and started getting things moving to be out by that time.

- *In the Interim* -

After going back to Seattle, I settled into getting my life ready to move to Miami. It all really seems like a blur right now because it happened so fast. It is unbelievable now that I'm looking back on it. One moment I'm a family man living in Seattle, and the next moment I was getting divorced and planning to live with a woman I had just met two weeks before. It seemed so incredible, but at the same time I felt as comfortable moving to Miami as I would be going to the corner store. Except in this case the corner store was 3500 miles away.

Over the next three weeks Alice and I called and talked to each other everyday, several times a day. Even though we also communicated online over the Internet, our phone bills seemed to be just as high. Alice would also send me these wonderful loving cards in the mail. She was never out of my thoughts during this time. We each even got in touch with our own poetic side. I wrote more poetry during that time than I had ever written before.

Because of the computer, we connected with a man online named Dr. Maurie Pressman. He was the co-author, with Patricia Joudry, of the book *"Twin Souls" A guide to finding your true spiritual partner.* This really helped us to define who we are. One night, about a week after I'd returned to Seattle, we were on line chatting and someone told us that Maurie was in a chat room discussing his book. He was talking about twin souls and how to recognize your own.

During this Internet speaking engagement, the public was invited to ask questions. I was in Seattle and Alice was in Miami, and we were both together in the chat room chatting with each other while also paying attention to Maurie's written words. We each were able to ask a question about twin souls as it related to us. We were also able to chat with Maurie after the lecture and he asked us to send him our story. That was the first time we had ever heard the term "twin souls" and it was our opening to the discovery of our twin-ness.

- The Scare -

It was the start of the 1996 summer Olympics in Atlanta, Georgia, and Alice called me because of the explosion that had just occurred there. Her son was then a photojournalism student at the University of Florida, and he had gone to Atlanta to get some pictures of the opening ceremonies. At that time he was working for *The Gainesville Sun* as a summer Intern.

I spent some time on the phone with her, and I felt she was overly worried about her son because she hadn't heard anything either way. I really felt that he was all right and I tried to let her know that. I was relying on my psychic abilities to "see" if he was ok. I was feeling very positive.

That was an intense time for me. Just that afternoon Justin had called to tell me that he and a group from the newspaper were driving from Gainesville, Florida to Atlanta to get some photos of the opening ceremonies and other Olympic festivities.

That night I was online, as I had finally become quite adept in "surfing the net". I was in a chat room when all of a sudden someone typed the words, "There's been an explosion at the Olympics in Atlanta!" The person went on to say that the news was on CNN, so I immediately got off the computer and turned on the TV.

I was alarmed and frightened, and I called Dennis. It was very late on the East Coast, and he was the only person I knew that I could call at that hour. He was also the only person other than Justin that I wanted to speak to at that time.

Dennis did calm me down somewhat as we both sat on opposite coasts and watched CNN together. He told me that Jackie, who is also very psychic, told him she felt Justin was safe, and all would be fine. After speaking some more to relax me, Dennis then went back to watching a movie he was enjoying with his kids, and I went back to watching CNN.

Within moments, I heard the announcer saying in an alarmed voice, "A photographer's tripod is down..." When I saw the film of the tripod lying in the street with all the commotion going on, naturally, I panicked. I called Dennis again.

I didn't know where Justin was staying, and I didn't know how to reach him. All I could do was wait for his phone call.

Thank God, my son has common sense as well as sensitivities. He couldn't even be certain that I knew about the explosion, but he called me anyway, just in case. I was still on the phone with Dennis when we heard the click to let me know another call was coming in. The first words I heard were, "Mom, I'm fine."

That was a very emotional time for both of us, but it brought us even closer than we were before, and we knew we needed to be together.

- Being Dad from 3,500 Miles -

During my final days in Seattle, Jackie and I sold the remaining large items we owned. We packed up everything else, my stuff in boxes to take with me; Jackie and the kids' things were packed in other boxes to go with them. All the boxes were separated into neat stacks and ready to move. On July 31st I was ready to move out, and was very nervous about how far away I was going to be from my kids.

All during this time I was focused on Alice and the life I hoped would be forthcoming. I didn't know how I could do it, but I just knew it would all work out for the best. I love my kids dearly and was always the kind of father that was there for them from the time they were born. I was never away from them for more than 10 days at any one time. How was I going to move 3500 miles away and still be a good dad? I didn't know. I just knew that this was something that I had to do and I would figure it out as I went. I know that there were lots of people judging me and that is ok. I am the only one who can really judge myself and make a difference, and I knew this was right. I love them and they know it. I have made sure during my time away to be as good a father as I can from 3500 miles away and I will always be grateful to them for their understanding, love and support.

This brings us to the end of July, 1996. Alice had decided to fly to Seattle and drive back to Miami with me. Part of the reason she decided to come was because I needed her financial help during the trip and she was glad to give it. She also came so that we could have a couple weeks alone together to get to know each other better. We always joke that by the time we got to Kansas, we would either be completely in love or she would be flying home to Miami and I would be headed back to Seattle.

- Revelations of Love -

The decision had been made, and now I had one more thing to do before I flew to Seattle. I needed to tell my parents that Dennis was moving to Miami and that we were going to live together. I was very concerned about what their reaction would be to the news. After all, I had only met Dennis six weeks earlier, and we'd only really been together for a total of seven days. Besides, they knew my track record regarding relationships, and they tended to doubt my judgment in that area. So, it was with great trepidation that I called them and said I'd like to have brunch with them the Sunday before I was to leave.

We had a pleasant and leisurely brunch, and after stalling for more time than I care to remember, I finally told my parents that I had something to tell them. There are perhaps two statements in relationships that always cause immediate concern. One is, "We need to talk." The other is, "There's something I need to tell you."

So, I asked my parents to please sit down, and they braced themselves for the worst. I said, "You know that Dennis and I are in love with each other, and I want to tell you something. I'm not asking for your permission; I'm asking for your blessing. I'm flying to Seattle on Wednesday, and Dennis is going to move here to live with me."

There was absolutely no negative reaction whatsoever. I think they were actually relieved that I was not the one moving away. I will always fondly remember what happened next. My mother turned to my father and coyly said, "Do you think we're twin souls?"

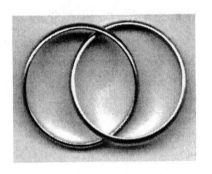

Chapter Fifteen

Journey to Paradise

- The Arrival -

Alice was arriving on a plane from Miami. We were going to drive back to Miami, taking our time and getting to know each other. As I drove to the airport the traffic was getting heavier by the minute. I hadn't known it when I left, but there was a lot of road construction going on between the airport and my house, and I was going to be late and this was not cool. I had gotten a late start, which made it even worse because now I was in a hurry. I knew she would be in on time and would be ok, but I had wanted to be there early to greet her. It took me about two hours to make the normal 45-minute drive to the airport.

When I arrived, it was at exactly the time that Alice's plane was to land. But the plane had arrived about 15 minutes early, and she was already waiting at the baggage area while I was heading toward the arrival gate.

As I made my way back to the baggage area, now about 30 minutes late, I saw Alice standing there looking very worried. She had been crying and was upset that I was late.

At that time we were still in the re-uniting phase of an age-old romance carried on into this life from many lives before. I really think she was afraid that I wasn't going to show up.

Silly girl, there is no way I wouldn't be there. She is my twin soul and nothing in heaven or on earth would keep me from being with her. When I took her in my arms and our lips met again in that special kiss that we have, we both knew that everything was perfect and our life was an incredible continuation from before.

I wasn't afraid that Dennis wouldn't show up; I was afraid that something might have happened to him on the way to the airport. We spoke to each other five times a day, so I knew he'd be there for me. But I was upset when he wasn't where we planned to meet. I really don't know why I began crying. Perhaps, because my life was about to change and neither of us knew what to expect. Well, I didn't, anyway. I'm not the psychic.

As we left the airport I had no idea what was going to happen next. Even though I am a psychic, it is very hard to read for myself. I was not ready to leave Seattle; I wasn't even finished moving out of my house, but I would be within the next 24 hours. We got a motel in Seattle and went next door for some dinner.

We spent the rest of the evening planning, with excited anticipation, the road trip to Miami. This was to be an adventure for both of us and we didn't really know what to expect, so we settled on a basic route and decided to just play it by ear. There were a couple important stops that I felt I needed to make on the way. One was to visit with my mom and stepfather, and the other was to see my uncle, who was about to die. I also wanted to take Alice to Yellowstone Park, and then show her the Grand Teton mountain range. She agreed and we went to bed early.

(Fade to black!)

- Finishing Up -

Over the next couple of days, I had to go to my house and finish packing up all my things. I had to finish cleaning the house and many other small odd-jobs. Alice didn't want or need to be with me while I completed these tasks and closed the chapter with Jackie.

So before I left, I took Alice to a nearby crafts store where she purchased some yarn and crochet supplies. She told me it had been twenty years since she'd done any craftwork, and so she spent the next day and a half at the motel relearning how to crochet, while I finished my tasks. She started making a blanket for one of her friends who was having a baby, and almost completed it by the time we arrived in Florida.

I had previously arranged to pick up a U-Haul trailer on Friday around noon. I asked Alice if she would like to come with me and she jumped at the opportunity to get out of the room for a while. We left to pick up my U-Haul trailer and then we went to the house to pick up all of my worldly possessions.

- The Twilight Zone -

When we arrived at the house, Jackie was there finishing up with some cleaning. After I had backed the trailer into the driveway, I said to Alice, "You don't have to get out and meet Jackie if you don't want to."

"Of course I will. I want to meet her, and besides, I have a ton of questions that I want to ask her about you," she laughingly joked.

"Great," I muttered and got out of the van.

The next hour and a half is possibly the strangest time that I have ever lived through in my life. Here I was, standing in a trailer, packing in all my worldly belongings, while my "girlfriend" and my "wife" were walking side by side, making small talk while bringing the boxes to the trailer.

It was very strange indeed and when what was

happening hit me, I asked them both, "Do you feel like you're in the 'Twilight Zone'? I'm asking because I certainly do."

They in turn looked at each other and Alice said, "Yeah, I sure do."

Then Jackie nervously laughed and said "Yeah, very strange indeed." Then we all broke into nervous laughter and finished packing the trailer. After the trailer was packed and we were done, Jackie and I needed to close out our bank account and she needed a ride to her sister's house.

For almost 23 years, Jackie and I were together and whenever she rode with me anywhere, she rode in the passenger's seat in front. Now Alice and I were together and it was a very strange feeling having her riding, not in the front, but in the back while chatting and laughing with us. Life is a very interesting ride.

Along the way I wanted to stop and get a diet coke, so I pulled into a small convenience store. It was really strange for me to see Alice, my girlfriend in the front seat and Jackie, my wife in the backseat, but the strangest part was that it didn't feel wrong. It felt perfect and we were not uncomfortable, and I know I owe that to both Alice and Jackie.

Although we had already filed for a divorce, it was still awkward. As I got out of the van, I just smiled and shook my head in disbelief.

Then I asked, "Alice, do you want to come in with me?"

"No, I think I'll sit here and talk to Jackie."

So I asked them both, "Would either of you like something to drink?"

They both responded in the negative and I went on into the store to get my pop not knowing what weird event might jump out of the corner.

After dropping Jackie at her sister's home, we went back to our motel. We needed to get some dinner and relax for the evening before leaving for Miami on Sunday.

Meeting Jackie really was a strange experience, but she never made me feel uncomfortable or unwelcome.

As a divorce lawyer, I have often counseled clients to make it a point to meet with the former spouse before they enter into a new relationship, and most definitely before considering a new marriage. So here was my golden opportunity. I had Dennis' wife in the same car with me, and we were sitting alone.

I turned to her and only half-jokingly said, "So, is there anything you'd like to tell me about Dennis? Promise me you'll only tell me one bad thing per week."

"Oh no," she quipped, "you'll have to find that out all by yourself."

The next day Alice and I spent the day with my three kids. We went to the Seattle Center, the site of the 1963 World's Fair, and just had a great afternoon of fun. Alice got to meet Joel, Leo and Andrea and spend some time with them. They seemed to get along well, and we all had a great time.

This was the last time I would spend time with my kids for about two months. I was planning to come back in October, but I wanted to connect with them and have some fun before I left. The last few months at home had been stressful. They needed to know that even though their mother and I were getting divorced, I still loved them and would always be available for them.

Dennis' children were quiet and reserved. They were obviously nervous and uncomfortable meeting me, so I tried to make our time together pleasant. My first thought was, "This is so different from being with Peter's kids. No past life karma here!" They truly are terrific and have allowed me into their lives and accepted me unconditionally, as I have them. That's the key. I finally learned to not place conditions or expectations on the new people coming into my life. The trick is to remember this as a mantra and to avoid old patterns of destruction. It really works when the intent is sincere and the love is genuine.

- The Start of Something Big -

The next morning was Sunday, August 3rd, 1996 and I left the Seattle area bound for Miami with my "twin soul". I was embarking on a life that is now what I would call incredible. I didn't know what to expect nor did I worry about it. I felt by this time that my life was going to be wonderful.

It was time for Alice to meet my family, so, the first day out of Seattle, we went to my mother's house in Moxee, Washington. We spent a couple hours with my mom and stepfather and then went on to spend the night with my sister Brenda in Sunnyside. Then we were off to Idaho.

I wanted to see Uncle Cecil, my mother's brother. He was Cecil to us, but everyone else knew him as Jim. We had been told that he was terminally ill and was not expected to be around much longer. I felt he was going to die soon so I needed to connect with him because I liked him very much and I also wanted Alice to meet him while she still could.

He was a flamboyant character and was well known and liked in the town of Ponderay, Idaho. He still holds the record for the largest Mackinaw trout ever taken out of

Lake Pend Orelle. There is even a lure named after him, it's called "The Gentleman Jim". Uncle Cecil was a man that many people loved. He enjoyed life and lived it like he wanted. In his younger days, he drank hard and played hard and was quite the hellion. He was what could be construed as a rebel, and he really didn't care what people thought of him because he was happy. I loved him because of who he was. In his retirement years he fished and hunted and basically enjoyed his time here on earth. He was also, as characterized by the lure named after him, quite a gentle man.

When we arrived at Cecil's house, another of my uncles, Lee, was there. Both he and I play guitar and Uncle Cecil wanted us to play for him. So for about an hour and a half, we played old country songs and had a great time singing and reminiscing. After a while Alice and I were both getting very tired so we said our good-byes, left and got a motel for the night.

I'm glad we took the time to visit him because he died two weeks later and has come to visit me spiritually many times since.

- The Interlude -

We left the town of Ponderay, Idaho, and headed east around the north end of Lake Pend Orielle. As we were traveling through the mountains of northern Idaho near the Montana border, we saw many deer and other wildlife. We decided to stop at one place along the road because it was so beautiful that we wanted to take some pictures.

We got out of the van and just gazed at the mountains and the water of the river we were beside. I had come up behind Alice and put my arms around her and was holding her close. She slowly turned in my arms and tilted her face toward me, offering her beautiful lips to mine. The energy was passing between us so strongly that, as I leaned down to connect our lips, a charge of electricity went from my lips to hers. As we embraced and kissed, I was taken back to a moment not too many weeks before in Baltimore when the first kiss passed between us. The feeling now was just as intense and strong as it had been then; it was wonderful. We stood there kissing for a few more moments. One car went by honking, the people whistling and waving their arms out the windows. We just smiled and continued.

After a few minutes, Alice went back to taking some pictures and I went back to the van. For some reason I sat in the passenger seat with the door open. The sun was warm and I was enjoying it while I was watching Alice. I was admiring her form and thinking about the many times that we had joined our souls and bodies together. I was thinking about how wonderful our lovemaking has always been. I guess that I was getting a little too deep in my thinking when I felt a hand on my upper leg.

"I guess my kisses have a wonderful effect on you?" Alice coyly questioned and pushed my leg to one side so that she could slide between them and hug me.

She was standing on the ground and I was in the seat. The way she was standing made it easy for her to lay her head on my stomach and put her arms around me without any trouble.

"You could say that," I softly replied and continued, "I was also remembering last night."

"I can feel what my kisses have done. Your kisses affect me like that too, honey," she cooed while adding, "It must be very uncomfortable in those tight jeans right now."

Then as she slowly started to unbutton my jeans, with a smile she asked, "Can I help?"

About an hour later we continued on down the road. Both of us were feeling very relaxed and ready to get nourishment for the body since we had nourished the soul.

The view __was__ magnificent.

- The Third Night -

Dennis is a musician, and we both are children of the 60's. Throughout our trip, we listened to tapes and CD's that Dennis has collected over the years. A recent addition to his collection was by the group, "The Eagles". Their reunion CD, "Hell Freezes Over", included a song called "Love Will Keep Us Alive". When the song came on the first time Dennis became quite emotional and when I looked at him, I saw he was crying. We played that song over and over until I knew every word, and we could sing it to each other, together.

The song "Love Will Keep Us Alive" was dear to my heart and I wanted to share it with Alice, as it was so special to me. I started listening to it during the "Onion Peeling" phase I went through, and I held on to the words "Love Will Keep Us Alive" like they were a life-ring in a hurricane. When I played it for her the first time, it hit me like a sledgehammer coming down on a rock, it smashed through and said to me...here it is in front of you, the love you have been searching for...those were tears of joy, not sadness.

We talked about our tastes in music, and when Dennis told me how he reacted when Jackie had played "Wind Beneath Your Wings", I told him what that song meant to me. After Sherril passed over, the movie "Beaches" was playing in the theaters. When I was about to go see it, Sandra told me that I shouldn't go yet, since Sherril's death was so recent and it might be too emotional for me. Whenever Sandra offered advice to me, I listened because

I knew my best interests were always her focus, and she never did or said anything without a good reason.

When I finally rented the movie, I watched it alone, and cried uncontrollably when the best friend died. Now, whenever I hear Bette Midler sing "Wind Beneath Your Wings", I think of my own best friend, Sherril, and know that she's with me when I do.

That night was spent in Missoula, Montana. We looked for a motel and after checking a couple different ones with no rooms available, we finally stopped at a Days Inn. The only room available in the entire place was the bridal suite! Was there a hidden message here? I don't think it was hidden in any way. We knew it was the Universe's way of giving us a message of things to come. Again, it was kind of like the big blinking sign in the movie "Field of Dreams". So we took the bridal suite, and since it was the first night officially on the road, it was appropriate.

The room was very nice. It had a Jacuzzi tub, a large walk-in shower, and bottle of champagne chilled and waiting. We were supposed to get chocolate roses but they were out of them. We enjoyed the Jacuzzi together, had a nice hot shower and went to bed feeling like newlyweds. It was one of the most wonderful days I had spent with anyone in my life.

The best part is that it was the first of many wonderful days to come. And, I never walked into a single shoe store!

- Where the Buffalo Roam -

When we left Missoula, Montana, we went to Yellowstone National Park. I had been there with Jackie and the kids, but I was starting a new life and wanted to create some new memories. Besides that, Alice had never been there and I wanted to show her everything. I really wanted to show her the world and experience it with her completely. When I looked at it that way, it made everything a new experience.

We took a lot of still pictures and videotapes. In the northwestern corner of Yellowstone is Mammoth Hot Springs. We decided to go there and check it out. When we arrived, there was a crowd gathered near the main area. We found a parking spot and this was no easy task with a trailer connected. Then we got out to explore and see what all the excitement was about.

Well, there on the lawn, was a herd of elk. There were a couple of bull elk with huge antlers. Alice decided she was going to get a close up picture of the big one. I started freaking out because what she didn't realize is that these are wild animals. As such, they are very unpredictable even though they seemed to be very docile at the time.

I tried to tell her this fact but she just said, "Oh, don't worry Dennis, they're laying down and seem to be tired."

"Yeah right," I said, adding, "the one you are taking the picture of is the leader and if you piss him off, there's no telling what he might do."

She didn't listen to me, but the postscript to this is that after we got to Miami, I showed her a video that I had from the Wild America series by Marty Stouffer. It showed a moose in Alaska that went berserk and attacked and killed a very big man. Alice has respect for the animals now.

I actually got some fantastic shots of these incredible animals. I had never before been that close to an uncaged wild animal, and I couldn't pass up the opportunity to take some photos. Dennis and I began our photo album from our time together in Washington, D.C., and I was planning to fill another album with photos from this cross-

country trip. In fact, all along the trip, we made sure to take a picture of each state's welcome sign as we crossed the borders.

Ok, I realize now that what I did was foolish, and I understand why Dennis was nervous when I went so close to the resting elk. I now have a lot more respect for the animals' privacy, and I know they will attack when they sense danger. But, I also know that being attacked by wild elk is not in my life's plan. After all, Dennis and I had just begun our lives together; no way were we going to be stopped.

The lesson here was that if it was meant to be, it would have. I live by that rule now and life is so much easier. I know that Alice and I were destined to meet and everything in my life is predestined. So I just enjoy it and get out of my own way.

After she finished trying to start a stampede, I dragged her away from the elk and we headed on toward the south. We saw the Paint Pots, lots of smaller hot springs and ended up at "Old Faithful".

Later in the afternoon, while driving through the park, we saw a huge herd of buffalo grazing off in the distance. Fortunately, we could not get too close to them, so Dennis agreed that we could get out of the van, and I took some more photos using the zoom lens.

It was so nice being with someone who enjoyed the same things that I did, and someone who enjoyed being with me. We still love spending all our time together, but we don't "need" to. We choose to be together each and every day and it is a conscious choice for both of us.

All during the trip, one of us would suggest something that the other was thinking at the same moment. It was really strange, but actually very comforting. I felt complete and was getting more in touch with "who I really am." I had finally found the person I was looking for. Me. When I found me, I also found the other part of my soul. I found Alice and she found me.

What we realized was that until each of us went through our individual processing and onion peeling, neither of us would have been able to recognize the other. It was the necessary first step toward the path to the twin soul recognition. I had also found "me", and I finally liked who I was. Now, I had found Dennis, and I liked who he was, too. But before we could love each other, we had to first like ourselves; then we had to also like the other person so that we could love unconditionally. The beauty of being with a twin soul is that the relationship doesn't complete your own "being-ness". We were each complete and content with who we were as individuals. Rather than completing, being with a twin soul enhances your life and your soul's journey.

We left the park, headed south and got to see the Grand Teton Mountain range. We had a sort of time frame to follow; we had to be in Miami by August 14th. Alice was a traffic magistrate and had to be back for traffic court that day.

- *Where the Deer and the Antelope Play* -

Wyoming is a very wide state and it has many antelope, which we found out first hand. After leaving the Teton National Park we headed diagonally, northwest to southeast, across the state toward Rawlins, Wyoming. This was a straight shot across the state and because of our time constraints, we drove well into the night as we did every night.

It had gotten very dark and as we were traveling along I started noticing, off to the side of the road, what I thought were eyes glinting in the headlights of my van. I mentioned it to Alice and she started watching for them with me. Suddenly, in the middle of the road stood a herd of eight to ten antelope. They were a good distance ahead and I had plenty of time to slow down and stop. I didn't want to hit one of them and be stuck out in the middle of Wyoming in a wrecked van. From then on we both were on guard watching for the antelope and because we had to drive at such a slow pace, it extended our trip by about two or three hours.

I couldn't believe what I was seeing! These were actually large deer and antelope roaming the countryside; just like in the song. Being a Florida girl, all I ever saw were signs saying "alligators crossing" or "key deer crossing". A key deer is found in the Florida Keys, and sometimes is no bigger than a German shepherd. And, I have yet to see an alligator in the middle of the road. But, these were animals I had only heard about and I was like a little kid watching them run around.

It was a very exciting night and Alice and I talked non-stop and laughed so much, I'm sure we enjoyed the antelope much more than they enjoyed us. As we arrived in Rawlins, right on the edge of town was a herd of about ten antelope grazing in someone's field. It was 2:00 AM and we were beat, so we found a motel and settled in for what was left of the night.

- Magical Trip Across Kansas -

The next morning we rose to a chill in the air and for some reason I felt that this was going to be a long day. It turned out to be the longest day of our entire trip.

After leaving Rawlins, we proceeded east over the crest of the Rocky Mountains, then south through Denver, Colorado and then continued east into Kansas.

Having been on the road for five days, we were not up on the news of the week. We'd been listening to tapes rather than the radio. What we didn't know was that this was the day before then-presidential candidate Bob Dole was to announce his running mate. It was big news, but we knew nothing about it.

We had been arriving in motels late at night, very tired and just wanting to take a hot shower and get to know each other better. We would leave early each morning, so we never watched anything on TV. So, when we got to Hays, Kansas and decided to get a room for the night, it came as a surprise when every single place was full.

It was very late when we arrived in Hays. We stopped into a local café to have some coffee and a snack once we had discovered there was no place available. We were so tired that we didn't even think to ask anyone why the local motels were filled to capacity. We just assumed that it was something specific for Hays and would be fine when we got to Russell, the next town.

I will never forget the moment we pulled into Russell, Kansas. After we exited the freeway, we pulled into the first motel to check for a room and none was available. As we pulled in, a car was leaving and it headed south on the main street. We decided to check out the next one, same story. It was then that I noticed about five cars, including the one that I had seen earlier, all in a caravan going from motel to motel, apparently looking for a room. That was when I realized we needed to find out what was up and pulled into a combination convenience store and gas station for some gas and information.

The man behind the counter told me that Russell, Kansas was Bob Dole's hometown. He said Senator Dole was in town to publicly announce his running mate the next morning. We were told that even Barbara Walters, along with the rest of the major media, was in town and it was rumored that private homes had been rented for the three days at exorbitant prices. Some lucky people in Russell were making a month's wages in a few days. It wasn't looking good for a room here.

This really was a very comical episode. We had to laugh when we tried to picture Barbara Walters or Katie Couric staying at a Comfort Inn or walking into the local Denny's for the buffet breakfast.

- Baring our Souls -

Alice and I had some coffee and decided to head on to Salina, Kansas. It was only about 95 miles and would take about 3 hours, or so I thought. Not only were we hauling a trailer, we had to stop often to have coffee to keep us awake, so our time was extended.

After driving about 30 minutes, I started getting really sleepy. This is when I asked Alice to talk to me. She had fallen asleep almost immediately after leaving Russell, which was ok most of the time, but I needed her to be awake right then.

"Honey, I feel like I am going to fall asleep," I said and continued by asking, "Can you talk to me and help me stay awake?"

"Sure, what do you want to talk about?"

Feeling really punchy and not expecting her to say yes, I jokingly said, "Why don't you tell me about every boyfriend you ever had."

Laughing out loud she said, "Fine," and with a short pause to think, she continued by asking, "Where do you want me to start?"

"How about as far back as you can remember?" I asked with a chuckle.

She laughed and said, "Well, when I was in second grade there was Bruce..." and she continued for the next three hours, telling in great detail about each one, because I had asked for it.

There's an old saying, "Be careful what you ask for because you might get it." However, one of my favorite philosophies has always been, "If you don't ask, you don't get." Dennis had asked, and I was happy to oblige.

We actually had a wonderful time telling each other about people who had been in our lives before we'd met...this lifetime. We learned more about each other that night than most people know about someone after being together for years! Dennis was genuinely interested in hearing the details of my single years and there was no sign of resentment or jealousy. The beauty of our relationship is that no one before we met each other mattered now. Those were only experiences we chose to have while waiting to find each other. The past is history and only serves to help make us who we are today.

Then it was my turn. I only had a little more than an hour to fill, which was perfect because we arrived in Salina at the exact moment I finished. We got a room at the first motel we found, all the while laughing playfully about what we had just shared with each other. After the two or three grueling days we had put on the road, we felt that we deserved and desired to reconnect our souls and our bodies. So we got undressed and, as we had become accustomed to, took a nice long hot shower together. The warmth of the water relaxed us and the soap and closeness of our bodies raised our awareness of each other to such a fever pitch that we made passionate love right there in the shower.

- *St. Louis Bound* -

The next morning, after a deep and restful sleep, we headed toward St. Louis, Missouri. It was a long trip across Kansas and Missouri, so when we got to St. Louis we decided to do a little research of my past life as Joshua Abram, the printer from St. Louis. We checked out old St. Louis and some old bookstores just in case there was something in print with his name on it. We didn't find anything about him then, but from the books, we gained some new and interesting knowledge about the old city.

I knew that Dennis had learned about one of his past lives through his regressions, and that he'd been a printer in St. Louis in the 1870's. When we arrived in St. Louis, I was hoping that, together again, we would have some sensation that we'd been there before.

I began to recognize the area even though I'd never been in St. Louis during this lifetime, and I was totally unfamiliar with the city. We walked down an old cobblestone street and the hair began standing up on our arms. I got a definite feeling that I'd been on that street at some other time, and Dennis described it as "chills of recognition". In the metaphysical world, chills and goose bumps are also described as a "psychic truth".

The name "Mary" came into my head, and we noted it for future reference. We agreed that we would explore this experience in greater detail, through regression work and research of the city's archives. While exploring the National Archives and the census of 1870 we found that Mary, as best we could tell, was not a member of the Abram clan. But a few months later, when Dennis facilitated a regression for me, she came up as a lady who lived in St. Louis and was Joshua's girlfriend and lover. We know there are many other lives that we will be discovering over the next few years and we hope to document as many of them as we can and present them in book form.

- Alice Doesn't Live Here Anymore -

When we arrived in Nashville, Tennessee, it was then that we were faced with the decision of which route to take. The question that Alice posed was, "Would you like to go through Chattanooga, or would you like to go through Knoxville and see the house I used to live in?"

I was not aware of the impact my next answer would have so I replied, "Sure, I would love to see your old house."

She said we could also go and see her friend, Susan, whom she hadn't seen in several years. Alice then told me that her ex-husband, Rob, still lived in her old house, and asked me if I wanted to meet him. Since meeting Alice, each day had been an adventure, so I knew this one would be nothing less.

So it was east toward Knoxville, Tennessee, about 180 miles from Nashville. It was a stormy, rainy night and we also had to fight many miles of construction along the Interstate.

I hadn't been to my old house since I got divorced in October of 1976. We purchased the house in early 1973, so I only lived there 3-1/2 years. It was a large home, about 4,000 square feet, and the back yard connected to the 6th green on the golf course in a beautiful subdivision called Fox Den. Justin was only two years old when we left Knoxville.

The most vivid memory I left for my neighbors was the large poster that my sister Diane made and placed on the front door. My former neighbors have told me they still talk about that story at the 19th hole in the Clubhouse.

Diane came to Knoxville in September of 1976, and stayed with me for about two weeks before I moved out. She helped me pack and was a tremendous comfort to me at that emotional time in my life.

She had urged me to take all the Lionel train sets that were stacked in the extra closet, still unopened in their original boxes, but I was afraid to take something that wasn't specifically written on my Settlement Agreement. What a fool I was! I spent seven years trying to get Rob to pay child support, and to give Justin the trains so that I could at least sell some of them. He did neither. He claimed that he had sold the trains, and no longer had them when my attorney filed contempt motions for support.

Well, since I had chosen to move back to Miami, Rob got the house and was going to move back in when I left. I'd had an incompetent lawyer and accepted a bad deal just so that I could leave the state with my son and my sanity. I wasn't about to leave quietly.

Diane, who has a sharp wit, decided to leave a note for Rob. So, she got a large piece of poster board, and when we locked the house to leave for the last time, we placed the poster on the front door. In large letters, she had written the title words from the 1974 Martin Scorsese movie, "Alice Doesn't Live Here Anymore".

So, here I was, exactly 20 years later, and I was about to drive up to the house and knock on the door. My thought was that we'd go by the house, and if anyone was home, we'd go in so Dennis could see the house. Meeting Rob would be the bonus.

Before we arrived, I had called Justin, my mother, and my friend Susan and told them where we were heading.

Justin said, "Mom! You can't do that; it's rude."

My dear mother saw it differently. She laughed and quipped, "Take a picture of his face when he sees you!"

Susan only said, "Omigod!"

We finally arrived in Knoxville at about 10:00 PM on Sunday night. I was just following verbal directions and amazingly, Alice, my love, who is geographically challenged, guided us to the house without any problem.

When we got there it was very dark and rainy. During the ride to Knoxville, Alice had regaled me with the whole story of her life in Knoxville and the details of the divorce. By the time we arrived, I knew all about everything that went on even after the divorce was finalized, including their battle over the Lionel trains.

When we were sitting outside in front of her former residence, Alice looked at me and asked, "Do you really want to do this?

I saw the look in her eyes and without hesitation said, "Sure, why not. I'm up for an adventure."

She had this surprised look on her face and then we both started laughing, got out of the van, and started up the driveway.

The house sat on a little rise above the road and it was a slightly steep incline. I had taken my big police style flashlight so that we could see as we were walking up the long driveway. When we got to the door, Alice again asked if I really wanted to do this.

I questioned, "Are you sure you want to do this?"

She answered me by ringing the doorbell.

When the door opened, a woman was standing there

talking on the phone. She said into the phone, "Just a moment, there's someone at the door."

Then she said to us, "Hi, can I help you?"

Alice said, "Yes, is Rob home?"

The lady said, "Yes he is, can I tell him who you are?"

"Hi, I'm Alice."

At which point the woman said into the phone with a nervous strain to her voice, "I have to go now. Bye." She then introduced herself as Charlene and invited us inside.

She said "Just have a seat in the kitchen and I'll get Rob." She then started to describe how to get to the kitchen. "It's right around…"

To which Alice quickly interrupted with, "I know where it is, I used to live here!"

Charlene then excused herself and said, "Well, ok, I'll go get Rob."

Moments later, Rob came around the corner into the kitchen and he had this very quizzical look on his face. It was as if to say, "What the hell are you doing here?"

But he was very cordial and said, "Hello Alice, how are you?"

"Just great. How about you, how are you doing?"

Very guardedly he said, "Oh, alright I guess. Just keeping my head above water." It was as if he was afraid that she was checking up on his assets to get something from him.

Alice then introduced me, "Oh, this is Dennis. We were just driving through town, and thought we'd stop by."

Then they had about fifteen minutes of what I would call trivial chitchat. It was really very friendly, with Alice asking questions about how Rob was doing, and Rob giving very sketchy details. It was awkward, but actually quite humorous to observe.

For me it was like being in the Twilight Zone again. Here I was in a house that Alice had lived in twenty years before, and we were sitting across from her ex-husband and his girlfriend. Both Alice and I were feeling in a very giddy mood, so the next thing out of Alice's mouth didn't surprise me in the least.

She asked Rob, "Do you mind if I show Dennis around the house? I've been telling him all about it and I'd love to show him." While she was saying this she was getting up, taking my hand and leading me down the hall toward the bedrooms, not waiting for an answer.

I could only imagine that Rob was thinking, "What does this woman want? I just know she is here to see what she can get from me."

What he didn't know was that even Alice didn't know why she had come there.

We wandered around the house looking in all the rooms, all the while with Alice making comments like, "Oh I remember that"; or "I bought that"; or, "Gee, Rob, this is the same carpeting and furniture we had when I lived here." At one point she said, "Rob, it doesn't look like you changed anything, these are even the same drapes that we had over twenty years ago."

He replied, I think a little sarcastically, and with an edge to his Southern drawl, "Oh no, I wouldn't change a thing. I wanted to leave it just like it was when you were here."

The four of us went downstairs and walked down the hall into the big rec room. I looked up on top of the tall cabinet on the far end of the wall and there they were. All the trains were there, still in their boxes and on display in full view. I was standing to Rob's right, and the trains were to his left. Alice had gone into the den, in front of him and to my right.

Knowing the story about the trains, I said, "Wow, those are very cool trains, Rob. How long have you been collecting them?"

He ignored me.

I tried again. I said, "Really, those are very cool trains. What are they, H.O. or H gauge?" Still he did not answer.

I tried one final time. "I'll bet you've been saving those for a long time, right?"

Finally, he responded, "Uh, yeah, H.O. gauge, yeah, a long time."

It was kind of cryptic in its delivery, but I could clearly feel he was getting more uncomfortable as the minutes ticked on.

It was then I heard Alice declare, "Oh Dennis, come over here, you have to see this. I made that!"

I looked at what she was pointing at, but the lights were off and the only light was from the adjoining rec room. The corner she was pointing toward was quite dark so I took the flashlight I was carrying, turned it on and pointed it at the object she was referring to. It was one of the ugliest lamps I have ever seen in my life, but I was not going to let on that I didn't like it.

I said, "Wow, you made that? It is so cool, I love it,"

while inside I was thinking, "Man, am I glad you left that thing here."

Alice looked at Rob and said, "I can't believe you still have that."

"Oh yes," he said, dripping with sarcasm, "it reminds me of you."

With that, we went back upstairs, thanked them for their hospitality, said good-bye, and left. As we were walking back down the driveway to my van, we were both having trouble stifling the laughter that wanted to break free. So when we got into the van we both busted out laughing full gut-wrenching laughs, the kind when you laugh so hard your stomach begins hurting.

Alice then said, "I'll bet that lamp is in the trash before we get to the main road."

As we were still laughing from this latest outrageous adventure we just created, I suddenly realized what had just occurred. I stopped laughing and said to Dennis very seriously, "I know why I had to go in there tonight."

"Why?"

"I needed to have complete closure with Rob," I replied pensively. For twenty years I've been angry about what he didn't do for Justin, and what good did it serve? My anger never hurt him; he never even knew or cared. It only bothered me."

I went on to explain what my feelings were right then. "We just spent 45 minutes in my old house, with things that belonged to me when I lived there. Nothing in that house has changed since 1973. Even Rob hasn't changed. That's sad, and I feel sorry for him. But I've changed, and Justin is grown and terrific. I don't need to have the anger now. It just doesn't serve me anymore."

I was now processing out loud and said, "Rob probably thinks we went there tonight so that I could check out the house to see if he has any money or assets. He's probably thinking I'm going to file papers next week!"

Dennis patiently listened while I continued to explain what was happening for me at that moment.

"Dennis, I just realized why Charlie came through in the reading you did for me in Baltimore. I needed to have closure with him, too. He'd always been such a thorn to me while I was married to Rob. I unknowingly carried anger against Charlie all these years."

"And, you know what else?" I said. "I'm a better divorce lawyer because of my bad experiences when I was going through a divorce myself. I promised myself when I went into family law that I would never allow people to have inadequate representation like I had here."

As we drove out of Fox Den, we began remembering the scene when Rob first saw me in the kitchen. I had to laugh again to think that he still didn't know why I'd been there that night.

- Continuing The Journey -

A day or so later, when we were approaching Columbia, South Carolina, I asked Alice to look at the map and let me know where to turn because I-26 had a jog in it. The next thing I know, we're coming to a traffic light. This was quite strange given the fact that I had just been driving on a freeway. We took the meaning of this to be there must have been something on the freeway that we were to avoid.

Actually, I prefer that explanation to Dennis' usual

quip that I'm just geographically challenged and can't read a road map. Even though it's true.

Life was becoming more enjoyable at every turn. Normally an event like that would have set me off and I would have been pissed and had a lot of anger come up. I was very calm and just started joking with Alice about it. In fact, all the way across the United States, we had been laughing and just having a great time enjoying each other's company.

- A Rose By Any Other Name -

As we traveled the highways, we talked about every conceivable topic. We were so comfortable with each other; as though we'd always been together as a couple. At one point I realized that I was having difficulty calling Dennis by his name. I fell into the ease of saying "honey" or "sweetheart" more often than "Dennis". I found myself actually having to think of his first name before I could say it to his face. Then the reason came to me...I didn't recognize this man as "Dennis". I knew his energy and his soul from so many previous lives. The face before me now was new and would take getting used to. Every now and then, we still get glimpses of past faces, and the recognition process is awesome.

Alice shared this with me some time after our trip. What she didn't know was that I, too, was having trouble remembering her name. After we had set up a home together in Miami, we were discussing our meeting...kind of reliving the feelings, and she blurted out, "You know, I was having a hard time remembering your name! I didn't recognize you as 'Dennis', and that's why I was calling you honey or sweetheart all the time."

"Well, as you can see, it didn't really matter because I thought it was great that you felt comfortable enough to call me honey. It felt perfect, but what is really funny is that I, too, was having a hard time remembering your name!" We had a laugh and continued to relive the wonderful parts of our connecting.

- Playfulness Abounds -

As we drove through Florida, I was in a playful mood because we were approaching Miami and our new life together. I was in love and looking forward to settling in and beginning my life with Alice.

Looming on the horizon, directly ahead of us, was a big black raincloud. It looked like one of the worst storms that I had ever been through.

I said to Alice, "Do you think we should pull off? That looks pretty bad."

To which she replied, "Oh, that little cloud? Don't worry about that. Besides, if you don't like the weather in Florida, wait five minutes. It'll change."

Then she started laughing and teasing me in a little girl voice, "Does that little ol' storm scare you, honey? Don't worry, I'll protect you."

All during the trip we had kept a cooler on the floor between the front seats of the van. In the cooler we kept all kinds of small things that needed to be kept cool, including my insulin. Mostly though, there was soda pop and water. I had just opened an ice-cold bottle of water and was about to take a drink.

Then I said, "Don't you worry your little self about me, you should just worry about the rainstorms coming, like the one coming right now. Look out, you never know when they will strike."

And with that, I pointed the open end of the bottle at Alice, and making a quick jerking motion toward her, half the ICE COLD water flew out and completely drenched her. She screamed, and at the same moment she threw the water in her water bottle at me and what ensued was a great, wild water fight.

It was so hot outside that it actually felt great. We both got cooled off and started laughing so hard we forgot about the storm "outside". It was then that I realized that the rain was coming down so hard, my windshield wipers couldn't keep up with the water. I slowed way down and pulled off the freeway at the next exit and pulled into a gas station,

I thought I might as well take this opportunity to fill up my tank. As I got out of the van and stepped down to the ground, my leg went into the water up to my knees. I turned around and looked at her. As the wind is blowing, the rain is coming down in sheets, and I am wondering what I have gotten myself into, Alice looks at me with her big beautiful blue eyes and says…

"Welcome to Florida!"

About the Authors

~Dennis Jackson~

Dennis is an internationally acclaimed psychic/ medium, clairvoyant, clairaudient, and clairsentient. He has traveled throughout the United States and Canada, and via radio and the internet, Dennis has become a much sought after medium by people around the world.

Dennis' path is one of service and is available for private sessions. The sessions can be over the phone or in person, both are equally successful. The sessions can consist of psychic reading and medium work, or strictly psychic or strictly medium, depending on client preference.

With energy and thought coming from a loving place, Dennis is able to put all of his gifts to work to help you in your search for your own truth. His readings are quite specific, whether in person or over the phone. With the help of his personal guide, HO, he will bring you information in the areas of love, relationships, money and career.

As a medium, Dennis is a channel for family and friends who have passed on to the other side. Dennis is especially gifted in being able to bring meaningful and healing messages to you and your family from loved ones and spirit guides from the other side.

Life has many messages for us and Dennis can assist you in your awareness of how your present life is related to your past life experiences. Using a deep but safe meditative process to tap into past lives through a past life regression, you may complete a much needed healing and be able to move forward in your present life.

~*Alice Best*~

Alice is an experienced Family Law attorney and is certified by the Supreme Court of Florida as a Family Court Mediator. She has an "AV" rating from Martindale-Hubbell, the highest professional level attainable based on her years of experience in Family Law and the endorsement by her colleagues in the areas of professional conduct, ethics and ability. She is licensed to practice law in Florida and Colorado, and has been admitted as a member of the Bar of the U.S. Supreme Court.

Alice has been a gubernatorial appointee to the Judicial Nominating Commission for the Third District Court of Appeal of Florida since 1995. The prestigious nine-member Commission investigates and interviews judicial candidates for appointment to the Appellate Bench for Dade and Monroe Counties. She also served as a Dade County Civil Traffic Infraction Hearing Officer from January 1996 through March 1999.

As a graduate of Barry University (B.S. 1983) and the University of Miami School of Law (J.D. 1986), Alice served as an Adjunct Professor at Florida International University in the Paralegal Studies program. Prior to practicing law, Alice spent 10 years as a legal secretary and Certified Legal Assistant.

Alice now considers herself to be a "recovering divorce lawyer" and is an active member of the International Alliance of Holistic Lawyers. After 10 years of handling only divorce and child custody cases, she closed a successful law practice, and limits her practice to mediations and uncontested cases. She finds it more enjoyable to work with people and assist them in solving their own problems, thus enabling them to regain control and power over their own lives, without placing blame on anyone. Holistic law looks at the totality of the picture and the consequences of actions, and is a focus of what Alice speaks about in her lectures to groups about relationships and how to handle family cases in a positive fashion.

Dennis and Alice lived together in Miami, Florida from August, 1996 through August, 1999. They now have Seattle, Washington as their home base, and travel all around the U.S. and Canada, promoting their book, facilitating special events and twin soul workshops.

Together, Dennis and Alice appear on radio, lecture and present classes and workshops on twin soul relationships, spirituality, and intuitive pathways. They have also produced a variety of meditation tapes that can be purchased via the internet or by phone. To receive more information on the tapes, schedule your private reading with Dennis, or to book Dennis and Alice for a speaking engagement, please call:

Toll Free (877) 595-4111

Or visit our website at:
www.denalilove.com

Watch for our next book:

The Psychic and The Lawyer